TROLLOPE'S PALLISER NOVELS

By the same author

THACKERAY: The Major Novels
JANE AUSTEN'S ACHIEVEMENT (*editor*)

TROLLOPE'S PALLISER NOVELS

Theme and Pattern

JULIET McMASTER
Professor of English
University of Alberta

First published 1978 by
THE MACMILLAN PRESS LTD
London and Basingstoke

Associated companies in Delhi
Dublin   Hong Kong   Johannesburg   Lagos
Melbourne   New York   Singapore   Tokyo

Printed in Hong Kong

British Library Cataloguing in Publication Data

McMaster, Juliet
Trollope's Palliser novels
1. Trollope, Anthony – Criticism and interpretation
I. Title
823' .8   PR5687

ISBN 0-333-23860-5

ع

TO MY PARENTS

Contents

List of Illustrations

Texts and Abbreviations

As my texts throughout I have used the Oxford World's Classics editions of Trollope's novels and autobiography. References are by volume number (in cases where the original issue was two volumes) and page.

A	*An Autobiography*
Critical Heritage	*Anthony Trollope: The Critical Heritage*, edited by Donald Smalley (London, 1969)
CYFH	*Can You Forgive Her?*
DC	*The Duke's Children*
ED	*The Eustace Diamonds*
Letters	*The Letters of Anthony Trollope*, edited by Bradford Allen Booth (London, 1951)
PF	*Phineas Finn, the Irish Member*
PM	*The Prime Minister*
PR	*Phineas Redux*
SHA	*The Small House at Allington*

Acknowledgements

I record here my gratitude to the people and institutions who have enabled me to write this book: to the John Simon Guggenheim Memorial Foundation and the Canada Council, for the fellowships which released me from teaching duties for a year; to the University of Alberta, for a research grant that enabled me to work on the Trollope papers in the Bodleian, and to the Bodleian Library itself and the Beinecke Rare Book and Manuscript Library, Yale University, for permission to publish some of my findings in their collections of Trollope manuscripts. Versions of my first two chapters have been published in *Nineteenth-Century Fiction* and *Studies in English Literature*, and I am grateful to the editors and to the University of California Press for permission to reprint.

My warm personal thanks are due to Robert H. Taylor, in whose splendid collection, housed in the Firestone Library at Princeton, I spent many (though too few) happy hours, and who not only gave me permission to publish my findings among his manuscripts, but also shared with me his enthusiasm as a Trollopian. I am also grateful to A. Walton Litz, J. Hillis Miller, Ian Watt, and Gordon N. Ray, for both personal and scholarly encouragement, and to John Johansen, for research assistance.

August 1977   JULIET MCMASTER

Introduction

Anyone who undertakes to write a book on Trollope's novels is in danger of biting off more than he can chew. I have chosen to examine only a group of novels, rather than the whole canon, because only in that way can I examine single novels in detail, as I believe they deserve to be examined. The Palliser novels present themselves as a convenient group not so much because of their recent serialization on television as because they have, until recently at least, not received the critical attention that has been accorded to the Barset series. I also prefer them to the Barset series, as will emerge, as I find them deeper in vision and more sophisticated in technique than the early Trollope.

To the six novels, from *Can You Forgive Her?* to *The Duke's Children*, and including *The Eustace Diamonds*, the two Phineas novels and *The Prime Minister*, I have annexed *The Small House at Allington* from the Barset series. The unfolding story of Plantagenet Palliser and Lady Glencora after all begins here; and besides, the Barset novel provides a convenient example by which to link and contrast the Palliser novels with the earlier series.

In a study of only seven novels, there is room to explore and elaborate on the meaning and the art of each one. My emphasis is on theme, for that seems to me to be one aspect of Trollope's art that has, for quite understandable reasons, not received as much attention as his much more visible concern with character. Because of his unemphatic tone and low-keyed, faithfully meticulous representation of all facets of the situations and characters he examines, it is often possible to read to the end of one of his novels, having been entertained from page to page by lively incident and lifelike characterizations, without having a sense that it is *about* anything, that it adds up to more than the sum of its parts. It is easy for the reader to conclude, like David Cecil, that "indeed, Trollope did not have the ideas with which to knit a story together. He

1

had a view of life – and a very sensible one – but it formed no part of his inspiration." Cecil also deplored, as have many other critics, Trollope's "irrelevant sub-plots."[1] But of course Trollope does incorporate a vision of humanity in his novels, and it is often through the relation of his main plot to his subplots that this vision is best comprehended. I have given more attention to the subplots than many of Trollope's critics, because one often finds in them the clearest indications of what his total subject is in a given novel. *The Small House at Allington* may seem at first glance a tangle of narrative threads about Dales, De Courcys, Pallisers, Crosbies and Cradells, but it has a consistent theme which is the common element in each story, and the minor characters become commentaries on the major one. *Can You Forgive Her?* would be in danger of falling into three pieces, and *The Prime Minister* of splitting in half, but for the careful system of parallels and contrasts that reminds us that the subject is still the same, even if the agents are frequently changed. It is when we superimpose the various plots that Trollope's figure in the carpet emerges.

Trollope indeed explained this procedure of the novelist: "Though his story should be all one, yet it may have many parts. Though the plot itself may require but few characters, it may be so enlarged as to find its full development in many. There may be subsidiary plots, which shall all tend to the elucidation of the main story, and which will take their places as part of one and the same work" (*A*, 205). It has been my intention to show how Trollope's subplots tend to the elucidation of the main story, as does often the imagery (another aspect of Trollope that has not received much attention), and thereby to identify the story's thematic thrust.

There is of course a danger inherent in my narrow focus: in pursuing the articulation of a theme in a given novel, it is easy to talk as though the other novels didn't exist. I should acknowledge at the outset that there is considerable overlap in subject matter between one novel and another; that, for instance, human perversity, and the quest for truth among lies, which I identify as the main themes in *The Small House* and *The Eustace Diamonds*, are perennial concerns of Trollope's, and are of import in many of his novels. But none the less I find that in a single novel he does present a particular subject, and elaborate it through plot and subplot, major characters and minor, action and incident, and often through imagery too, so that his subject is ultimately incorporated into the total pattern of the book.

In the last chapters I depart from the practice of a consideration of a single novel at a time to examine in general certain recurring issues in Trollope's work – the relation of the sexes, the importance of location and setting, and our sense of the authorial presence in the novels. Here, though I do not restrict myself to a consideration of the Palliser novels, they remain my major concern. Amidst such plenty, one must select.

1 *The Small House at Allington*: The Moth and the Candle

"Lilian Dale, dear Lily Dale – for my reader must know that she is to be very dear" – did not remain as dear to her author as she was at first.[1] She is the heroine who has most charmed and most irritated Trollope's readers in successive generations, and he seems himself to have had mixed feelings about her.[2] How are we to view her great passion for Crosbie and her determined rejection of Johnny Eames? To answer that question she needs to be examined not on her own, but as one piece of the larger pattern of the whole novel, a pattern which spreads from main plot to subplot, and then leads back again.

For all the apparent fortuitousness of the various plot lines in *The Small House*, and the seeming distance of, say, Palliser's story from Johnny Eames's, Trollope has constructed a set of relationships with careful symmetry. The main plot, of course, is his usual one of the woman between two men. At the apex is Lily Dale of Allington, with her two suitors, one successful and faithless, the other faithful but unsuccessful. Each of these has temptations in another world than Allington; Crosbie is attracted to high life, and engages himself to the earl's daughter, Lady Alexandrina De Courcy; Eames is seduced by low life, and succumbs to the doubtful charms of the boardinghouse-keeper's daughter, Amelia Roper. The parallel is emphasized by many small touches: in each case, for instance, the fatal commitment to these sirens is made when they have let down their hair (I; 80, 331). In their respective country house and boardinghouse circles, each encounters a young man, shading off into the upper reaches of the aristocracy in one case, into the lower reaches of shabbiness in the other, who is carrying on a dangerous flirtation with a married woman; and so the stories of Palliser and Cradell are lightly connected with each other and with Lily Dale's, and the marriage of the vulgar Mrs. Lupex and her gin-tippling husband is a gloss on the other threatened alliance, of Lord and Lady Dumbello. (For perfect symmetry, Trollope could finally have married off Palliser, after his abortive flirtation with Lady Dumbello, to the abandoned Lady Alexandrina, as he paired Cradell with Amelia; but fortunately he reserved Palliser for better things.) To this main structure – a triangle with flourishes, as it were – Trollope adds another fainter triangle, in which Lily's sister Bell, the other "pearl of Allington," is courted by *her* two suitors, Bernard Dale, who is rich but unsuccessful in his suit, and Dr. Crofts, who is poor but carries off the prize. It is all very neat, even diagrammatic.

But the various stories belong to each other not simply by reason of this symmetrical system of parallels and contrasts, but by the common element in the behaviour of the characters – by the fact that they all belong to Trollope's major theme. He ventures to be most obvious about this theme in the stories which are furthest from the main action: that is, in the parts concerning Cradell and Palliser, the two young bachelors who get themselves involved with married women. Cradell pursues Mrs. Lupex, in spite of the fact that she is old, gross, vulgar and malicious, and that he is likely to get in trouble with her drunken husband. Trollope thus describes this perverse attraction:

> When the unfortunate moth in his semi-blindness whisks himself and his wings within the flame of the candle, and finds himself mutilated and tortured, he even then will not take the lesson, but returns again and again till he is destroyed. Such a moth was poor Cradell. There was no warmth to be got by him from that flame. There was no beauty in the light, – not even the false brilliance of unhallowed love. Injury might come to him, – a pernicious clipping of the wings, which might destroy all power of future flight; injury, and not improbably destruction, if he should persevere. But one may say that no single hour of happiness could accrue to him from his intimacy with Mrs. Lupex. He felt for her no love. He was afraid of her, and, in many respects, disliked her. But to him, in his moth-like weakness, ignorance, and blindness, it seemed to be a great thing that he should be allowed to fly near the candle. (I, 144)

It is a central image, and applicable, in one way or another, to all the major characters in the novel, and many of the minor ones. Indeed, here Trollope expands the image to include his readers, and by implication society and humanity in general: "Oh! my friends, if you will but think of it, how many of you have been moths, and are now going about ungracefully with wings more or less burnt off, and with bodies sadly scorched!" It is the unifying theme of the novel. Cradell and Palliser, Johnny Eames and Crosbie, and Bell and Lily Dale – all in one way or another consciously devote themselves to ruin and unhappiness; they are all excited by what they know will damage them, all perversely enamored of pain.

Cradell knows that "no single hour of happiness could accrue to him from his intimacy with Mrs. Lupex"; she is physically repellent, though he tries to rationalize his attraction to an ugly and slatternly female by telling himself she is a fine figure of a woman (I, 52); and he lives in constant terror of a fracas with her husband. Nevertheless, the affair is all-important to him. "Think what a time I have of it – standing always, as one may say, on gunpowder," he says to Johnny Eames, simultaneously boasting and bewailing his fate (I, 401).

Palliser in his pursuit of Lady Dumbello is the aristocratic parallel to Cradell. Trollope makes it clear from the outset how much he has to lose: "We may say that he had everything at his command, in the way of pleasure, that the world could offer him. He had wealth, position, power. ... He was courted by all who could get near enough to court him. It is hardly too much to say that he might have selected a bride from all that was most beautiful and best among English women" (I, 318). And yet so much the more does he feel the necessity to put all this in jeopardy by the pursuit of a married woman in the teeth of his uncle's prohibition. In fact the Duke of Omnium's opposition is what determines Palliser to persist, though he is not in the least in love. When the Duke takes it upon himself to warn his nephew of Lady Dumbello, Palliser is the more determined to persist in his pursuit, although he has everything to lose and hardly anything to gain:

> Mr. Plantagenet Palliser received everything he had in the world from his uncle. He sat in Parliament through his uncle's interest, and received an allowance of ever so many thousand a year which his uncle could stop to-morrow by his mere word. ... Nevertheless, the nephew immediately felt himself aggrieved by this allusion to his private life, and resolved at once that he would not submit to such surveillance. (II, 173)

Lady Dumbello is no Mrs. Lupex, certainly; but he finds making advances to her "really very hard work" (II, 178), and her cold beauty never attracts him until he sees in it a possibility of his own ruin. Before he enters the affair he is already lamenting the joys of married life that this liaison will make impossible, and when he finally makes his bid for her, he goes about the business "twittering with expectant love, and trembling with expectant ruin" (II, 353–54).[3] Fortunately for him, however, Lady Dumbello, one of the few characters in the novel who fully knows her own interest and is able to follow it, is not similarly enamoured of disaster, and hence we know in advance "that Mr. Palliser's chance of being able to shipwreck himself upon that rock was but small, and that he would, in spite of himself, be saved" (II, 349).

Trollope's view of human nature here, expanded and varied through many characters and situations in a long novel, is like Dostoyevsky's, which is concentrated in a single figure in *Notes from Underground*.[4] Here the narrator's perversity amounts to madness, but his fascinating articulateness about his own malady would make him a shrewd commentator on, say, Johnny's pursuit of Amelia Roper. For Johnny is like the man he describes who is perfectly clear and lucid about his own interests and determined to follow his own rational resolutions, and yet

> within a quarter of an hour, without any sudden outside provocation, but simply through something inside him which is stronger than all his interests, he will go off on quite a different tack – that is, act in direct opposition to what he has been saying about himself, in opposition to the laws of reason, in opposition to his own advantage, in fact in opposition to everything.[5]

And he goes on to conclude, "does not man, perhaps, love something besides well-being? Perhaps he is just as fond of suffering? Perhaps suffering is just as great a benefit to him as well-being? Man is sometimes extraordinarily, passionately, in love with suffering, and that is a fact."[6] Johnnie Eames subjected to Amelia, Crosbie attracted to Lady Alexandrina, Lily Dale with her "Apollo," like Cradell and Palliser fluttering around *their* candles, are all aware that they are damaging themselves; few of them even derive much pleasure from their dangerous liaisons, and yet, "unfortunate moths" as they are, they cannot resist casting themselves into the flame.

Johnny Eames's entanglement with Amelia dates from before the action of the novel begins, so we do not see how it started. It is only clear that he regrets it, and longs to extricate himself. Trollope makes it clear how Johnny detests Amelia, physically, emotionally and rationally. He is aware that "life with such a wife as that would be a living death" (I, 138), he thinks of her as a millstone round his neck, he shudders with revulsion when he recalls the way she looks, he is moved to writhing disgust by her love letter. And he lives in fear of her. "The prospect of Amelia in her rage was very terrible to him; but his greatest fear was of Amelia in her love" (I, 394). There is in this relation, in fact, some suggestion of the sexual dimension of Trollope's theme, for there is an element of masochism in Johnny. He keeps recalling her appearance at his bedroom door with her hair down over her ample shoulders, and her fierce eyes and vigorous gestures make thim think of her as a Judith (I, 404).

He longs to escape from her, and yet when he is offered the chance he cannot take it. Knowing the kind of hold she has on him, Amelia offers to release him from his promise. "Only say the word," she urges; but he is unable to say it (I, 59). On another occasion we hear "his only wish was to escape, and yet his arm, quite in opposition to his own desires, found its way round her waist" (I, 405). And when in a transparent bid to make him jealous she flirts with Cradell, "she succeeded in the teeth of his aversion to her and of his love elsewhere" (II, 215). Against all his own interests and desires, Johnny must burn himself in the smokiest and least attractive of candles. In *The Last Chronicle of Barset* he does it again, this time with the more sophisticated Madalina Demolines, whom he finds neither pretty nor amiable. "He did see plainly enough that he was getting into trouble; and yet, for his life, he could not help himself. The moth who flutters round the light knows that he is being burned, and yet he cannot fly away from it" (*Last Chronicle*, II, 411–12).

Crosbie's case is parallel. His dilemma has been seen as the standard choice between love and the world, between the joys of domestic felicity with Lily Dale of the Small House and the glitter of social success as an earl's son-in-law.[7] And indeed this is the way he himself rationalizes his behaviour. But it is not as simple as this; for Lady Alexandrina is not really a good catch from any point of view, worldly or otherwise, as Crosbie knows very well. Trollope makes it clear that he knew her before he went to Allington, and in the previous spring "the intercourse between them had almost been tender" (I, 236, 308) – to the point that, as the narrator acknowledges, "Under such circumstances Mr. Crosbie should not have gone to Courcy Castle" (I, 225). He seems to have been aware that he could probably have had her then if he had wanted her. But he apparently did not want her – until his engagement to Lily gave him the chance to ruin his life by jilting a woman he did love for another whom he didn't, and to bring on himself social opprobrium and domestic misery. He does not find Alexandrina physically attractive – she is older than he, somewhat tarnished by her prolonged and un-successful campaigning in the marriage market, and hardened by con-tact with her dreadful family. Amelia does exert a certain physical magnetism over Johnny, but Alexandrina has scarcely any for Crosbie. Of their first lovers' tête-à-tête Trollope relates succinctly: "Then the countess went away, and Alexandrina was left with her lover for half an hour. When the half-hour was over, he felt that he would have given all that he had in the world to have back the last four-and-twenty hours of his existence" (I, 334). And when, just before their marriage, he tries to take her hand, her response is a single syllable, "Don't" (II, 145). So much for their sexual relation. As for the match from a worldly point of view, Crosbie tries to convince himself that he is making a catch, but, like Palliser making love to Lady Dumbello, he finds it hard work. "He had almost taught himself to believe that a marriage with a daughter of the house of Courcy would satisfy his ambition and assist him in his bat-tle with the world" (I, 310). It is not that Crosbie makes a mistake out of ignorance and then lives to regret it. Trollope is careful to insist how ful-ly he is aware of his own interest, and yet how all the same he deserts it.

While he is still at Courcy Castle and as yet uncommitted to Alexandrina, he reflects,

> As to the daughters, he had ridiculed them all from time to time – even Alexandrina, whom he now professed to love. . . . He could measure the whole thing at its worth, – Courcy Castle with its privileges, Lady Dumbello, Lady Clandidlem, and the whole of it. He knew that he had been happier on that lawn at Allington, and more contented with himself. . . . He knew that there was something better [than the Courcy world], and that that something better was within his reach.
>   But, nevertheless . . . (I, 240).

Nevertheless, he jilts Lily and engages himself to Alexandrina. In fact as he finds out later but essentially knew all along, his marriage to the Earl's daughter is very far from advancing his interests in the world: it only binds him to a portionless woman of blue blood and expensive habits, and an arrogant, rapacious set of in-laws who so tie up his income and spend his money that he is financially and professionally crippled. His income would have gone much further with Lily to husband it, and Lily would no doubt have made for him something of a social success in London.

Crosbie has not as much self-awareness as Eames. Johnny knows his entanglement with Amelia is irrational and against all his interests; whereas Crosbie, finding himself unable to resist Alexandrina, rationalizes his conduct and tries to believe that the marriage to Lily would be the disastrous one. At Courcy Castle he tells himself that "soon after making that declaration of love at Allington he had begun to feel that in making it he had cut his throat" (I, 312).

Presently, however, we hear him saying irritably to his club acquaintance, "Yes, . . . I shall marry Lady Alexandrina; – that is, if I do not cut the whole concern, and my own throat into the bargain" (I, 344). Crosbie does not physically enact that threat, but in marrying Lady Alexandrina he does figuratively cut his own throat. For Crosbie, the narrator insists, "had seen and approved the better course, but had chosen for himself to walk in that which was worse" (II, 211).

With considerable conceit, he casts himself in the roles of ambitious man of the world, Lothario, even Satan, telling himself that he is not cut out for the simple joys and goodness of the Allington world: "It was of no use for him to tell himself that the Small House at Allington was better than Courcy Castle. Satan knew that heaven was better than hell; but he found himself to be fitter for the latter place" (I, 240). "I never do like Paragons," he once says jokingly (I, 118). It is a common and even modish perversity to reject the perfect; and here Trollope touches on one of Tennyson's themes in *Idylls of the King*. Guinevere despises

Arthur, thinking that in preferring Lancelot she is choosing warmth, colour, and humanity, and she has to learn

> We needs must love the highest when we see it,
> Not Lancelot, nor another. ("Guinevere," II. 655–56)

But Trollope's characters seldom learn (the burned moth "even then will not take the lesson"), and he spends this novel showing how, like the unreformed Guinevere, like Satan, they deliberately choose the worse alternative and reject the good, so determining their own misery.

As for Lily Dale herself, it is no doubt her surface perversity that so endears her both to the characters around her and to many of Trollope's readers. It shows itself as liveliness and charm in her everyday discourse and behaviour. But Trollope's intention is perceptible on close reading. When she is packing her mother's effects and finds she is holding an heirloom she says cheerfully, "Oh, dear, what should I do if I were to break it? Whenever I handle anything very precious I always feel inclined to throw it down and smash it" (II, 265). It is a light touch, but a significant one. For this is just the surface manifestation of a perversity that goes much deeper, and decisively affects the course of her life.

It is most evident, of course, in her persistent rejection of Johnny. It has often been noticed how many of Trollope's heroines are peculiarly persistent in saying no to their suitors. In the Barset series alone, Mary Thorne, Lucy Robarts, Grace Crawley and Lily Dale, as Hugh Walpole pointed out, "do nothing else for hundreds and hundreds of pages but refuse their patient and persistent lovers."[8] Mario Praz suggests, "all of them reach the point of lacerating their own hearts by professing not to love their lovers. To put it shortly: there is in them a considerable degree of masochism."[9] It was of course not Trollope's intention to portray Mary Thorne or his favourite Lucy Robarts as masochists, though perhaps a shade of masochism, which he would rather have called self-denial, is included in his view of a good woman. (I will be discussing this question in more detail in a subsequent chapter.) But an examination of Lily Dale, set as she is in the centre of a set of self-tormentors, shows the degree of consciousness in Trollope's depiction of this element. For Mary Thorne and Emily Warton and Grace Crawley and the rest say no, for good if not quite sufficient reasons, only up to the penultimate chapter, but Lily says no right to the end of two long novels, and for no reason at all. Like Crosbie, she tries to rationalize her rejection of Johnny in various ways, both in *The Small House* and in *The Last Chronicle*: she still loves another man, or Johnny is fickle, or he gets too many people to plead for him, or she doesn't love him. But all these reasons crumble away, and in the second novel at least Trollope makes it plain not only that she now despises Crosbie but that she has come to love Johnny, though not with the rapture of her first love. Indeed, even within *The Small House*, Bell's words suggest the possibility of a happy outcome of a love between Lily and Johnny. "She is fond of him, – very fond. In a sort of a way she loves him – so well, that I feel sure she never mentions his name without some inward reference to her old childish thoughts and fancies" (II, 315). And her mother reflects of the proposed match, "if the thing could be done, Lily would be a happy woman" (II, 372). But Lily is vigilant, and steadfastly opposes all schemes to make her happy.

The publicity of Johnny's courtship, which she seems to resent, actually gives her an audience for her spectacular espousal of spinsterhood, and the more people urge the match the more she is determined against it. The anonymous letter from Madalina Demolines, asking "Is Miss L. D. engaged to marry Mr. J. E?" which might have given her the chance to show some loyalty to Johnny, rather stimulates her to commit herself again to a negative: " 'No,' said Lily, out loud. 'Lily Dale is not engaged to marry John Eames, and never will be so engaged' " (*Last Chronicle*, II, 198). But even at Johnny's first proposal, Lord De Guest is perhaps right when he comments on the news, "So the young lady has been perverse" (*SHA*, II, 391). Johnny's suit may be too early for an acceptance at this stage, but Lily need not have committed herself to a refusal in perpetuity, and she is altogether too vigorous in her rejection of any attempts to bring them together. Johnny's last proposal is phrased appropriately: "Lily, cannot you say yes?" But she cannot, though at this stage her only reason seems to be the barren determination not "to be talked out of the resolution of years" (*Last Chronicle*, II, 381–82). Lily refuses not because Johnny is not good enough for her, as some critics have suggested,[10] nor because she is not good enough for Johnny, as others contend,[11] but because she is constitutionally incapable of grasping at happiness; she is enamoured of suffering. Trollope makes this clear, I think, by placing her in the central role in a novel where all the characters, more or less obviously, are constantly acting in direct opposition to their own interests and well-being.

Even when we turn to her love affair with Crosbie, in which she was certainly ready enough to say yes, there is something of the same element in operation. This is the point of Trollope's emphasis on Lily's adverse judgement of Crosbie in the first scene of the novel. "But Mr. Crosbie is only a mere clerk" – those are the first words we hear of Lily's, and the first speech of the novel. And then, " 'I'll tell you what he is, Bell; Mr. Crosbie is a swell.' And Lilian Dale was right; Mr. Crosbie was a swell" (I, 12–13). She is in fact shrewd enough to perceive the social-climbing side of him: and she might have been shrewd enough to know that a clerk who gives himself airs, or a swell, is a man on the make, and not the kind to be faithful to a dowerless and unsophisticated country girl. It is not too much, I think, to postulate that with some part of her mind Lily knows, in fact, that he is likely to give her pain, and she gives herself to him for that reason. Indeed, after his desertion, when she is settling down to her life as jilted maiden and perpetual spinster, she ruefully recalls to her sister, "Don't you remember, when I called him a swell? Ah, dear! so he was. That was the mistake, and it was all my own fault, as I had seen it from the first" (II, 190). To see and acknowledge her mistake of the past is no gain for Lily, however, as she will not regulate her future conduct by her knowledge.

There is a great deal of harping on how she is burning her boats in her engagement, and a suggestion that even while she triumphs in Crosbie's love she is anticipating its withdrawal:

> And yet she knew that there was a risk. He who was now everything to her might die; nay, it was possible that he might be other than she thought him to be; that he might neglect her, desert her, or misuse her. But she had resolved to trust in everything, and, having so trusted, she would not provide for herself any possibility of retreat. (I, 171)

Hugh Walpole thought that Trollope had not made Crosbie sufficiently attractive. "He should have given him *some* attractions – or what are we to think about the desperate infatuation of the so-particular Lily?"[12] But I think this is Trollope's point – Crosbie *doesn't* have the kind of solid worth and likability that Johnny has, but he has about him, as it were, a smell of infidelity, a waft of the heartbreaker, that itself attracts girls like Lily. Other characters, including Bell, Bernard and Johnny, have intimations of his desertion well before he has given them outward cause. Lily's story is to demonstrate that "Love does not follow worth, and is not given to excellence; – nor is it destroyed by ill-usage, nor killed by blows and mutilation" (II, 2). Another case of the moth and the candle.

It is certainly true that when Crosbie does jilt her she wallows in her misery: "Lily declared that she still loved the man who had so ill-used her" (II, 2–3); Trollope might have said, if he was being as explicit here as in his subplots, that to some extent she loved him *because* he had so ill-used her. There may be some pathos in Trollope's account of "the wounded fawn," but there is also a good deal of shrewd assessment of a woman who is not only lying in the bed she has made for herself, but luxuriating in it. On the day of Crosbie's marriage to Lady Alexandrina – ironically on Valentine's day – she consecrates her morning to a kind of mental enactment of the ceremony. And she says at one point of the bride,

> "I should so like to see her. I feel such an interest about her. I wonder what coloured hair she has. I suppose she is a sort of Juno of a woman, – very tall and handsome. I'm sure she has not got a pug-

nose like me. Do you know what I should really like, only of course it's not possible; – to be godmother to his first child." (II, 191)

That fantasy is echoed in *The Last Chronicle*, this time by the outrageously self-dramatizing Mrs. Dobbs Broughton, who perpetually indulges in a kind of emotional masturbation as she promotes the match between her beloved Conway and Clara Van Siever:

> In one moment she resolved that she would hate Clara as woman was never hated by woman; and then there were daggers, and poison-cups, and strangling cords in her eye. In the next she was as firmly determined that she would love Mrs. Conway Dalrymple as woman never was loved by woman; and then she saw herself kneeling by a cradle, and tenderly nursing a baby, of which Conway was to be the father and Clara the mother. (II, 101)

It is an illuminating parallel. Lily's character is conceived with a great deal more delicacy, but there is in her something of Mrs. Dobbs Broughton, something of chosen martyrdom.

A parallel of a different kind is James's Isabel in *Portrait of a Lady*, another girl who spends much time rejecting eligible suitors and then accepts one who makes her miserable. Isabel is altogether a finer creature than Lily Dale, conceived on a larger scale and operating in a wider range, psychologically as well as geographically, than the provincial and missish Lily. But, at least according to one possible reading of the novel, Isabel's behaviour can be interpreted similarly. She seems to have an aesthetic sense of her own destiny that precludes her settling down to a comfortable and unspectacular life as Lord Warburton's wife. She sees herself, one suspects, as a heroine of tragedy, and it is partly this that makes her devote herself to a diabolical egoist like Osmond in the teeth of all her friends' opposition to the match. Early in the novel she hankers to see the ghost of Gardencourt, which Ralph tells her appears only to those who "have suffered first, have suffered greatly, have gained some miserable knowledge" (Ch. 5). She achieves at least this, and at Ralph's death at the end of the novel she has the sense of a spirit near her bed, for "she apparently had fulfilled the necessary condition" (Ch. 55).[13] Lily has evidently longed to see the same ghost, and like Isabel takes steps to fulfill the conditions.

Lily very sturdily refuses to be consoled. She suggests that to accept Johnny afterwards would be a kind of bigamy, since she considers herself virtually married to Crosbie. "If she died, and he came to me in five years' time, I would still take him. I should think myself constrained to take him," she says (II, 379); yet in the next novel, when this actually happens, she refuses to marry Crosbie, though she has forgiven him and still loves him, only because, she says, he would despise her for doing so.

"I *will* drown, and nobody *shall* save me" is the proverbial expression of this kind of behaviour.

A question arises here whether Johnny, in his pursuit of Lily, is not being almost as perverse as in his pursuit of Amelia. Does he sense, as Lily does of Crosbie, that here is someone who will make him unhappy, and so dedicate his life to her? It is an arguable point, but I think that in Eames, despite his temporary entanglements with Amelia and Madalina, Trollope has given us an essentially healthy man. Lily for him is happiness, and he does all he can to attain her; Johnny for her is happiness, too, but she spends her youth rejecting him.

No wonder Trollope did not share his readers' enthusiasm for this "female prig" (*Autobiography*, 154).[14] Lily's fans were always begging him to unite Lily with Johnny, but as he shrewdly observes, "Had I done so, however, Lily would never have so endeared herself to these people as to induce them to write letters to the author concerning her fate. It was because she could not get over her troubles that they loved her" (154). Trollope's readers, in fact, are like the characters in his novel, longing for what they would in fact be sorry to have.

Many minor characters, too, belong to Trollope's theme of perversity. Squire Dale, who likes to "indulge in that solace which an injured man finds in contemplating his injury" (II, 108), always makes it a grievance that Mrs. Dale does not come to his house, yet "Had he known his own wishes he must have acknowledged to himself that he was better pleased that Mrs. Dale should stay away" (I, 34). It is the same with Lady De Courcy and her awful husband. "The countess, in former days, had been heard to complain of her lord's frequent absence. But it is hard to please some women, – and now she would not always be satisfied with his presence" (I, 219). When one thinks of the savage and disgusting old earl, with his blackened, gnashing teeth, one sees why. His presence allows her to look back "with bitter regret to the happy days when she was deserted, jealous, and querulous" (I, 358). (In a novel where everyone is engaged in the pursuit of misery, "happy" is a word that Trollope uses with deliberate irony, as in the chapter on the Crosbie's separation, which is headed: "Showing how Mr. Crosbie became again a happy man" [II, 360]). The earl too is energetic about making himself unnecessarily uncomfortable by his excessive niggardliness. "It must be supposed that his self-imposed sufferings, with regard to money, rose rather from his disposition than his necessities" (I, 357). Even as peripheral a character as Mrs. Boyce, who hardly appears at all, is characterized when she does by her determination to complain. She is angry because her husband did not walk her home, but "if Mr. Boyce had gone home with her, she would have grumbled because he walked too fast" (II, 31–32).

Some self-imposed suffering, of course, takes the form of a morally laudable altruism, and Trollope examines this kind too, particularly in

1. Mrs. Dale indulges her gloom: Millais' illustration for *The Small House At Allington*, chapter 3

the "good" and loving sphere of Allington, which is opposed to the selfish world of Courcy Castle and London. Mrs. Dale is a generously self-sacrificing mother; and yet there is a certain air of self-congratulation about her when she resolutely stays at home, lonely and out of things, while her daughters go out to enjoy themselves. And she is surely more scrupulous in avoiding influencing her daughters than she need be. Though squire Dale asks her only to mention her predilection in favour of Bernard as a husband for Bell, she steadfastly refuses, and quarrels with him for asking. Bell's marriage to Bernard, we hear, would give Mrs. Dale "a realization to all her dreams of future happiness. . . . But, as she said to herself over and over again, all that must go for nothing" (I, 264). And in *The Last Chronicle* it is of her that the narrator comments, "mothers . . . can bring themselves to welcome the sacrifice of themselves with something of satisfaction" (I, 236).

Bell Dale, too, is a true relative of Lily, as she shows by her readiness to fall in love with Crosbie. Trollope reflects, "It is almost sad to think that such a man might have had the love of either of such girls" (I, 70). In refusing the rich Bernard whom she does not love and marrying the poor Dr. Crofts whom she does, she is acting like a normal healthy girl; and yet there is a kind of vehemence about her rejection of all considerations of money that makes her belong to Trollope's theme too. As Bernard reasonably argues, "surely the fact that our marriage would be in every way suitable as regards money should not set you against it" (I, 180). But Dr. Crofts's poverty is, in her mind, definitely a point in his favour, though his solicitude about his ability to support her in moderate comfort angers her. "As if a woman cannot bear more than a man!" she says, with a curious pride (I, 127). And, like Lily with Johnny, she finds it difficult to accept a worthy man whom she loves. At Crofts's declaration, "Bell started back from him. . . . She probably loved him better than any man in the world, and yet, when he spoke to her of love, she could not bring herself to understand him" (II, 123). And, merely because of the way he phrases his proposal, she finds herself, at the first asking, unable to say anything but "no" (II, 124). Even when they are engaged, and Crofts explains to her mother, "We shall not be rich –" Bell interrupts him vehemently, "I hate to be rich" (II, 278). And she can look on a period of prolonged separation from him with stern equanimity. There is something daunting about so much self-abnegation. Mrs. Dale and her daughters take the virtues of self-sacrifice, fidelity, and financial disinterestedness to a fanatic extreme, and perversely indulge in them.

This emphasis on the self-inflicted suffering of the individual characters in the novel expands into a vision of a perverse society, where manners and social forms, everyday discourse and gossip, the whole system of social distinction, even religion, all afford opportunity for further pursuit of the ugly and the painful, of much that is "past reason

hunted, and no sooner had,/Past reason hated, as a swallow'd bait."
Crosbie, who finds the earl's family with which he was so eager to unite
himself a humiliating burden rather than a passport to high society, is
only one of a number of characters who go through some agony to gain
what is not worth having. Trollope adapts Thackeray's theme of *vanitas
vanitatum* to his own purposes by showing to what an extent his social
climbers are conscious of the worthlessness of their aspirations even
while they are aspiring. The whole system of snobbery, which requires
that you crawl before your superiors and bluster to your inferiors, is
part of man's perversity, for Trollope's view of the snob here is of a man
who is nightmarishly conscious that he is humiliating himself. Sir Raffle
Buffle, in claiming a warm intimacy with Lord De Guest to Johnny,
knows that he is lying, and knows Johnny knows. Yet he keeps asking
him, "And how's my dear old friend?" – as one imagines, with a fixed
smile of agonized patronage on his face. "There are men who have the
most lively gratification in calling lords and marquises their friends,
though they know that nobody believes a word of what they say, – even
though they know how great is the odium they incur, and how lasting is
the ridicule which their vanity produces" (II, 409). Gazebee similarly
humiliates himself for Lady De Courcy, who makes it quite plain that
she despises him. He is always pressing her to be his guest, "and yet her
presence in his house would have made him miserable as long as she
remained there" (II, 129). And so with many kinds of social event, including formal dinner parties: "The owners of such houses . . . dread
the dinner which they resolve to give quite as much as it is dreaded by
their friends. They know that they prepare for their guests an evening of
misery, and for themselves certain long hours of purgatory which are
hardly to be endured. But they will do it" (I, 325). Social forms are
recurrently seen as giving pleasure to no one, and annoyance to most.
Hospitality is an imposition, entertainment produces ennui, and men
court intimacies that they do not enjoy. "Crosbie did not like such men
as John de Courcy; but nevertheless, they called each other old fellow,
poked each other's ribs, and were very intimate" (I, 228). By the accumulation of such small touches Trollope reiterates his major theme.

Religion too becomes a matter of self-inflicted and unreasonable discomfort. Old Mr. Harding's brief appearance reminds us, as it reminds
Crosbie, of a possible world of wholehearted love and a faith that is
combined with hope and charity and the pursuit of beauty and happiness. But the dominant vision is very different, and the self-castigating
Lady Rosina De Courcy, with her puritan conviction that one must
suffer in order to be devout, is the representative of religion in the world
of this novel. (She has much mellowed by the time she re-appears in *The
Prime Minister*.) She reigns over the ménage at Courcy Castle until "that
so-called day of rest, . . . under her dominion, had become to many of
them a day of restless torment" (I, 223).

There is also the standard background chorus of outraged morality in the novel, noticeable particularly in the part concerned with Palliser. Society is perpetually raising its hands in righteous indignation at the predicted indiscretion of its members, and, needless to say, gloatingly excited when its gossip about sin and ruined reputations comes true. Palliser perseveres in his uphill work with Lady Dumbello to some extent because his reputation paradoxically demands that he should compromise himself; for Lady Clandidlem and the other members of the chorus accord a certain admiration to those who gratify their expectations by sinning. So there is some advantage after all in the perverse pursuits in the novel. Cradell's affair with Mrs. Lupex does increase his reputation, and his landlady, who had mistakenly suspected him of eloping with her, is disappointed when her fears are not fulfilled: "As her suspicions subsided, her respect for him decreased. Such was the case also with Miss Spruce, and Amelia, and with Jemima" (II, 153). This is the boardinghouse version of the high society chorus when Palliser abandons his courtship of Lady Dumbello: "He never attempted to make love to her again, utterly disappointing the hopes of Lady De Courcy, Mrs. Proudie, and Lady Clandidlem" (II, 357). So Johnny in his affair with Amelia, and Crosbie in jilting Lily, hope for a certain social distinction in their roles of Don Juan and Lothario. There may be some rewards for the individual's perversity, but only because of the perversity of society, which like its members finds delight in what it also abhors.

Lily too has her gains from suffering: as the narrator in *Notes from Underground* says, perhaps suffering is just as great a benefit to her as well-being. But in the moral world of Allington, society's admiration for those who break its laws becomes rather an exaggerated deference to the sufferer. By being jilted and having her heart broken Lily achieves considerable status in her home and her community, and swiftly establishes her mastery over her mother and sister. "Ill-usage and illness together falling into her hands had given her such power, that none of the other women were able to withstand it" (II, 187). And her prolonged and determined spinsterhood gives her a license to say and do many things which would not have been allowed to her as a young girl, or as Mrs. Crosbie or Mrs. Eames either. When her mother urges her to go out for a walk with Johnny, telling her persuasively, "It would do you good," Lily evidently has her reasons for replying, "I don't want to be done good to, mamma" (II, 334).

Allington as a moral sphere, idyllic though some consider it, certainly has its drawbacks; and its inhabitants, solidly principled and well-meaning though they are, show considerable talent in making themselves and each other uncomfortable. Squire Dale and his sister-in-law are both as sensitive as if they were made without skin, with all their tissues raw. And it is not only the Squire who nurses his grievances and fingers his bruises: Mrs. Dale and her daughters do too. The whole part of the book on the proposed removal of the ladies from the Small House to lodgings in Guestwick is a history of how people may heap inconvenience and embarrassment on themselves for no sufficient cause. Nobody wants them to move, least of all themselves, and yet the process of packing relentlessly proceeds. It is the best sign of health and the human capacity occasionally to set things to rights after they have been put awry that at last Mrs. Dale and Lily are able to accomplish this little exchange about the decision to move: "Lily; I think I do repent. I think that it has not been well done." "Then let it be undone" (II, 323). But Lily has been incapable of applying that instruction to her own misjudged pledge.

Allington may not be entirely idyllic, but Courcy Castle, which also has its moral atmosphere, is almost a hell, where inhabitants pause in their self-torment only to torment each other. It is Trollope's equivalent of Gaunt House in *Vanity Fair*, where all the inmates are at each others' throats, and intent on making each other suffer, simply for the suffering's sake. Trollope departs to some extent from his habitual low mimetic mode to show how this heaven to which the socialite aspires is more like a hell to its inmates. The Earl De Courcy, referred to as "Old Nick," and the "Prince of Darkness" has the lurid colouring of a Dickensian character: "'I will have no bills, d'ye hear?' snarled the Earl, gnashing and snapping upon his words with one specially ugly black tooth" (II, 133); and his wife is in constant terror that he will strike her with his crutch. After the manner of many of Trollope's aristocrats, he hates his son and heir with a bitter hatred – and the son reciprocates. All the sons and daughters of the family are rivals, and many of their actions are undertaken simply to spite each other. Porlock, we hear, decides to marry as soon as he hears his younger brother's wife is about to give birth to a new potential heir, just "to cut him out" (I, 229). And as for the youngest brother, the ne'er-do-well hanger-on, "Where will John be when the governor goes off the hooks? Porlock wouldn't give him a bit of bread and cheese and a glass of beer to save his life; – that is to say, not if he wanted it" (I, 236). The final qualification conjures up the unpleasant picture of Porlock's gleefully thrusting cheese and beer between his dying brother's teeth in the event that he does *not* want it. Likewise the Countess, with quite gratuitous malice, rejoices in and promotes the misfortunes of others: "Whether Crosbie should eventually become her own son-in-law or not it came to her naturally . . . to bowl down the stumps of that young lady at Allington" (I, 246). All this Crosbie and the world well know, "yet none knows well/To shun the Heaven that leads men to this Hell."

Of course perversity is a recurring theme of Trollope's, part of his view of human nature, as Cockshut, for instance, points out.[15] In a passage that has been quoted more than once,[16] Trollope wrote:

They who do not understand that a man may be brought to hope that which of all things is the most grievous to him, have not observed with sufficient closeness the perversity of the human mind. (*He Knew He Was Right*, 364)

One of his favourite structuring images is that of Hamlet's two portraits, and he frequently portrays women, Like Alice Vavasor in *Can You Forgive Her?* and Emily Wharton in *The Prime Minister*, who have a perverse predilection for the satyr over Hyperion. And critics, particularly since Cockshut's emphasis on Trollope's studies of obsession and delusion in the later novels, have stressed his understanding of morbid psychology in single characters like Josiah Crawley, Cousin Henry, and Mr. Scarborough. But it is in *The Small House at Allington*, I think, that perversity becomes most definitely Trollope's theme, rather than simply one element in his view of human psychology. Here it operates not just in a single character, but in all the main figures, who thus illuminate the operative force in one another, and in the whole society. Perversity, the moth's attraction to the destructive flame, is the structuring principle, the common element that links the stories of Cradell and Palliser, Eames and Crosbie, and the crowd of minor characters from high and low life that form society, and makes them indeed "tend to the elucidation of the main story" of Lily Dale's self-devotion to pain and misery. Thackeray unifies a long novel about many different characters, families, and levels of society by making them all visibly belong in the world of Vanity Fair. Trollope, in his less emphatic manner, nonetheless presents a unified vision of human psychology and the relation of individual to society. In that each has to some extent resolved "evil, be thou my good," all his characters belong in some self-tormenting pandemonium, and one of its chambers is the Small House at Allington.

2 *Can You Forgive Her?*: The Meaning of Words and The Nature of Things

In a study of the Palliser series as a group, it is tempting to concentrate on the Glencora subplot of *Can You Forgive Her?* at the expense of the main plot, that which concerns Alice Vavasor.[1] The Glencora plot is the beginning of great things, whereas the Alice plot is the end of something not so great, Trollope's rejected play of years before, *The Noble Jilt*. But if Trollope, like his public, liked the novel chiefly as the initial appearance of Lady Glencora Palliser,[2] he had nonetheless brooded long over his noble jilt, Alice, and felt the need to get her story told: "The story of the struggle has been present to my mind for many years," he explained, within the novel itself (I, 474).

According to Hugh Walpole, Alice Vavasor is "one of the stickiest and most stupid in all the ranks of Trollope's heroines";[3] and she has similarly irritated readers and critics since the original appearance of *Can You Forgive Her?* The *Spectator* reviewer called her "uninteresting and unintelligible,"[4] and her vacillations about whom she should marry were dismissed as "a subject for mere drawing-room gossip" by the young James, who went on rather irritably, "The question is, Can we forgive Miss Vavasor? Of course we can, and forget her, too, for that matter."[5] Nevertheless, *Can You Forgive Her?* was popular, and sustained Trollope's reputation at its highest – his publishers paid him more for this novel than for any other in his career[6] – for Alice's failings were redeemed by Lady Glencora's attractions. "We do not fear to dogmatize when we say that by rights Lady Glencora is the heroine of the book," said James with authority.[7] Twentieth-century critics have by and large agreed with him. In this novel we have "an obvious case of the sub-plot swallowing the principal story," said Walpole; Robert Polhemus has

20

found the novel to be "maddeningly contradictory" because the Alice Vavasor story does not live up to the Lady Glencora Palliser story;[8] and, though he treats the main plot sympathetically, Stephen Wall in his introduction to the Penguin edition also asserts, that "what is really important in *Can You Forgive Her?* is the situation of the Pallisers."[9]

Alice's, it would seem, is a hopeless cause. In relation to Glencora she is undoubtedly the "heavy" – Amelia to Becky Sharp, or Elinor to Marianne Dashwood. She is serious to the point of prudishness in her pronouncements, and restrained and drearily unleavened in her dramatic reactions – she has none of Glencora's roguishness and sparkle. Glencora, without doubt, upstages her because she is charming and Alice is not. However, in discussing a novel in which the question of women's rights is to the fore, one may well point out that critics who are disposed to admire all kinds of intractable male characters *as creations* still tend to demand of female characters that they be charming *people* before they will grant tham applause, as though they were one's hostess or one's dinner companion rather than an imaginative creation. Who ever found Josiah Crawley charming? – yet nobody doubts he is one of Trollope's great achievements in characterization. But most of the young women that Trollope's readers have been disposed to admire have had to be vivacious and captivating, like Lily Dale or Lady Glencora. Alice Vavasor is certainly neither vivacious nor captivating, but then it is worth remembering that she was not intended to be. Trollope, though not elated, was quite satisfied with his performance in her characterization: "The character of the girl is carried through with considerable strength, but is not attractive," he wrote of her in the *Autobiography* (155).

Alice is not meant to be attractive – Trollope is quite clear about that. She is "gloomy", a word he had used definitively for her counterpart in the play, *The Noble Jilt*;[10] and she has no facility in being happy. At the end, when she is to be united with John Grey after all, Glencora says that if she were to give her joy, "you would put on a long face at once, and tell me that though the thing is to be, it would be much better that the thing shouldn't be. Don't I know you, Alice?" (II, 439). Yes, Glencora does know her, and so does Trollope. It is all part and parcel of Alice's problem that she should be morbidly gloomy.

Alice is a girl with a problem – as T. H. S. Escott pointed out, this novel shows Trollope to be a pioneer of the modern problem novel[11] – and at a time when Trollope's reputation has received a boost because A. O. J. Cockshut[12] and others have focused on his explorations of morbid psychology, I believe Alice deserves her share of attention as a psychological study. Her fiancé John Grey is aware that in dealing with her he must in some sense be ministering to a mind diseased: he resolves "to treat all that she might say as the hallucination of a sickened imagination, – as the effect of absolute want of health" (I, 143). But Alice's sickness is important in the ideological structure of the novel too, for her malady is an extreme version of one that is afflicting many of the characters, and which Trollope sees in this novel as shaking the very nation's grasp on reality.

Trollope has carefully described the environmental factors that would be likely to make Alice a "case.'" She lost her mother in infancy, and was reared by a Calvinistic old snob, Lady Macleod, who sent her to school abroad. Having financial independence and a taste for using it, she then settled with her father in London, sharing the household expenses with him. But John Vavasor is a weak and irresponsible parent who, having spent years as a bachelor, cannot bring himself to change his habits when his daughter moves in with him; and so he neglects her shamelessly, leaving her alone night after night while he dines and socializes at his club. This paternal neglect is an important factor in Alice's development – she has grown to distrust love and to be proud of not relying on it. Usually Trollope emphasises the strong bond between father and daughter, returning to it almost as often as to the antagonism between father and son. His quiet chronicling of the several key points at which Alice is unable to turn to her father in time of need has some force by contrast.

Her financial independence is an extra strain. Unlike most women of her age, she has complete control of a competent income, but though she values her independence, and resents any attempts at influence, it is a burden to her, for she is without anything to do with her money or her leisure. The women's "work" at which she is so often employed, stitching at unspecified embroideries in her drearily tidy sitting-room, surrounded by useless ornaments, is for her only a substitute for basket-weaving.[13]

Lonely and unoccupied as she is, she becomes hyper-conscious, brooding, even morbidly obsessed. And her vacillating and seemingly irrational decisions reflect this. As Glencora phrases it, what a wild game she plays with her lovers! Here is a woman who was initially almost engaged to marry her cousin George; then, after he breaks faith with her, she loves and engages herself to the worthy John Grey, but sub-sequently breaks that engagement, though apparently without ceasing to love him. Next, she re-engages herself to George; next, that engage-ment too is broken; and finally she re-engages herself to Grey, and at last marries him. And all this is done by a girl who, we are to believe, is constant in her affections and rigidly principled in her behaviour. What can be the explanation for such a contradiction? Again, the characters within the novel are bemused, as well as the readers. Lady Midlothian, virago though she is, acts as an on-stage chorus for our reactions: "The thing was so inscrutable!" (II, 498). It is the puzzle that the *Spectator* critic gave up in despair when he dismissed Alice as unintelligible and uninteresting. But Trollope has given the reader sufficient guidance to solve it for himself, and in the process by which Alice becomes intelligible she also becomes interesting. Her behaviour, so curiously at odds with her character, gives the clue to the operative forces in other characters, and accounts for other situations, both personal and political.

So, in spite of the main current of critical opinion, I take Alice to be properly the heroine of *Can You Forgive Her?*, the central character whose dilemma is echoed and amplified in the rest of the novel, and becomes indeed its major unifying theme. Lady Glencora, bless her, is no doubt the heroine of a larger unit, the whole of the Palliser series. But in this novel she is, however attractive, the heroine only of the secondary plot.

Can You Forgive Her? has three distinct plots, two of them, Alice's and Mrs. Greenow's, imported directly from Trollope's old play, and one, Glencora's, invented for the occasion. George Bartley, in the criticism of the play which Trollope resolved to consider as gospel, had complained that there was no really sympathetic character;[14] and Glencora may have been created to supply the deficiency. Certainly she succeeded in upstaging Alice.

Trollope has constructed his three plots as a set of more than usually obvious parallels. He shows a girl, a wife and a widow each hesitating between two suitors – "the worthy man and the wild man," as Alice calls them (I, 23), – and concerned not only with her own emotional preferences in the matter, but with the just and equitable disposal of herself and her fortune. The question of choice, with the factors involved in it, is thus the major theme of the novel. Of course the mind in process of decision is perennially interesting to Trollope, but here more than usually he makes the hesitation the major action of the novel, as well as the common factor in the three plots.

Here again Trollope employs the image from *Hamlet* of Gertrude's two husbands. Kate Vavasor, trying to persuade Alice to marry George instead of Grey, tells her, "It is Hyperion to a Satyr," but Alice asks pointedly, "And which is the Satyr?" (I, 77). Later, when Alice has sent the Apollo-like Grey packing, and committed herself to her Satanic cousin, she has learned the difference: "As the mental photographs of the two men forced themselves upon her, she could not force herself to forget those words – 'Look here, upon this picture – and on this' " (I, 458). The claims of beauty and ugliness, and of moral worth and worthlessness, are balanced and interacting. Alice's worthy suitor is beautiful and godlike, her wild one is marred by his Cain-like scar. But so much the more does she feel she ought to devote herself to the disfigured and imperfect one. In Glencora's men, however, appearance belies the reality, and it is the unworthy one, the ruined wastrel Burgo Fitzgerald, who is beautiful, while her worthy husband is totally undistinguished in appearance. The widow Greenow, the only one who does finally commit herself to the wild suitor, is similarly balanced between the portly, well-heeled Mr. Cheeseacre of Oiley-mead(!) and the flamboyant scamp Captain Bellfield. All three women have, in one form or another, that characteristic vice or virtue of so many Trollopian ladies, the desire to sacrifice themselves, and by so doing to redeem their fallen men. A great part of the attraction of George, of Burgo, of Bellfield, is that life with them would involve danger and self-sacrifice, whether in the form of lost fortune, lost reputation, or lost love. This is the way Glencora, for example, contemplates union with Burgo:

> She knew Burgo Fitzgerald to be a scapegrace, and she liked him the better on that account. She despised her husband because he had no vices. She would have given everything she had to Burgo, – pouring her wealth upon him with a total disregard of herself, had she been allowed to do so. She would have forgiven him sin after sin, and might perhaps have brought him round, at last, to some life not absolutely reckless and wretched. (II, 363)

Thrown into the scale of decision for all three women, to complicate the choice between the physical and moral alternatives, is the financial factor. All the worthy men are well off (in Cheeseacre's eyes his wealth indeed constitutes his worth), and for perfect symmetry all of them even subsidize the wild suitor at some point or other. But the wild men are all short of cash, and each is in need of his lady's. It is a set of love affairs in which emotional and financial considerations are inextricably entangled.

In his depiction of the Satyrs, the wild men, Trollope is voicing the common-sense Victorian reaction to Romanticism. George Vavasor's scar, like his moody and violent behaviour, relate him to Cain and Ahab, and other Satanic heroes dear to the Romantic imagination. Burgo is surely a recreation of the popular image of Byron:

> He was as handsome as ever; – a man whom neither man nor woman could help regarding as a thing beautiful to behold; – but not the less was there in his eyes and cheeks a look of haggard dissipation, – of riotous living, which had become wearisome, by its continuance, even to himself. (I, 369)

And his dreams of life with Glancora are sardonically compared with Byron's account of Juan and Haidée (I, 373). The significant locations for these relationships are heavy with romantic associations. Alice is first induced to consider giving up Grey for George on a balcony overlooking the Rhine at Basle on her first trip to Switzerland, and resolves

to marry George in Wordsworth country, among the fells in Westmorland. Glencora can best re-kindle her love for Burgo among the
ruins of a mediaeval Priory in moonlight. The good men, Grey and
Palliser, with their sensible notions about comfort and sufficient in-
comes and domestic tranquility, are to the romantic dreadfully dull. So
Glencora says to Alice of Palliser:

'He is so good; – isn't he?'
'Very good,' said Alice. 'I know no one better.'
'And so dull!' said Lady Glencora. 'But I fancy that all husbands are
dull from the nature of their position.' (II, 334)

Yet George is a would-be murderer, and Burgo little better than a
burnt-out firework; and both of them have a very unromantic concern
for their ladies' bank balances. The women are, in fact, able to estimate
them truly with one part of their minds throughout the book, and finally, like Tennyson's Guinevere, to understand that the "good" man is
also the *best*, from all points of view.

But Trollope was trying to do something more subtle than simply
watch three women balance the pros and cons and come to a decision
according to the result, intricately though he has complicated their
problems. He is alert to the unpredictability of the human mind. Alice
can and does add up and subtract and compare and contrast the debits
and credits of her two men, and she can always come to the right
answer: Grey is physically and morally, as well as economically,
George's superior; moreover, she loves him, not George, and is
engaged to marry him, not George. Duty and inclination should unite
to make hers a simple story of a girl happily united to the man she loves.
And yet she breaks her engagement to him and betrothes herself to
George. Her conduct is totally at odds with her character. *Why?*

It seems that Alice's lonely and brooding life has made her almost two
people. She has come to think differently from what she feels, and she
has lost the ability to reconcile the various contradictory impulses of her
consciousness. Alice has a *theory*, and to that theory the realities of the
relative values of the two men, and of her own feelings for them, are
made to bend. Grey is accurate in his diagnosis when he says that Alice
has been a jilt because she has "halted between two minds" (II, 433).
Alice's mind has been divided; but as halting between two minds she is
only an example of a besetting malady in humanity at large. In this
novel Trollope is exploring the discrepancy between theory and fact,
and between language and reality. People make for themselves out of
their own minds artificial constructs about the way things are, and formulate them in language, and believe in them. Words have been

wrenched from things, and expression belies the feelings that are meant to be expressed. Promises are far from performance, and profession from conduct. The gap between profession and conduct is not a simple matter of hypocrisy – though in Mrs. Greenow's lamentations over her "dear departed" Trollope approaches the traditional satire on the Blifils and the Pecksniffs of the world – but a more complex study of the almost schizoid propensity of human beings to live separate lives in their minds and their hearts. It is almost as though language constituted a different sphere of experience, instead of being primarily a means of expression.

The force of language is a constant concern at many levels of the novel, and words, and what is said, or written, are all very much part of the subject matter, and under discussion by the characters as well as by the narrator. Alice's "word," considering how many times she gives it, is of major import in the plot, and she indulges in much agonized specula-tion of the kind: "Could she permit it to be said of her . . . that three times she would go back from her word?" (I, 475). Miss Palliser makes much ado about the "word" she is to say to Glencora (I, 427–428), Grey pleads with Alice, "those words should not be spoken" (I, 141), George demands "one word of love" from Alice, as though the word were a perfectly acceptable substitute for the love (I, 449), and so on. Close to the end of the novel the narrator comments sadly, a propos of an attempted explanation between Grey and Palliser, "We all know that neither of them would put the matter altogether in a true light. Men never can do so in words, let the light within themselves be ever so clear" (II, 463). The characters themselves take up the chorus, and la-ment the difficulties of expression: "There are some things that won't get themselves told," says Glencora (II, 270); "It is not always easy for a man to show what he thinks by what he says," laments her husband (II, 225); "There are things which happen in a day which it would take a lifetime to explain," comments Grey (I, 464). And Alice writes in a letter: "I must tell it you all, though it is dreadful to me that I should have to write it" (II, 172). A character's mode of interpreting "the meaning of words and the nature of things" becomes, in fact, that which most fully defines him (II, 274).

The disjunction between language and reality, which affects so many lives, becomes Trollope's major concern, and he dramatizes it chiefly through Alice's almost double life. With her the separation between the two realms has become such as almost to incapacitate her for conduct-ing her life. There is a sense in which she has made war on words. She resents the obligation which is involved in her original engagement to Grey. She is a woman who values freedom, and she finds that this promise, this verbal commitment to future action, stultifyingly limits her. See for instance this exchange with Lady Macleod soon after her engagement:

'A young woman that is going to be married, as you are – '
'As I am, – perhaps.'
'That's nonsense, Alice. Of course you are. . . .' (I, 15)

Constituted as she is, Alice sets about proving her power for independent action. And again when Grey writes with confidence of their coming marriage, she reacts: "She had no husband; – not as yet. He spoke
of their engagement as though it were a betrothal, as betrothals used to
be of yore; as though they were already in some sort married" (I, 28).
The tyranny of her own given pledge oppresses her, and she rebels
against it.

As she promises that which is unwilling to perform, so she does that
which she hates to hear put into words. When her grandfather refers to
her "jilting Mr. Grey" she acts as though the proverbial "names" do
have the power of sticks and stones to break her bones. "Poor Alice! It is
hard to explain how heavy a blow fell upon her from the open utterance
of that word! . . . She was a jilt; and perhaps it may have been well that
the old man should tell her so" (I, 414). Again we hear of her similar
reaction when her father comments on her latest decision not to marry
the last man she said she was going to marry: " 'Things of that sort are
so often over with you!' This was very cruel. Perhaps she had deserved
the reproach, but still it was very cruel. The blow struck her with such
force that she staggered under it" (II, 257). It is true that such a speech
from her father is hardly sympathetic; for of course there is a delicacy
and gentleness necessary in human relations that consists in *not* saying
much of what is undoubtedly true – and that too is part of Trollope's
vision of human nature here. Yet we are reminded again of the curiously
double life that Alice leads, which makes her particularly aware of the
injury of having her conduct named in words.

So Alice in some sort drives a wedge between the word and the thing,
and a whole series of elements of life that should be inextricably related
are disastrously wrenched apart – theory and practice, language and
reality, head and heart. In the important chapter in which Trollope accounts for her decision to break her engagement to Grey, he explains
that she is a girl who has *thought* too much about marriage, and about
an abstract idea of her lot in life. "She had gone on thinking of the
matter till her mind had become filled with some undefined idea of the
importance to her of her own life. What should a woman do with her
life? There had arisen around her a flock of learned ladies asking that
question" (I, 134). Trollope's attitude to the cause of women's rights was
complicated: he seems to have had a rare sympathy with women who
were stifled in their domestic roles, while being hostile to the
movement: the two Misses Palliser, in this novel, who are of the stuff
that suffragettes are made of, are stuffy and ineffectual spinsters, quite

unsympathetically drawn. But he is meticulous in showing just how Alice's mind is affected by the fashionable talk:

> She was not so far advanced as to think that women should be lawyers and doctors, or to wish that she might have the privilege of the franchise for herself; but she had undoubtedly a hankering after some second-hand political manoeuvring. She would have liked, I think, to have been the wife of the leader of a Radical opposition, in the time when such men were put into prison, and to have kept up for him his seditious correspondence while he lay in the Tower. She would have carried the answers to him inside her stays, – and have made long journeys down into northern parts without any money, if the cause required it. She would have liked to have around her ardent spirits, male or female, who would have talked of 'the cause,' and have kept alive in her some flame of political fire. (I, 136)

It is clear from the reference to the Tower and the messages in the stays that Alice's political ambitions are really fiction, the mere stuff of romance and idle daydream, which should be recognized as such. "As it was," Trollope continues, "she had no cause." Alice is not really politically minded, even if she does dare to mention the Ballot at Mr. Palliser's dinner table. She craves a bit of excitement, but the political ambition that she thinks she has is all simply a fabrication, a theory that she must fulfil herself by doing something with her life instead of burying herself as John Grey's wife in Cambridgeshire. So she denies her genuine love for Grey to unite herself to George, trying to convince herself that George is to be a moving spirit in the world, and that she, as the woman behind him, will thus do her part in bettering it. When George in fact attains his ambition and becomes a member of Parliament, she is hard put to it to raise any enthusiasm.

Some readers, who have not been able to understand how completely she can delude herself by thus believing in an entirely theoretical construct instead of the present reality of her own love, have tried to account for her conduct by suggesting that, as George himself believes, she really loved her cousin all along, with a deep and guilty passion: that George is the libidinal figure, as Grey is the embodiment of the super-ego, and hence that here we have the familiar conflict of passion with duty.[15] But this is not the story that Trollope has written. He is not only emphatic in his commentary that Alice's love for Grey – and it is a sexual love, even if it is combined with "esteem" – never wavers, but he powerfully dramatizes her physical revulsion from George's sexual approaches. When he visits her after receiving her written acceptance of his written proposal, "He was standing close to her now, and she could not escape from him. She was trembling with fear lest worse might betide her even than this. ... At this moment he inspired her with disgust rather than with love" (I, 445–446). But Alice is by no means "sexless," as Polhemus has called her,[16] for within the bounds allowed him Trollope is quite explicit about her sexual attraction to Grey. "The memory of John Grey's last kiss still lingered on her lips," we hear (I, 443); and she recalls how he "had come and had touched her hand, and the fibres of her body had seemed to melt within her at the touch, so that she could have fallen at his feet" (I, 473).[17] That may not sound much like D. H. Lawrence, but it is still pretty strong stuff for a novelist writing in the prudish sixties.

It is significant that George's proposal to Alice, and her acceptance of it, are both in the form of letters, for clearly it is only because the offer is made in this way, at a distance, in words alone, and with no physical presence to enforce a direct and personal reaction, that she is able to accept it. She can do in written words what she cannot do in deed – give herself to a man she does not love. Indeed letters play an indispensable part in this novel, since there is an indirection in this method of communication that matches the hiatus between expression and essence. Trollope (naturally enough, considering his work with the Post Office) regularly fills his novels with letters, and the timing of the collection and delivery of the mails is frequently of import in the action. One thinks of Lily Dale's pathetic interception of the postman who day after day brings no love-letter from Crosbie, or the masterly correspondence of Lady Carbury that initially defines the world of *The Way We Live Now*. But the letters in *Can You Forgive Her?* advance the action in a different way, since they are not just communication but almost action in themselves. In a kind of parody of his own subject Trollope introduces the Misses Palliser, a pair of avid correspondents. According to their cousin, "They write wonderful letters" – but the letters they write are to people they do not know, on totally impersonal subjects, and they never read the answers they get. "No; their delight is in writing. They sit each at her desk after breakfast, and go on till lunch" (I, 291–2). It is an image of how communication can become an end in-itself, and totally separate from what it is that is to be communicated. A great deal of trouble is occasionally taken to do by letter what ought to be far more simply dealt with in an interview. So George, who lives within easy walking distance of his fiancée in London, goes all the way to Westmorland to bully his sister into writing to Alice from there to ask her for the use of her money. This elaborate indirection allows people to live double lives, and to create sets of relations that are impossible to maintain in the light of the realities of human feelings.

The letters between Alice and George essentially constitute all there is of their engagement, which is definitely suspended when they are in each other's presence. After she had actually seen George in the flesh again, Alice realizes the impossibility of consummating the pledge she has made to become his wife: "Must she submit to his caresses, – lie on his bosom, – turn herself warmly to his kisses? 'No,' she said, 'no,' – speaking audibly, as she walked about the room; 'no; – it was not in my bargain; I never meant it.' But if so what had she meant; – what had been her dream? Of what marriage had she thought, when she was writing that letter back to George Vavasor?" (I, 473). Of course she had been thinking of the marriage of George the Radical Errant and Alice the English Joan of Arc, the figures of her political romance, not of the actual physical Alice Vavasor of Queen Anne Street and her scheming cousin. She begins to be aware of how totally she has separated the two realms of experience, and the impossibility of reconciling her deeds to her verbal undertakings. Well may George ask, when she won't let him touch her, "Did that letter which you wrote to me from Westmorland [her acceptance of his proposal] mean anything?" Alice can only plead, "George, do not strive to make me think it meant too much" (II, 73). Trollope neatly sums up: "She had said that she would become George Vavasor's wife, but she wished that the saying so might be the end of it" (I, 443).

Bradford Booth, citing Michael Sadleir in the same context,[18] has found fault with the novel because of its infringement of poetic justice: Alice, for all her vacillations and breaches of promise, gets off very easily, being happily united with the noble John Grey after all. But this objection overlooks Trollope's calculated chapter "Showing How Alice Was Punished." Here Alice tells her cousin Kate of George's violent words and actions on his last visit. "He swore . . . that he would punish me for my perfidy with some fearful punishment," she relates; and then, turning the threat over in her mind, she goes on, "Punishing me, indeed! What punishment can be so hard as that which he has already inflicted?" (II, 172–173). This seems at first glance somewhat hysterically exaggerated. He has not actually struck her, or publicly shamed her, or administered such poetic justice as may be required for a woman who has thrice jilted a fiancé. This is the worst that he does: "Then he came and sat by me, and took hold of my arms. Oh, Kate; I cannot tell it you all. He put his mouth close to my ear, and said words which were terrible, though I did not understand them" (II, 174). It is enough. Alice has sinned in words rather than in deeds, and in words she is punished. Her delusion in living a disjointed existence is now ended. The whispered obscenities, and the enforced physical contact with the man she has been able to consider only at a distance and in theory, have the force to jolt her back to an awareness of the proper relation of words and things.

One further instance of how Alice contributes to Trollope's theme is her dual role in the novel, protagonist in her own plot and mentor in Glencora's. It is one of her unattractive characteristics that while she can be making a disastrous mess of her own life, with her broken pledges and misjudged decisions, she can be astonishingly sentimous in her judgments on Glencora's behaviour, and in the very matters in which she is herself most at fault. When Glencora asks her, " 'Alice, you are very wise. What am I to do?' ... Alice had no doubt as to what her cousin should do. She should be true to her marriage-vow, whether that vow when made were true or false" (I, 353). *She* can talk! – one feels inclined to interject hotly. She is vehement that Glencora should by no means renew the connection with Burgo by meeting him at Monkshade, but she had herself utterly rejected Lady Macleod's advice that she should not renew *her* connection with George on the trip to Switzerland. And when Glencora says that the watchfulness of her two "duennas" makes her the more determined to give them reason to disapprove, Alice tells her gravely, "I think, if I had been you, I would not have allowed their presence to make any difference to me" (II, 272) – when Alice has throughout been remarkable for reacting perversely from any attempt at guidance from *her* moral supervisors. The disjunction between her advice and her conduct is a cause for some irony at her expense. As Glencora tells her affectionately, "You are so wise. Only you haven't brought your own pigs to the best market, after all" (II, 270). And in fact Alice's erratic conduct is perhaps the main reason why someone like Glencora can accept her as a friend as well as a mentor: "I can manage to put myself on a par with a girl who has played such a wild game with her lovers as you have done," she tells Alice (II, 277). Alice is of course perfectly convincing in this very contradition between principle and practice. Most of us have at some time irritably responded to cavillers, "Don't do what I do, do what I say!" And indeed, Glencora neatly sums up Alice's character with a proverbial expression: "That is very easily said, my dear, but by no means so easily done" (II, 272).

Glencora too belongs to the theme, though since her troubles in her marriage are real, and her love for Burgo is undoubtedly a fact, and no mere exhalation from a brooding, over-active mind, her delusion is not as great as Alice's. Delusion, however, her great temptation no doubt is, as Trollope makes clear. Again his critics have wished Trollope had been more daring, and had actually let Glencora elope with Burgo, as she contemplates: "If Mr. Trollope," the *Spectator* critic speculated, "had had the heart (shall we say the nerve?) to ruin Lady Glencora, he might have given (what is rare with him) a genuinely tragic interest to his story."[19] But again they were wanting Trollope to write a different story from the one he was attempting. For in fact Glencora, speculate about it though she certainly does, is never really close to committing adultery.

In this novel Trollope is constantly visualizing his characters as vocal beings. In the first scene of our introduction to Glencora, when she rattles away to a tongue-tied Alice, she defines herself accurately as a "talker." (Her taciturn husband she classifies as one of the "non-talkers" of the world, though this does not preclude his being a "speaker" – "for Mr. Palliser has plenty to say in the House, and they declare that he's

2. Glencora broods over her lost love: Taylor's illustration for *Can You Forgive Her?*, chapter 58

one of the few public men who've got lungs enough to make a financial statement without breaking down" [I, 275]).

Glencora is indeed a talker – Alice on one occasion reproves her for lacking "the reticence which all women should practise" (I, 319) – and she almost talks herself into an elopement with Burgo Fitzgerald. But, really, talk is all that there is of the project.[20] Trollope maintains suspense, and makes the reader think she is closer to the abyss than she is, by introducing the side issue of the two "duennas," male and female, whom she determines to shock; but really they, rather than her own real inclination, are the reason she goes even as far as she does in capitulating to Burgo.

She is certainly emphatic in talking of her love, though she is to remain far from consummating it: "I would give everything I have in the world to have been true to him. They told me that he would spend my money. Though he should have spent every farthing of it, I regret it; though he should have made me a beggar, I regret it. They told me that he would ill-use me, and desert me, – perhaps beat me. I do not believe it; but even though that should have been so, I regret it. It is better to have a false husband than to be a false wife" (I, 351). "Glencora, do not speak like that," interposes Alice; and the speaking is perhaps the major extent of the sin. Glencora's outburst certainly rings truer than Alice's cerebral fantasies about imprisoned Radicals and messages stowed in stays, but the heiress's references to farthings and beggars suggest that here too there is an element of romanticizing. Similarly she can best contemplate elopement with Burgo in the Priory ruins by moonlight – her dream vanishes in a drawing room in the ordinary light of day. She has had her genuine love for Burgo, and there has been a romance between them, but their relationship belongs in her irrecoverable past, and her verbal revivals of it do not constitute a real alternative to the present and consummated fact that she is *now* and in reality Palliser's wife. Burgo's letter, the invitation to elope, she keeps with her as the palpable extension of their love, but unlike Alice, who is so convinced by the written proposal from George Vavasor that she writes an assent, Glencora never answers it. She waltzes with Burgo, she exchanges some tender words as a last testament of their past love, she allows him to kiss her – and she dismisses him. When it actually comes to the point, she has no hesitation. Her passionate speeches and speculations vanish away, and reality, and the romantic construct that she has substituted for it, bear again their proper relation. Trollope is explicit about his theme at the climactic moment of her decision:

'Cora,' he said.

But she had now recovered her presence of mind, and understood what was going on. She was no longer in a dream, but *words and things bore to her again their proper meaning*. 'I will not have it, Mr. Fitzgerald,' she answered, speaking almost passionately. '. . . Do as I bid you. Go and leave me, and do not return.' (II, 129; my italics)

And when this dream has vanished away, and been recognized as no more than a dream, Trollope thus analyzes the essentially artificial nature of her temptation: "She had had courage enough, – or shall we rather say sin enough, – to think of going with him, – to tell herself that she would do so; to put herself in the way of doing it; nay, she had had enough of both to enable her to tell her husband that she had resolved that it would be good for her to do so. But she was neither bold enough nor wicked enough to do the thing. . . . Therefore, knowing now that it was so, she tore up the letter that she had carried so long, and burnt it in the fire" (II, 234). To have kept the letter proposing elopement in her pocket, secretly, has been her most palpable crime; and so by burning the words of the proposal, she effectively exorcises the temptation. So she comes to know herself. "I can think of it, scheme for it, wish for it; – but as for doing it, that is beyond me. Mr. Palliser is quite safe," she concludes reconciledly (II, 343). Palliser, when Glencora is pregnant with the long-awaited heir and all their troubles are over, reflects exuberantly, "Burgo Fitzgerald was a myth" (II, 415). The myth, like other myths, has its own power, however, and it is to figure as a definitive component in Glencora's consciousness throughout her married life and beyond, as we discover in *The Duke's Children*. But for practical purposes he is right – Mr. Palliser is quite safe, as Glencora says.

Alice, too, when she has recognized that she could never in fact bring herself to marry George, is amazed that she "had been mad enough to think and talk of such a marriage" (II, 285). Theirs are both stories not so much of a conflict between passion and duty as of a recognition of the fictions they have perpetrated on themselves and of the process by which they have almost speculated themselves into infidelity and misery. Like Alice, though to a lesser degree, Glencora has manifested herself as a different person in expression from that she is in essence.

Trollope carefully describes the two worthy lovers as men who are aware of the dangers of language, and mindful of the necessity of keeping it properly related to reality. Of Palliser we hear at the outset that "he was very careful in his language, labouring night and day to learn to express himself with accuracy" (I, 303). He distrusts oratory and flourishes of rhetoric as the politician's counterfeit; as a "speaker" his main wish is to communicate his knowledge. "He desired also to be honoured for his knowledge. But he had no desire to be honoured for the language in which his knowledge was conveyed" (I, 303). Trollope makes the distinction carefully. Palliser's worthiness resides partly in the fact that he is "not prone to give words a stronger significance than they should bear" (II, 242).

Palliser is however somewhat stunted in his humanity because of his inhibition in expression: "It is not always easy for a man to show what he thinks by what he says," he comments sadly (II, 225); and his marriage is no joy to himself or his wife until he learns to communicate more than mere facts and figures. Grey too cannot make Alice understand that he loves her because he has no flourishes of language or gesture, but he is more articulate and has a fuller understanding of the dangerous dichotomy of language and reality than Palliser. He is right to appeal to Alice before she comes out with her speech of dismissal, "Do not say to me the words that you were about to say. . . . I think I know what those words were to be. If you love me, those words should not be spoken" (I, 141); for Alice's words are essentially untrue in being without a real referent. And unlike Alice, who reacts agonizedly to the appelatives "jilt" and "prude," he is unmoved by his rival's name-calling. He refuses to let George's blustering and threats move him to extravagant action – that is, he will not allow an exchange of words to become an exchange of bullets – and when George taunts him, "Then you are a coward," he replies calmly, "Perhaps I am; – but your saying so will not make me one" (II, 404). Not dashingly romantic, this, but Grey is the appropriate hero of the novel in refusing to let words betray him into a contradiction of essence.

As for the villain: – George Vavasor is in a sense deluded in the same way that Alice is. He too, being solitary and brooding (though in his case this is from choice rather than necessity), has "taught himself some theories of a peculiar nature" (I, 384), and he too constructs mental pictures of himself in certain fictional roles, and acts against his character and against the realities of his circumstances, to try to realize them. When, by smothering his scruples and taking his fiancée's money, he has actually gained his seat in Parliament, he finds he is totally uninterested in the proceedings. By this time his mental picture of himself as Radical leader has given way to that of injured outcast and master criminal, and "in the House he sat all the night with his hat over his eyes, making those little calculations [of murder] of which I have spoken" (II, 254). So much for the use he makes of the seat in Parliament for which he has sold himself. His various roles displace each other, allowing none to become the real expression of himself. His violence is real and dangerous; but even here many of his threats and gestures are mere posturings. When he tells his mistress he intends to blow out his brains, and shows her the pistol, "She knew enough of his usual manner to be aware that his threats of self-destruction were probably unreal" (II, 399). A reviewer like James wished that Trollope had finished off his villain with a courageous splash of blood,[21] but again it was not Trollope's purpose to allow this egoistic self-dramatizer to fulfil any of his fantasies of political brilliance, heartbreaking, murder, or suicide, and George simply fades unspectacularly out of the picture, emigrating to America.

In the realm of language, George is unlike Alice in being a deceiver.
"He must be a very clever sort of man, I think," comments his grandfather, "when he has talked you out of such a husband as John Grey" (I,
415). His "talking" is not a matter of direct lies or hypocrisy, but he
speaks for effect, and frames his propositions craftily with an eye to the
person he is trying to persuade, deliberately suspending his own spon-
taneous feelings in order to speak what will most get at his listener. He
uses both his recklessness and his want of money in such a way as to
appeal to Alice's zeal for self-sacrifice and her self-image. "For myself I
know that there is much in my character and disposition to make me
unfit to marry a woman of the common stamp," he writes with apparent
humility, but in fact with a conceit that is also calculated to reach her
peculiar vanity (I, 387). And he manages to speak occasionally with passion as though he loved her, though all he has of genuine emotion to
work with is his own desire that she should adore *him*. His letter of
proposal is strictly an exercise in rhetoric; it is not winning Alice that he
cares about, but success in the enterprise of persuasion, once he has undertaken it: "Whether or no he cared to marry his cousin was a point so
little interesting to him that chance might decide it for him [he literally
sends the letter on the toss of a coin]; but when chance had decided that
he did wish it, it was necessary for his honour that he should have that
for which he had condescended to ask" (I, 402). So George like Alice
separates the expression from the thing expressed; only he is the
manipulator and she, for the most part, the one who is manipulated.

George's election campaign to sit as member for the Chelsea districts
gives a political dimension to the theme. He runs on the slogan "Vote
for Vavasor and the River Bank," and pledges himself to the project of
embanking the Thames from Westminster to Pimlico, by which much
profit would accrue to Chelsea:

> 'But it will never be done' [he points out to his election agent].
> 'What matters that?' and Mr. Scruby almost became eloquent as he
> explained the nature of a good parliamentary subject. 'You should
> work it up, so as to be able to discuss it at all points. . . . If it were
> done, that would be an end of it, and your bread would be taken out
> of your mouth." (II, 46)

What matters is not that the project should be completed, but that the
campaigning politician should have a "subject" to make speeches
about. The talk is an end in itself. And so it is with speeches in the
House. During an address delivered with blistering indignation, it
becomes "evident that, in spite of his assumed fury, the gentleman was
not irate" (II, 15). Such are the protestations of the men who govern the
nation – full of sound and fury, signifying nothing. There is no doubt a
need for the authorial aphorism directed at the political aspirant:

"There are many rocks which a young speaker in Parliament should avoid, but no rock which requires such careful avoiding as the rock of eloquence. Whatever may be his faults, let him at least avoid eloquence" (II, 14). And when the Duke of St. Bungay is discussing the qualities desirable in a member of the Cabinet, he too testifies to the duality in the mind's operation: "Now, in politics, I would a deal sooner trust to instinct than to calculation" (II, 237). Alice learns that the same maxim applies to her personal life.

Trollope is in pursuit of an idea, and he follows it through many variations in the different strands of his novel. As a political satirist he glances at the hot air that is blown off on the hustings and in the House, and the verbal flourishes which politicians, though with the best possible faith, substitute for performance. As an observer of the human mind he focuses on the schizoid propensity of human beings to believe and do and say different and incompatible things, to deceive themselves about their own needs and feelings until they so complicate their lives as to leave themselves almost no return to reality. As a philosopher (and I use the word in its widest sense, for Trollope does not habitually express his ideas in terms of abstracts) he is examining the construct of language, and its relation of experience: the novel is his contribution to the old *res/verba* conflict of classical philosophy, and shows his awareness of the problems of expression that are explored more amply by modern structuralists (the phrase I use for my title in this chapter is echoed in Michel Foucault's *Les Mots et les Choses*).

Trollope does not, as Sterne did, pursue this concept into the very texture of his own narration, making the process of verbal creation itself a subject of the book; as a novelist his chief interest is rather in the question of what constitutes character. His study of Alice Vavasor, and of those elements in her make-up that are mirrored in various other characters, is his way of dramatizing this conundrum. How can one define a man? Not by his words; not by his actions; not even by his thoughts or his conscious feelings; for all these may be at odds with one another. It is because he is hovering on the edge of producing a theory of the unconscious that he writes a problem novel, with a central character who is in effect mentally disturbed. His sense of the separation of the various strands of human character is no doubt one reason why he was opposed in principle to the technique of limited point of view in his novels,[22] and why *The Noble Jilt*, as a dramatic version of Alice's story, did not succeed as a play. Alice could neither tell her own story in words, nor act it out – we need an omniscient narrator to explain the curious disjunction between her words and her actions. Only thus can he make us understand how it came to pass that "No woman had a clearer idea of feminine constancy than she had, and no woman had sinned against that idea more deeply" (II, 429).

3 *Phineas Finn*:
The Politics of Love

As so often in the *Autobiography*, Trollope undersells himself in his description of the composition of *Phineas Finn*. It was written at the time of the emergence of his own political ambitions, and to some extent as a substitute for a political career of his own; but he doubted that politics alone would be of sufficient interest to his readers; "If I wrote politics for my own sake, I must put in love and intrigue, social incidents, with perhaps a dash of sport, for the sake of my readers" (272). Such an admission suggests that large stretches of the novel were mere grudging concessions to the public, and one gets as usual the impression that artistic considerations were the last thing to occur to him. But the novel is of course far from being the kind of left-over stew of love, intrigue and sport in a matrix of politics that he insinuates. The "politics for me and love for the public" formula, however carelessly conceived, becomes a novel that subtly explores the relation of the professional and the personal life. The elements are not slapped together as he suggests, but intricately interwoven through character, action, language and imagery. It is the skilful integration of the various elements that gives the book its solid structure and sustained interest. In his editor's introduction to the *Saint Pauls* magazine, in which *Phineas Finn* first appeared, Trollope announced his intention "to describe how love and ambition between them may cause the heart of a man to vacillate and make his conduct unsteady."[1] That is a clear enough statement of subject.

In a perceptive and favourable review of *The Small House at Allington*, the *Spectator* reviewer praised Trollope for his skill in the depiction of what he called "social tactics."[2] No other writer, he says, has Trollope's eye for seeing relationships, even the most trivial and insignificant ones, like that between Lily Dale and Hopkins the gardener, in terms of power. So it is in *Phineas Finn*, but here the vision becomes pervasive rather than incidental, and Phineas's political aspirations are so interwoven with his matrimonial ones that a book conceived out of the love of politics becomes one about the politics of love.

Hugh Walpole, with his usual vigour and vividness, has suggested that these novels are not really political at all – that though we get a great deal of detail about the people and the externals of political life, 'it is all concerning nothing at all. . . . We see the benches filled with figures, the gallery crowded with spectators, the hats and the papers and the trousers and the cuffs, but in spite of all this moving life, nothing occurs.'[3] M.P.'s are forever coming in and going out of the House, but nothing gets done inside. Bradford Booth agrees that "of political philosophy there is virtually none."[4] And he takes Trollope at his own estimate in assuming he hadn't dared, for fear of boring his public, to include as much political doctrine as he would have liked.

Now, it is true that Trollope does not discuss the rights and wrongs of the various issues that confront his ministries. We can't even be sure where he himself stands on such matters as the Ballot – an issue so hot that Alice Vavasor is considered as highly advanced and very brave for even mentioning it at a dinner table (*CYFH*, I, 290). But these are political novels nevertheless: – it is just that Trollope is not a politician but a novelist. "Men not measures" may be an outrageous doctrine for politicians – though even they practice it constantly without preaching it – and so it is considered by Gresham's opponents in *Phineas Redux* when he commands his party to vote against the conservative Church reform bill not for itself but because it is introduced by the wrong party; but it must be the very breath of the nostrils of a novelist (to use a Trollopian phrase).

The principles of legislation do not concern Trollope nearly so much as the *process*. Walpole's image of "the doors of the House of Commons ever swinging backwards and forwards" is appropriate enough here. It must be the process of arriving at the decision, the ways to and from it, rather than the decision itself, that will occupy the novelist. If it were not so, we would be quick enough to accuse him of propagandizing. The ballot, and Irish tenant right, and Church disestablishment are neither achieved nor ultimately rejected in the two *Phineas* novels, but the personalities of the legislators, the question of procedures, – so important in democratic legislation, as we who sit on committees all know – have meanwhile been very thoroughly explored.

The procedural issue that most interests Trollope in the world of politics is the question of the individual politician's relation to his party. It becomes for him an analogue for more familiar concerns of the novelist, the relation of the wife to the husband in marriage, or of the individual to his society. Phineas's relation to his party is a parallel with that other uneasy union of individuals, the marriage of Mr. and Lady Laura Kennedy; and major and minor characters in the political world

are fitted in some place in the scale of allegiance to the self or allegiance
to the corporate structure.

The story of Phineas's political career turns on this issue.[5] He is first
selected and encouraged to stand for Parliament because his friend
Barrington Erle has represented him as "a safe man, one who would
support 'the party' " (I, 7). And though he is easily and cheaply elected
for Loughshane, his lack of an independent income forces him to look
to politics as a career, and that means being given office and a salary by
his party when it is in power. He has high ambitions and considers an
office in the government to be an honourable though necessarily
precarious career, and when office is offered him he is triumphant. But
he is constantly twitted for his enforced dependence on party favour,
and grows to think of his required vote for his party as something like
prostitution. "Voting black white" comes to be the recurrent image for
those obedient members whose vote is at the service of their party. His
old tutor Mr. Low tells him that political office is "at the best slavery and
degradation, – even if you are lucky enough to achieve the slavery" (I,
56). And Violet Effingham, when the party whip is calculating the liberal
majority, mocks him:

> 'Mr. Ratler has been explaining to me that he must have nineteen next
> session. Now, if I were you, Mr. Finn, I would decline to be counted
> up in that way as one of Mr. Ratler's sheep.'
>   'But what am I to do?'
>   'Do something on your own hook. You men in Parliament are so
> much like sheep! If one jumps at a gap, all go after him, – and then
> you are penned into lobbies, and then you are fed, and then you are
> fleeced.' (I, 142)

For a while, however, Phineas toes the line. When a radical measure is
introduced to disenfranchise his own constituency, the pocket borough
of Loughton, his party opposes it, though he as an advanced Liberal
approves of the reform on principle. So here he has the additional
humiliation of knowing that a vote for his party also looks like a vote in
his own personal interest, and he "recorded his vote in favour of the
seven boroughs with a sore heart" (II, 96). Loughton is abolished, but
Phineas, that child of good fortune, is safely elected for Loughshane
once again. And now with an access of national loyalty he pledges
himself in various speeches to support Irish tenant right. When the issue
comes up he finds himself bound to resign his post and vote against his
party. His last piece of business is to vote for his party and with his principles, but against his own interest, in a further reform bill that disen-
franchises Loughshane. "And very dirty conduct I think it was," says
Lord Tulla, the peer whose pocket Loughshane has been in. Trollope

here moralizes, "It never occurred to Lord Tulla that a member of Parliament might feel himself obliged to vote on such a subject in accordance with his judgment" (II, 422). And so Phineas's political career ends, at least for this novel.

The other political characters are fitted in to the same central concern. Phineas's friend and mentor, and perhaps Trollope's ideal member of parliament, Mr. Monk, is in the same dilemma, though higher up in the party. He is a Radical who tries to further his cause by joining the government rather than opposing it, and so he accepts office in the Cabinet. If you can't beat them, join them. One of the scenes in Phineas's political education is a dinner party with Monk and Turnbull whereat he witnesses "a pleasant sparring match between the two great Radicals, – the Radical who had joined himself to the governing powers, and the Radical who stood aloof" (I, 199–200). Trollope's sympathies are very definitely with Monk, and he represents Turnbull as a charlatan, the arrogant extreme of "independence," and his independence of party is bought at the expense of subservience to popular adulation; but even Monk has found no satisfactory *via media*, and at one point he sadly reflects that "he had contributed but little to his country's welfare by sitting in Mr. Mildmay's cabinet" (I, 335).

If Turnbull represents the independent member, Barrington Erle is the party man *par excellence*. One of the original reviews of the novel accused Trollope – and made this a general reflection on his quality as a novelist – of failure in character definition, of offering us only the externals of behaviour and neglecting the inward and spiritual motions. "He gives us no strictly individual life, – no life beneath the social surface, – at all."[6] I think at a first reading this must strike many readers: the Barrington Erles, Laurence Fitzgibbons, Ratlers and Robys, sometimes even Phineas himself, are seen so entirely in their social and official roles that one doubts of their having genuine private lives of their own. The case of Phineas is a special one, and I shall discuss him later. But for the others it is completely appropriate that they should have, as it were, only an official existence – it is only in their official existence that we are concerned with them. They are sufficiently differentiated, like "Rosencrantz and gentle Guildenstern" or "Guildenstern and gentle Rosencrantz," but otherwise they are so many counters to be moved about, or, in Violet's phrase, so many sheep to be penned and fleeced.

For Barrington Erle, it is easy to believe, his official existence *is* his existence. He is the Prime Minister's sister's son, and the party is all in all to him. An early conversation between him and the youthfully idealistic hero is reminiscent of Pendennis's enthusiastic rehearsal of commonplaces about "truth" to the cynical Shandon, who has heard it all before (*Pendennis*, Ch. 35). Phineas boasts that he intends to go into Parliament "not to support a party, but to do the best I can for the country."

Barrington Erle turned away in disgust. Such language was to him simply disgusting. It fell upon his ears as false maudlin sentiment falls on the ears of the ordinary honest man of the world. . . . He hated the very name of independence in Parliament, and when he was told of any man, that that man intended to look to measures and not to men, he regarded that man as being both unstable as water and dishonest as the wind. (I, 17–18).

He knows that there are occasions, on the hustings, or in speeches delivered away in constituencies and not under the tutelary eye of the Treasury Bench, when members of Parliament have to commit themselves as individuals, and he makes it his business to repair the damage they inevitably do. When Phineas imprudently comes out in favour of tenant right in his speeches in Ireland, Erle tries to persuade him to forget all about it:

'All that Irish stump balderdash will never be thrown in your teeth by us, if you will just go on as though it had never been uttered' (II, 338).

And if a man makes a promise on the hustings that turns out to conflict with party policy, Erle's principle is "D– the hustings" (*PR*, I, 143). So much for loyalty to the constituents, who certainly don't have much respect accorded them either by the party men or the members who maintain their "independence."

Amidst all this, there is a good deal of humorous incident. At the beginning of the novel, when division between the parties is a very near thing, we hear how the party whips are lashing the aged and the infirm out to vote. Sir Everard Powell is so bad with the gout that he screams in his paroxysms, –

'But Sir Everard is a good man, and he'll be there if laudanum and bath-chair make it possible.' . . .
'Poor Sir Everard!' said Lord Brentford. 'It will kill him, no doubt, but I suppose the seat is safe.'
'Oh, yes; Llanwrwsth is quite safe,' said Barrington, in his eagerness omitting to catch Lord Brentford's grim joke. (I, 67)

And since parliamentary reform has become part of the Liberal party platform, the aristocratic members of the old Whig families have a bitter pill to swallow in obeying party orders and abolishing the comfortable boroughs they have been used to keeping in their pockets. A Tory aristocrat like Lord Tulla can gloat over their predicament:

'They've clean swept away Brentford's seat at Loughton, haven't they? Ha, ha, ha! What a nice game for him, – to have been forced to help to do it himself! There's nobody on earth I pity so much as a radical peer who is obliged to work like a nigger with a spade to shovel away the ground from under his own feet.' (II, 128)

Phineas's task is to preserve his integrity in such a world. He recognizes that there must be a party if work is to be done; and he certainly is ready to work. Though Gresham as the Prime Minister is a *parti pris*, his argument when he accepts Phineas's defection at the end of the novel carries force, both for Phineas and the reader:

> 'I think you are wrong, you know, not so much in your views on the question itself, – which, to tell the truth, I hardly understand as yet. [So much for convictions!] ... I think that Mr. Monk was wrong in desiring, as a member of the Government, to force a measure which, whether good or bad, the Government as a body does not desire to initiate, at any rate, just now. ... He failed to comprehend the only way in which a great party can act together, if it is to do any service in this country.' (II, 407)

Barrington Erle is certainly able to render this kind of service to the country; but then the Erles of the world are available as willing tools and can become the arms and legs of a Nazi party. Phineas, with his noise about his convictions, certainly would never do that. He makes his gesture and declares his independence and displays his conscience in the question of tenant right; but the gesture is an expensive one that costs him his job and, as far as he knows, his career. And inevitably in his reflections "he did wish that he had been a little less in love with independence, a little quieter in his boastings that no official considerations should ever silence his tongue" (II, 339). His independence has turned out to be a hollow luxury. But he does not deserve Walpole's comment that "with the affairs of the nation he has little concern."[7] It is true that he spends more time talking about his convictions than defining them, and he is subjected to some irony for his blustering; but when it comes to the crunch he does, however regretfully, stand on a principle in a matter of legislation and so end his career. It is also true that we ourselves learn little more about the rights and wrongs of tenant right than Gresham – Trollope sarcastically passes over Phineas's climactic speech thus: "Of what further he said, speaking on that terribly unintelligible subject, a tenant-right proposed for Irish farmers, no English reader will desire to know much" (II, 420). But he is probably right. In a novel we want men and not measures, and even in a political novel the process of legislation, involving men rather than doctrine as it does, must be more interesting to use than political dogma.

Deliberations about the curtailment of personal liberty in accepting office under a party are constantly paralleled in the women's world by deliberations about the curtailment of freedom in entering marriage. Phineas's three women in London all have other suitors, their ranks increasing as do Phineas's own prospects. Lady Laura Standish is courted by Mr. Kennedy, a commoner though a very rich one; Violet Effingham by Lord Chiltern, heir to a seat in the House of Lords; and Marie Goesler by the Duke of Omnium himself, the most socially prestigious man in England, royalty hardly excluded. Each of these women, with more and less reason, contemplate in marriage a surrender of individual identity, a condition of subjection as galling as Phineas's subjection to the party whips. And in fact their men are tyrannical in various ways. Kennedy, "a rigid martinet in all matters of duty" (I, 188), is a moral tyrant. Chiltern, the fiery red Lord, is for Violet a physical threat (though the bark of the lover turns out to be worse than the bite of the husband). And the Duke of Omnium, who offers Marie power, would also subject her to a kind of social tyranny, requiring her to be Duchess of Omnium rather than herself, and involving her in a bitter society battle with his family. Moral, physical and social tyranny: Trollope works out his patterns carefully.

Each of these women chafes under her limitations as bride, or proposed bride, as Phineas chafes under party discipline. Violet fears Chiltern more before marriage than after it, and once married, as we see in *Phineas Redux*, she is able to settle down to a happy married life, after her beast has been tamed by the channelling of his energies into hunting rather than bullying. But Lady Laura, who chooses to marry Kennedy rather than Phineas because she is confident that in that way she can maintain her sphere of influence as a woman behind the political scenes, finds after marriage that she has entered a trap. Some of the most moving scenes of the novel are those that show how her large spirit – and her love of power is not mean; there is something fine in it – and her ample life are progressively pared down and curtailed in her marriage. When she tells her husband, "There are moments, Robert, when even a married woman must be herself rather than her husband's wife" (II, 25), he can no more understand the proposition than Barrington Erle can understand that a man may want to vote on the side of his conscience rather than of his party. She has disastrously misjudged her man. Kennedy's self-righteous Calvinism is simply not amenable to her influence; and the dreary walls close in around her. It is interesting to compare the chapter, "Sunday in Grosvenor Place" with Dickens's description of London on Sunday in *Little Dorrit*. The comparison illumines what the two novelists have in common, as well as the degree to which they differ. Dickens evokes the inexpressible dreariness of the seventh day:

> Nothing to see but streets, streets, streets. Nothing to breathe but streets, streets, streets. Nothing to change the brooding mind, or raise

it up. Nothing for the spent toiler to do, but to compare the monotony of his seventh day with the monotony of his six days, think what a weary life he led, and make the best of it – or the worst, according to the probabilities. (Ch. 3)

Trollope's rhetoric is less emphatic, and his context is more specific; but Lady Laura is equally with Clennam a weary soul in a joyless puritanical desert:

> Then the Sundays became very wearisome to Lady Laura. Going to church twice, she had learnt, would be a part of her duty; and though in her father's household attendance at church had never been very strict, she had made up her mind to this cheerfully. But Mr. Kennedy expected also that he and she should always dine together on Sundays, that there should be no guests, and that there should be no evening company. After all, the demand was not very severe, but yet she found it operated injuriously upon her comfort. The Sundays were very wearisome to her. (I, 254)

The Sundays, and her nervous "headaches," come to be typical of the joyless subjection of her married life. After bowing to her husband's command that she should not read novels on the Sabbath, she reflects on her life:

> Then he left her, and she sat alone, first in the dusk, and then in the dark, for two hours, doing nothing. Was this to be the life she had procured for herself by marrying Mr. Kennedy of Loughlinter? (I, 260)

I wonder if a memory of this passage stirred James when he wrote that magnificent forty-second chapter of *The Portrait of a Lady*, where Isabel Archer, another free spirit who has submitted herself to another kind of martinet, sits on into the darkness to meditate the disaster of her life: "She has taken all the first steps in the purest confidence, and then she had suddenly found the infinite vista of a multiplied life to be a dark, narrow alley with a dead wall at the end." So with Trollope's trapped wife: "More than a shadow of truth had come upon Lady Laura herself. The dark cloud created by the entire truth was upon her, making everything black and wretched around her" (I, 376).[8]

Her eventual separation from Kennedy parallels Phineas's separation from his party. When her husband threatens that he will use the law of the land to make her return to him, she retorts, "Is a woman like a head of cattle, that she can be fastened in her crib by force?" (II, 374). The image recalls Violet's party sheep again.

When Lady Laura groans, "The curse is to be a woman at all," Violet replies, "I have always felt so proud of the privileges of my sex" (II, 143). There is that great difference between them; and then Violet is not so strong on "ideas," but she is more skilful in practice. She says plainly of Chiltern, "I am afraid to be his wife" (I, 117). When she looks at him, "there was something in his eye that almost frightened her. It looked as though he would not hesitate to wring his wife's neck round, if ever he should be brought to threaten to do so" (I, 125). But nevertheless, though she holds him off a long time while she makes up her mind, at last she submits to him. And she knows that her acceptance is a submission, in spite of his assertion that he would do whatever she bids him:

> 'Bid you indeed! As if it was for me to bid you. Do you not know that in these new troubles you are undertaking you will have to bid me in everything, and that I shall be bound to do your bidding? ... My wonder is that any girl can ever accept any man' (II, 153)

– as Turnbull's wonder is that any man can accept government office. Accept him she does, however, even if with this touch of irony. She has "rendered herself to the conqueror" (II, 191). Before she is engaged, she is capricious and independent in an attractive girlish kind of way; and during the engagement she tries to be a moral influence on Chiltern, with the result that they quarrel. At the reconciliation it is she who retracts: having meant to be "very wise" in her advice to him about his conduct, she promises "I never will be wise any more" (II, 403). And eventually she is to become the model wife as we see her in *Phineas Redux*, making her husband's interests her own, and, though not without power, confining her activities and her influence to the woman's sphere.

We are told near the outset of our acquaintance with Marie Goesler that "she was highly ambitious" (II, 210). Hers is the kind of ambition that rises to meet a challange. The respectable British public is difficult to placate, so she placates it. The Duke of Omnium is difficult to attract, so she attracts him. The course of her relation with the Duke is perhaps determined by that little incident at Matching where on being introduced to her he slights her. Thereafter he must be made to stoop. And stoop he does, until he is fairly on tenterhooks as to whether she will accept him or not. Like the other women, she hesitates, and compares him with Phineas. Lady Laura, who had Phineas at her feet, chose Kennedy instead; Violet, who almost decided to marry him, still decides against him by a narrow margin; Marie, who is not sure of Phineas's availability at all, yet rejects the alternative, because by her principle she must make her "leap in the dark" (II, 254). But the power of the Duke is attractive: "what if she caught this old man, and became herself a duchess, – caught him by means of his weakness, to the inexpressible dismay of all those who were bound to him by ties of blood?" (II, 250).

The decision is a difficult one, especially as, though she recognizes that
life with the Duke might be tedious, she knows that life without him is
tedious also. The featherweight incident that decides her, between rising
on the morning on which she must write him her answer and going
downstairs to breakfast, is a little exchange with her maid:

> 'I would never rest till I had a title in this country, [the maid en-
> courages her,] if I were a lady, – and rich and beautiful.'
>   'And can the countesses, and the ladyships, and the duchesses do as
> they please?'
>   'Ah, madame; – I know not that.'
>   'But I know. . . .' Then Madame Goesler had made up her mind.
> (II, 269)

Trollope says that this matter of liberty is not the only consideration that
determines her refusal, but yet preserving her independence has been
the final decisive factor. "She had decided, and the thing was done. She
would still be free, – Marie Max Goesler, – unless in abandoning her
freedom she would obtain something that she might in truth prefer to
it" (II, 272). So too has Phineas hesitated between the attractions of
political independence and the temptations of party office. And,
through Marie, Trollope neatly integrates his theme as it pertains to the
woman and to the man. In Marie's bold offer of her hand and her fortune to Phineas she is ready to sacrifice her independence that he might
gain his. Their marriage would involve the loss of her freedom; but her
money would end Phineas's dependence on office under the Government. The love interest and the political interest have been made one.

I have been speaking of Phineas's women in their relations with their
other men, and the extent to which Trollope works out those relations
in terms of power so as to align their stories with the political action.
Now I come to Phineas and *his* relation to the women.

At a first reading of the novel I think it is common to be exasperated
at Phineas, not for his fickleness, to which, indeed, many characters
within the novel draw attention, or for any other moral failings, but
because of his lack of self-awareness. The *Spectator* reviewer to whom I
alluded before complained that we don't see enough of his inner life –
"We never see him as he would see himself even for a chapter."[9] Hugh
Walpole calls him a hollow drum. "Trollope beats upon him constantly,
a fine noise is produced, but we are well aware that there is nothing inside."[10] James Pope Hennessy finds him convincing only as belonging
"to that gigantic category of passive persons with little volition to whom
things merely happen."[11] But Phineas has positive features, even if they
are the possession of negative qualities. In fact he is positively
characterized as a being lacking self-consciousness. (His attainment of
that quality is to be painfully dramatized in the trial in *Phineas Redux*.)

Trollope deliberately contrasts him with Kennedy, Chiltern, and the Duke of Omnium, whose wills are iron, in making him infinitely adaptable in his personal relations. Chiltern is at perpetual loggerheads with his father, and the world, and the woman he loves, because he cannot bring himself to concede an inch; Phineas, with no effort at all, charms Chiltern's father and accepts the family seat quite naturally. Kennedy discourses stiffly on duty until his wife is bruised by his very rigidity; Phineas submits to Lady Laura in all things, and so becomes utterly her master. This is the kind of power usually wielded by women in Trollope's novels, and it is appropriate that there should eventually be a debate in *Phineas Redux* on whether or not Phineas is "womanly." Lady Laura is conscious that he has "enough of the feminine side of a man's character" to be unusually sensitive to a woman's feelings (*PR*, I, 68).

It is this combination of a lack of self-consciousness with flexibility that gains him his success, both in love and in politics, and that also maintains our sympathy for him, once we see what Trollope is about. The flexibility, if it were deliberate, would make him a time-server, a cynical Vicar of Bray figure. And the innocence without the intelligent adaptibility would make him awkward – and he is never that, as the ladies admiringly agree. Lady Laura describes him to Violet: "He is so honest and so naïve without being awkward! And then he is undoubtedly clever" (I, 132).

There is a shrewd passage in *Vanity Fair* where Thackeray comments on the natural propensity of affection to cling to status: "People in Vanity Fair fasten on to rich folks quite naturally. . . . Their affections rush out to meet and welcome money. Their kind sentiments awaken spontaneously towards the interesting possessors of it" (Ch. 21). Trollope touches on the same subject in *Can You Forgive Her?*, though with a milder irony. Mr. Vavasor advises his daughter that "Rank and wealth are advantages," and that "men and women ought to grow, like plants, upwards."

> 'If I had a choice of acquaintance between a sugar-baker and a peer, I should prefer the peer. . . . I don't call that tuft-hunting, and it does not necessitate toadying. It's simply growing up, towards the light, as the trees do.' (*CYFH*, I, 266–7)

Phineas could never formulate this advice, but his *practice* is certainly to grow upwards towards the light. To Mary Flood Jones, his Irish love, he says naïvely of Lady Laura Standish, his London love, "I [admire her], because she possesses such an appearance of power" (I, 25). And so he attaches himself to her, as naturally as the ivy to the oak. She and his career are inseparably linked in his mind. A passage early in the novel, in which we are privy to his rather boyish meditations about courting Lady Laura, is a marvellous example of the combination of his matrimonial and political ambitions:

> His great desire would be to support his own wife by his own labour. At present he was hardly in a fair way to do that, unless he could get paid for his parliamentary work. Those fortunate gentlemen who form 'The Government' are so paid. Yes; – there was the Treasury Bench open to him, and he must resolve that he would seat himself there. . . . And then he remembered that Lady Laura was related to almost everybody who was anybody among the high Whigs. She was, he knew, second cousin to Mr. Mildmay . . . [there follows a long rehearsal of her influential family connections.] Simply as an introduction into official life nothing could be more conducive to chances of success than a matrimonial alliance with Lady Laura. Not that he would have thought of such a thing on that account! No; – he thought of it because he loved her; honestly because he loved her. He swore to that half a dozen times, for his own satisfaction. But, loving her as he did, and resolving that in spite of all difficulties she should become his wife, there could be no reason why he should not, – on her account as well as on his own, – take advantage of any circumstances that there might be in his favour. (I, 46–7)

It is subtly done, that naïve reasoning: 'I want to marry her, therefore I must be successful in order to support her; her influence will help me to success, but of course that's not why I want to marry her; but one might as well take anything that's going.' One is reminded of Tennyson's Northern Farmer's principle, "Doänt thou marry for munny, but goä wheer munny is!" (The line was a favourite with Trollope, and he expatiated on it in *The Eustace Diamonds*.) And there is some irony at Phineas's expense as he repeatedly swears to himself that it's the lady he loves and not her influence. But nevertheless we are to believe that he is honest. He is entitled to that moment of sad self-congratulation when, at a much later stage in his career, he reflects on the misery of the Kennedys. "After all, was not the world much better with him than it was with either of those two wretched married beings? And why? He had not, at any rate as yet, sacrificed for money or social gains any of the instincts of his nature. He had been fickle, foolish, vain, uncertain, and perhaps covetous; – but as yet he had not been false" (II, 375). It has simply come naturally to him to "luvv [the] lass an' 'er munny too."

Phineas's career is like the climbing of a ladder of which the verticals are political advancement and the rungs are people. Yet he himself is not really aware of the difference or of the ladder itself as an instrument. It is as though all he has in mind is the view from the top.

And, through Lady Laura, he gets invited to Loughlinter where he hob-nobs with Cabinet Ministers and plays chess with the future Prime

Minister; he becomes intimate at her father's and her husband's houses as well, and after a dinner with her father becomes the hero of the hour by rescuing Kennedy from the garrotters, so that as the family saviour he is given the seat at Loughton.[12] Here, when he is off with the old love and beginning to be on with the new, the seat becomes the occasion of a *crise de conscience*. Is he being disloyal to the family in taking Loughton and using his success there as an asset in the courting Violet, whom the family intend for Lord Chiltern? Lord Brentford's son-in-law saved is balanced against the daughter-in-law lost, and Phineas reconciles his conscience to the new suit, after duly informing Chiltern of his intentions. Through Violet Effingham he gets involved in a duel, and this, like the incident with the garrotters, greatly increases his prestige, and becomes a factor in his promotion, as he, the principal in the duel, displaces Laurence Fitzgibbon, who had been his second. Through Marie Goesler he confirms himself in friendly relations with powerful families, this time the Pallisers. But the great asset for his career that she offers him, her money and herself, he has at this stage to reject, because he has engaged himself to Mary Flood Jones. As for Mary, she is not a rung in the ladder at all, and marriage to her automatically – for Phineas – goes with resignation from his post and surrender of his political ambitions. He never even tells his London friends of her – this love is incompatible with politics as his other loves have been inseparable from them.

And through it all – through incident, and motivation, and phrasing – Trollope intricately weaves his propostion that love and power and politics are a package deal. Lady Laura, balked in her love for Phineas, espouses his political interests with a zeal born of a need for sublimation: "Perhaps there was a feeling on her part that having wronged him in one way, she would repay him in another" (I, 303). And she can make a passionate avowal of her lasting loyalty to his cause instead of a declaration of her continuing passion: "I have never swerved. . . . I have ever been true to you" (II, 362–3). Phineas in his social life finds himself star-struck by the glare of women and politicans together: at a gathering in Lord Brentford's house – "manifestly a meeting of Liberals, semi-social and semi-political" – he basks in the combined glow: "There were there great men, – Cabinet Ministers, and beautiful women, – the wives and daughters of some of England's highest nobles" (I, 433). As he finds himself a place in the affections of the beautiful women, so he finds his confidence in himself and his stock in the world at large increase; at one point we find him reflecting indignantly when he has been addressed with undue familiarity by the editor of *The People's Banner*: "He, who had Lady Laura's secret in his keeping; he who hoped to be the possessor of Violet Effingham's affections, – he to be called 'dear Finn' by such a one as Quintus Slide!" (I, 387). And we are told that the happiest moment of his life is when he receives Lady Laura's letter of congratulation on his successful speech in the House – it is not just the political success itself that elates him, nor success in love, but the combination of the two (I, 425).

Trollope has arranged that through all this tangle of mixed motives Phineas can still retain our sympathy because of that naïveté that makes him unaware of the rather sordid implications of his simultaneous pursuit of women and of professional success. We forgive Tom Jones for being a gigolo, because he is one in effect but not in intention – the money Lady Bellaston gives him is the welcome result but not the motive of his attentions to her. So it is with Phineas. "There had been no stain of premeditated mercenary arrangement upon him at any time" (II, 408). He is lucky enough to have been rather slow at any premeditations whatsoever.

Why is Phineas so successful, in politics as in love? Trollope takes pains to explain, and to dramatize his appeal to men as to women, which is the secret of his success. He has a "peculiar power of making himself agreeable." Many people study this art, but with Phineas it is not art: "It was simply his nature to be pleasant" (I, 144). And again, "Nature had been very good to him, making him comely inside and out" (II, 26). To be able to say something nice to the right person at the right time is no doubt a very useful accomplishment, but Phineas has the more special gift of being able to say it and mean it too. He is pleasant because he is responsive and adaptable. So the same qualities that make him a great asset to the government when he is filling his post as under-secretary for the colonies – he can grasp a situation swiftly, and work tactfully with people – make him susceptible and attractive to the women. Indeed, this is why Phineas can maintain so many close relations with different women at the same time – he is so responsive and adaptable as to be virtually a different person in each relationship. This is most evident in his concurrent tendernesses towards Mary Flood Jones in Ireland and Violet Effingham in London. Here a change in location aids him in the change in identity:

> Now that he was in Ireland, he thought that he did love dear Mary very dearly. He felt that he had two identities, – that he was, as it were, two separate persons, – and that he could, without any real faithlessness, be very much in love with Violet Effingham in his position of man of fashion and member of Parliament in England, and also warmly attached to dear little Mary Flood Jones as an Irishman of Killaloe. (I, 401).

"He was aware, however, that there was a prejudice against such fulness of heart," Trollope adds, with irony. But by implication this state of mind can be extended to all his relations. Phineas's acute responsiveness to the situation of the moment makes him, to a sometimes shocking and often hilarious extent, a different person to each of his women, and, by extention, in his various roles as radical, party member, under-secretary, Irishman, and so on. He is an extreme version of the Johnny Eameses, Crosbies, and Harry Claverings of Trollope's novels who are tossed to and fro on the winds of other people's appeals to them. It is not that he has *conflicting* allegiances – the allegiances in his own mind actually co-exist. The conflict is not in his mind, but in the rules of society that make certain alliances incompatible with one another. And in the end, he has to sort out the allegiances according to the external necessities of his position; he votes on tenant right as an Irishman *rather than* as a party member; he is forced, for the first time in his life, to say no to a woman, because he has induced another woman to say yes to him. So he makes his concession to the "prejudice against . . . fulness of heart."

But meanwhile Trollope carefully chronicles Phineas's changing roles in his relations with women, and dramatizes the difference in his behaviour to them as, chameleon as he is, he matches himself to the image each has of him. The greatest care, of course, is expended on the depiction of his relation with Lady Laura, – one that lasts through two long novels and outlasts both their marriages. Such a relation necessarily progresses and changes, but there are certain constant features in it. For Lady Laura at the outset he is to be her "political pupil," her Telemachus, and she is to be his Mentor. They establish that highly aphrodisiac situation, a pedagogic relationship – like that between Swift and Vanessa, Emma and Mr. Knightley, Charlotte Brontë and Monsieur Héger, and all the others; but here the usual roles of the sexes are reversed, and the woman is the instructor while the man is the pupil. Phineas is soon brooding, "And was it possible that a female Mentor should love her Telemachus, – should love him as Phineas desired to be loved by Lady Laura?" (I, 152).

The scene at Loughlinter in which Phineas declares his love is a splendid piece of work, in that it sets the tone for so much that is to come. Here Telemachus must take the initiative and propose, and he is quite ready to do so; but the Mentor turns the tables on him by announcing she is already engaged to Kennedy, that they must remain good friends, that it is all for the best, and so forth. She is the one who is cool and rational and fully in control of the situation; and he is boyish, and impetuous, and heart-broken. Yet the durable impression is made on Lady Laura, not on Phineas. Very soon he is courting another woman, and can hardly remember he had been in love with Lady Laura – "That now was ages ago, – eight months since" (I, 252); whereas she, through her marriage and her separation and her widowhood and all the suffering and guilt they have involved, cannot shake a detail of the scene out of her memory. In *Phineas Redux* she is still agonizing over the recollection of how "you blurted out your short story of love that day over the waterfall. . . . Ah, how well I remember it" (*PR*, I, 123). There is certainly

"I wish to regard you as a dear friend,—both of my own and of my husband."

3. Phineas and Lady Laura by the Linter: Millais' illustration for *Phineas Finn*, chapter 15

a memorable kind of pathos in Phineas's declaration, when he blunders
on in spite of her announcement about Kennedy:

> 'I, poor, penniless, plain simple fool that I am, have been ass enough
> to love you, Lady Laura Standish; and I brought you up here today to
> ask you to share with me – my nothingness. . . . It was like a child
> wanting the moon; – was it not?' (I, 168–9)

Phineas certainly has boyish attributes at this stage of his career: the day
before Lady Laura and Mr. Kennedy had caught him, in a moment of
embarrassment, throwing stones into the river like a listless youth (I,
147). That image of the child stays with Lady Laura. Telemachus is after
all just a boy, and Phineas in his relations with her retains a boyish
charm and innocence. Long after he has gained experience enough to
know better, he cannot help going to Lady Laura, as a child goes to its
mother, to blurt out his troubles. When he finds it almost certain he will
lose his seat at Loughshane, he tells her about it with a pathetic show of
bravery; " 'I've made up my mind to give it up,' said he, smiling as he
spoke. . . . 'Of course it makes me a little down in the mouth.' And then
he smiled again" (I, 354). Laura's eyes, one can imagine, can almost see
the lips tremble. At any rate, like an indulgent mother, she resolves at
this moment that if he is to lose Loughshane he shall have Loughton,
and so she arranges it. Even when he has the enormous tactlessness to
make her his confidante in his suit of Violet,[13] he wins her over to plead
his suit for him. She does it because, she explains, "There are moments
in which we try to give a child any brick on the chimney top for which it
may whimper" (II, 206). Trollope shows this irresistible appeal of the
boy to the mother as a constant component of the relationship, and that
brave smile that is the front of anguish is its signal. In *Phineas Redux*
Phineas still finds himself living up to the same image of himself. When
he realizes the new government does not intend to offer him a place, he
confides again to her: "Phineas smiled, and tried to smile pleasantly, as
he answered, 'I don't know that they'll put themselves out by doing very
much for me' " (*PR*, I, 413). Again, even when he is in prison on trial for
his life: " 'I cannot understand it [she cries, distraught]. They cannot
really think you killed him.' He smiled, and shook his head" (*PR*, II,
166). And when she makes her declaration at Königstein of "my strong,
unalterable, unquenchable love for you," she pathetically jokes: "I shall
fret about you, Phineas, like an old hen after her one chick; and though
you turn out to be a duck, and get away into waters where I cannot
follow you, I shall go cackling round the pond, and always have my eye
upon you" (*PR*, I, 124–5). In her extremity, when her passion has
become evident to her brother, she admits, "I love him, – as a mother
might love her child, I fancy" (*PR*, II, 116). This is of course only a part
of the truth, as she loves him in other ways too. Her love for him, since

that scene at Loughlinter when she had been so calm and controlled, has been a constant quantity which she has tried to repress and to sublimate, but which has emerged uncontrollably in various forms – as her zeal for his career, as her sisterly affection when she welcomes him at Dresden, as a guilty adulterous passion in which she nevertheless takes a luxurious pride, as a widow's fantasies about eventual union with him by the falls of the estate she has inherited from her deserted husband. But Phineas has lived up mainly to that role of the boyish Telemachus, who must blurt out his triumphs and troubles to her, cost her what it might.

For Violet, happily for the reader, Phineas plays a more mature role, and also a more light-hearted one. He can exchange jokes and badinage with her, and he is on a more equal footing with this rebellious young heiress than with the serious-minded Lady Laura. But for Violet too he is invested with some special interest, and she finds something heroic in him, something of the Paladin: his suit of her coincides with his rescue of Mr. Kennedy from the garrotters:

> 'Why, what a Paladin you are! But you succour men in distress instead of maidens.' 'That's my bad luck,' said Phineas. 'The other will come no doubt in time,' Violet replied; 'and then you'll get your reward.' He knew that such words from a girl mean nothing, – especially from such a girl as Violet Effingham; but nevertheless they were very pleasant to him. (I, 347).

And he lives up to this heroic image in the affair of the duel – fought, naturally, for Violet's sake. In that affair his chivalrous conduct in shooting to miss, when Chiltern has every intention of killing Phineas if he can, eventually becomes public knowledge, and Violet is impressed. Years later when she is safely married to Chiltern, she recalls enthusiastically, "That was the grandest thing of all" (*PR*, I, 153). However, the role of Paladin is a little too difficult for a Victorian Member of Parliament to sustain, and Phineas cannot quite live up to Violet's expectations of him. She comes close to accepting him, but decides against him at last partly because of his being so adaptable, so much everybody's man: "Mr. Finn was just half an inch too short. He lacks something in individuality. He is a little too much a friend to everybody" (II, 381). It is a fault that the touchy and aggressive Chiltern could certainly never be accused of.

As for Mary Flood Jones – for her of course he is a hero, a "black swan," the only man in the world. Their relation doesn't need analysing. Phineas at the beginning kisses her as a matter of course, and at the end takes her similarly because she is so completely there to be taken. She is one of the girls who is "like water when one is athirst, like plovers' eggs in March, like cigars when one is out in the autumn. No one ever dreams of denying himself when such temptation comes in the way" (I,

37, 23). He does refrain from taking her during the course of the novel, because in London there is metal more attractive. She is the only one of the women that has no other suitor, no hesitation, no complication. As soon as he deigns to take her, she will be his. Naturally, such an attitude on the part of the woman begets a certain patronage on the part of the man, and Phineas lives up to his role of black swan, as to the other roles, with his usual natural grace.

The difference of the sexes is not nearly so noticeable a component in Phineas's relation with Marie Goesler as it is in those with his other women. She looks on him not as a mother on her son, or a damsel on her Paladin, or a little girl on a hero, but as one person who has made her own way in the world looks on another, and admires his success. She overlooks the conventional barriers between the sexes by proposing to him herself. She rejects union with a man who is far above her in age and social standing to attach herself to an equal. In making this bold Jewish adventuress one of the most sympathetic women in the Palliser series, Trollope shows himself to have become much more liberal in his racial and sexual attitudes than he was in the Barsetshire series, with its array of self-abnegating Anglo-Saxon maidens.[14]

As Robert Polhemus has pointed out, there are certain parallels in the characters of this hero and heroine[15] (for Marie is definitely the heroine of the two Phineas novels, if not unequivocally of *Phineas Finn*). They are both highly ambitious, and highly scrupulous. Both find adaptibility to be the secret of success, – though Marie is deliberate in using her adaptability as a tactic, where Phineas is unconscious. As Phineas is torn between being a safe party man and the more attractive and dangerous alternative of acting independently, she hesitates between becoming a duchess and offering herself to Phineas. Like Phineas, she chooses the romantic alternative, and like his, her gesture is ineffectual. Phineas resigns from his party, but in the process he ends his career, so that his "independence" is cancelled out; and she refuses the Duke and proposes to Phineas, but she doesn't get him, so that she too is back where she started.

In a chapter labelled "Madame Goesler's Politics" she outlines her philosophy to her suitor, the Duke of Omnium: "The safest way in the world is to do nothing. . . . Much the safest. But if you have not sufficient command over yourself to enable you to sit in repose, always quiet, never committing yourself to the chance of any danger, – then take a leap in the dark" (II, 254).[16] She genuinely admires repose, and is capable of it herself, as her controlled behaviour, calmly eating grapes while the Duke frets, is designed to show. And she genuinely admires the Duke, finding in his after all rather useless life not just social prestige but something approaching natural grandeur: she compares him to a snowy Alpine peak, glorious and dignified in its quiescence; whereas Phineas is "an express train at full speed." When Phineas argues that the Duke has done nothing to earn his dignity, she replies earnestly that if he can earn his glory by his own efforts, "I too may be able to see that the express train is really greater than the mountain" (II, 296). And so, to mix her metaphors, she takes her leap in the dark, but she misses her express train, at least at this particular stop.

And so Phineas plays his parts – and keeps several women in the air at once, like a skilful juggler. Though a scrupulous Victorian gentleman and no Macheath (though like that cheerful polygamist he might well say "I love the sex!"), he nevertheless manages to maintain tender relations with two or three women concurrently, and without feeling faithless to any of them.

Trollope's depiction of Phineas and his women is a subtle study in the shifting and elusive nature of identity. It has been traditional, from the contemporary reviews through the twentieth-century studies like Walpole's and Polhemus's, to praise Chiltern and Kennedy as creations – and fine creations they are. But to find interest primarily in them and react to the two novels as though Phineas wasn't there is to miss Trollope's more careful and subtle portraiture. For Kennedy and Chiltern life is very simple, and decisions are dictated by some internal mechanism that they do not question. It is not so with Phineas, whose delicacy and responsiveness make life infinitely more complicated, even if they also make him appear to be lacking in decision and definition. Trollope was perhaps reacting to his readers' response and setting the matter straight when, in a memorable image, he compared Chiltern and Phineas in the later novel:

> The Master of the Brake hounds himself was a man less gifted than Phineas Finn, and therefore hardly capable of understanding the exaggerated feelings of the man who had recently been tried for his life. Lord Chiltern was affectionate, tender-hearted, and true; – but there were no vacillating fibres in his composition. The balance which regulated his conduct was firmly set, and went well. The clock never stopped, and wanted but little looking after. But the works were somewhat rough, and the seconds were not scored. (*PR*, II, 301)

In a character like Phineas's, the seconds *are* scored, and it would be a pity to ignore the fine distinctions. The "vacillating" in a man's composition were as we know endlessly interesting to Trollope, though, to outward appearance at least, he himself conducted himself more like a Chiltern than a Phineas.

Not that in *Phineas Finn* there is not plentiful comedy at the expense of Phineas's responsiveness. To Phineas at the time his passions are of tragic dimensions, but in context the narrator, and the other characters too, ironically undercut Phineas's passionate pretensions. A short while after his heart-break at Loughlinter we hear, "As he was still violently in love with Lady Laura, any other love was of course impossible; but, nevertheless . . ." – nevertheless he finds himself becoming jealous of the affections of Violet Effingham (I, 191). When he gets the news that Violet is engaged, there is much talk about how his "back was broken," and he sees himself as totally incapacitated for intercourse with society and the world; however, he drags himself out to dine with Madame Goesler that night, and manages to behave almost as usual; and by the following Wednesday, he is having one of his consolatory heart-to-heart talks with the new love about the old, with ironic authorial commentary:

> It is not, I think, surprising that a man when he wants sympathy in such a calamity . . . should seek it from a woman. . . . But it is, perhaps, a little odd that a man when he wants consolation because his heart has been broken, always likes to recieve it from a pretty woman. One would be disposed to think that at such a moment he would be profoundly indifferent to such a matter. (II, 178)

And when Marie Goesler, with her bright eyes and her soft hand, sympathizes with his love, "Then Phineas of course told her that such sympathy from her was all and all to him. But the reader must not on this account suppose that he was untrue in his love to Violet Effingham. His back was altogether broken by his fall, and he was quite aware that such was the fact" (II, 199). Lady Laura is not quite so accommodating – "I think your heart is a sham heart" (II, 20), she says shortly. Which goes to show that a man can expect consolation about the old love from the new, but not about the new love from the old. Violet at last compares the impressions on Phineas's heart with "an inn-keeper's score which he makes in chalk. A damp cloth brings them all away, and leaves nothing behind" (II, 383). And Violet doesn't even know of the existence of Mary Flood Jones. Nevertheless, Phineas is sore beset by his scruples and his responsiveness together, and we scarcely know whether to be amused or agonized at his predicament when Lady Laura makes her various avowals: "he hardly knew how not to throw himself at her feet, and swear, that he would return now and for ever to his old passion, hopeless, sinful, degraded as it would be" (II, 207).

Phineas's women interlock with each other as they and their concerns interlock with his political progress. Phineas, his career and his women, and the interweaving of them, provide an integrated framework for a novel that is at first sight rather loose and episodic. In this novel there is no subplot, except insofar as the women who revolve around Phineas create their own minor centers of gravity, and have their own satellites. Otherwise everything radiates out from the hero, with his curiously malleable heart and his concurrent and diverse aspirations. The unity is largely thematic, as the issues of love and power, independence and obedience, and rigidity and flexibility are pursued through the patterning of lovers and rivals, allies and opponents, success and failure, that impinge on Phineas's public and personal life.

4 *Phineas Redux*:
The Law's Delay,
The Insolence of Office

Phineas Finn and *Phineas Redux* "are, in fact, but one novel," said Trollope (*A*, 274). Hence my departure from the chronological sequence in discussing *Phineas Redux* before *The Eustace Diamonds*, which actually preceded it.

The second Phineas novel is not just a sequel to the first: it is its complement. There is a sense in which we seem to be travelling over the same ground again, but looking with new – or rather older – eyes. Lawrence Durrell in his Alexandria series tells over many of the same events, but differentiates one novel from the other by seeing the events from the point of view of a different character. Trollope doesn't do anything as tricky as that – the external events of the two novels are different, and the action of *Redux* is set some two or three years later. Yet he has the events, though literally different, closely parallel those in the first novel, so that Phineas seems to be going through it all again; only it has all turned sour. The first Phineas found himself on this goodly frame the Earth; Phineas recalled finds himself on a sterile promontory. The first Phineas has a joyous confidence that man is noble in reason, infinite in faculties, express and admirable in action; Phineas recalled discovers him to be no more than a quintessence of dust. This cheerfully unself-conscious young man, like Hamlet, goes through a trauma that triggers a crisis of self-consciousness. He becomes unbalanced if not mad, and in his breakdown after the trial he finds how weary, stale, flat and unprofitable seem to him all the uses of this world.

The young Phineas's career had not been without its trials and troubles, of course, but he faced them with confidence, and the world was his oyster. But that same world has changed in the vision of the

4. Phineas bereaved: Holl's illustration for *Phineas Redux*, chapter 6

Phineas who returns to it, and he finds "It is not now as it hath been of yore." Trollope said particularly of these two novels, though he spoke also of the whole series, that he had been concerned to portray "the state of progressive change" (A, 273), that he had occupied himself with imagining how certain people will behave differently at different stages in their career, or before and after a certain experience. It is so with Phineas. He has changed.[1] And equally the world he enters again has changed from the world he entered before.

In the first novel, as we saw, Phineas was always changing – his fickleness and his adaptability and his consequent lack of a stable identity were among his most distinctive characteristics. But this change is different, and not just one in a series so long as to make change almost a constant rule. Between the novels something has changed permanently; and in the course of the second we are to see the confirmation of the change in the shattering experience that puts Phineas agonizingly and lastingly in contact with his own consciousness.

The event that has happened between the two novels has been Phineas's marriage to good insignificant little Mary Flood Jones. Trollope owned that he had bungled in marrying off his hero to Mary at the end of *Phineas Finn*, when he intended to bring him back to the scene in a later novel. "When he did return I had no alternative but to kill the pretty simple Irish girl, which was an unpleasant and awkward necessity" (A, 273). (He had been similarly callous with John Bold between *The Warden* and *Barchester Towers*, so that he could lead his favourite Eleanor through the matrimonial tangle again.) And there are signs that he was embarrassed about Mary, and would fain have his reader forget she had existed. Characters like Mrs. Bunce make brief reference to her, and then hastily pursue "well, then, I won't mention her name again" (I, 62) – as though Phineas's wife by dying had committed some sort of unmentionable indiscretion, like running away with the coachman. And Violet Effingham says cheerfully when she meets him again, "Why should you be altered? It's only two years. I am altered because of Baby. That does change a woman" (I, 24) – as though a man is to take his wife's death in childbirth without batting an eye. Nevertheless, Trollope has made more out of that sad little episode than he perhaps meant to. He is cursory about the facts of the short marriage, but still the reader becomes compellingly aware that *something* has happened to Phineas. "I feel to be changed in everything," he had said to Violet, before that rather unfeeling speech of hers. To return to my Hamlet analogy, he too is a young man in black, with the present awareness of death upon him.

Here is a case, by the way, where the illustrations are peculiarly fitted to the text. Trollope had reason to be grateful to Millais for the fine work he did in illustrating *Phineas Finn* and others of his novels,[2] but Frank Holl's work for *Phineas Redux* is often more sensitive and dramatic

5. Kennedy fires at Phineas: Holl's illustration for *Phineas Redux*, chapter 23

than Millais'. Holl was an engraver and the son of an engraver, and moreover had training in the great tradition of *The Graphic*, when *Phineas Redux* had its serial run. His inspiration was to provide dominantly dark designs. In our first view of Phineas his back is turned in grief, and he seems to be in mourning; subsequent plates, like those of Phineas at Loughlinter,[3] Phineas being shot at by Kennedy in the dreary Judd Street hotel room, Phineas in prison, are gloomy enough to rival the famous "dark plates" of *Bleak House*. These, perhaps, are "but the trappings and the suits of woe," but like Hamlet's inky cloak they are appropriate.

Trollope dramatizes his theme of change by apparently covering much of the same ground and reviewing the same territory – only, as we find, with quite different effect. The external action in *Phineas Redux* quite closely parallels that in *Phineas Finn*, so that one can find equivalents for many episodes. But the change is nearly always for the worse.

In the first novel Phineas Finn sought the love of Lady Laura Standish, and though he was rejected by her he became the intimate friend of her and her husband and reaped the benefit of such influential connections. In *Phineas Redux* Lady Laura, withered and possessive, torments him with seeking *his* love, and his part in the triangle does him considerable political damage. Loughlinter, which had been the locus of so many of his aspirations, amatory and political, progressively deteriorates from a scene of hope and prosperity to the utterly dreary and comfortless retreat where Phineas visits the deserted and demented husband. In the first novel he rescued Kennedy from the garrotters, and Kennedy thought him a saviour; in the corresponding violent episode in *Phineas Redux*, Kennedy curses him as his wife's paramour, and shoots a pistol at his head. In *Phineas Finn* there was a duel, a romantic episode where rivals in love faced each other on the field of honour, and Phineas chivalrously aimed to miss, and was wounded by an honourable opponent who became his close friend and ally, and Phineas was regarded as a hero. The parallel action in *Phineas Redux* is the murder of a mean-minded official in a dark alley, and Phineas is put on trial for his life. In both novels Phineas is the ladies' favourite, but where in *Phineas Finn* their influence had been beneficial, in *Phineas Redux* the women's conspiracies simply make mischief: Gresham, detecting "some woman's fingers in the pie" (I, 435), determines not to advance Phineas, and Phineas has the additional humiliation of being publicly excoriated as "The good-looking Irish Member of Parliament who had been put in possession of a handsome salary by feminine influences" (II, 30). In *Phineas Finn* seats fell into Phineas's lap like ripe plums: Loughshane, Loughton, and again Loughshane at the moment of his need became miraculously available. But in the second novel Phineas has to fight a hotly contested election, and it is a dirty fight; and when the electors of

Tankerville *are* ready to return him enthusiastically, it is for reasons which he considers contemptible. It is the same even with his sporting life. Phineas's first exploit was to ride the dauntingly-named Bone-breaker, which he does with such success that he has a fine day's hunting, and would have been in at the kill but for his gallant rescue of Chiltern. In the next novel, his horse balks at a jump and throws him, and then continues to balk until his rider is utterally frustrated and is left behind by the hunt. (An emblematic little incident this: it is Marie Goesler who rescues Phineas, and is patient with him, and compensates him with her company for his lost opportunity, as she is to do in the larger action of the novel.) To sum up: in *Phineas Finn* Phineas was the child of fortune, and all doors open to him; in *Phineas Redux* he finds himself "more ill-used by Fate than had been any man since Fate first began to be unjust" (II, 127), and all doors close, including the door of the prison.[4]

As with the action so with the themes. In the political realm, there had been a certain tension and excitement about the *crises de conscience* of Phineas and his colleagues that were caused by the conflict between their personal principles and their loyalty to their party, and there was a touch a nobility about Phineas's final gesture of resignation that was recognized even by those who disagreed with him. But in the later novel that same gesture is denounced by Bonteen and acknowledged by Monk to have been a "scuttling of the ship." And the whole tension of con-science has relaxed into an accepted cynicism. The main political issue of the novel, the movement to disestablish the Church, and the manner in which it is introduced, require everyone to forsake his principles as a matter of course. The process of one party's stealing the other's thunder cancels out the reasons for any individual to belong to a given party. Daubeny accuses Gresham of "depending upon faction, and upon fac-tion alone" (I, 361), but of course he is himself tarred with the same brush, and forces his party members to do what they abhor simply to make political mileage. "It is no good any longer having any opinion upon anything," the M.P.'s groan in their clubs (I, 367).

Phineas himself is early disgusted at the turn of events. Having enthusiastically advocated disestablishment in his own campaign speeches, he finds that Daubeny's minority government, for reasons of policy rather than principle, have moved in on his territory: "No doubt he had advocated the cause, – but he had done so as an advanced member of the Liberal party, and he regarded the proposition when coming from Mr. Daubeny as a horrible and abnormal birth" (I, 96). From the outset his principles have been set at odds with his party; and such is the general condition. The progress of hopeful ascent to success to regretful resignation that was the graph of Phineas's political career in *Finn* is in *Redux* one of progressive estrangement from his party and disillusion with political process to a final rejection of his once coveted place on the Treasury bench.

As a light-hearted analogue to the issue of the individual's relation to his party and the furore over Daubeny's introduction of a bill to disestablish the Church, Trollope introduces the hunting world of Lord Chiltern, M.F.H., and the hue and cry about Trumpeton Wood. Trollope talked about having "dragged" hunting into his novels, but nevertheless he is careful, as with his subplots, to integrate the hunting sections into the structure of the novel in hand. The Master of Fox Hounds, seen in solemn conference with his huntsman, kennelman and whips (II, 16), is a kind of parody of a Prime Minister with his Cabinet and *his* party whips (the metaphor was to this extent ready made), and Chiltern's concern in running a hunt is as serious as a dedicated politician's in running the country's finances: "To kill a certain number of foxes in the year, after the legitimate fashion, had become to him the one great study of life; – and he did it with an energy equal to that which the Duke devoted to decimal coinage" (II, 376). Such parallels are made explicit more than once. Chiltern feels that the old Duke, as the owner of Trumpeton wood, is "bound to find foxes for the Brake hunt. It is almost a part of his title deeds" – just as a party man like Barrington Erle feels a man is bound to vote for his party. When, instead, a man allows the foxes on his property to be destroyed, "It's as bad as voting against the Church establishment," Madame Goesler jokes. She finds it "so odd in this country that the owner of a property does not seem at all to have any exclusive right to it" (I, 163–4). "The Duke's property indeed!" – is Chiltern's contemptuous reaction to such an argument – "Surely all that was understood in England by this time" (II, 377). The issue of Trumpeton Wood is the issue of the claims of the individual against the group. As the matter is argued in the sporting papers, it sounds like the "scuttling of the ship" quarrel that Phineas and his party opponents are arguing in the clubs and lobbies:

> Is a landed proprietor bound, or is he not, to keep foxes for the amusement of his neighbours? ... Many things are, no doubt, permissible under the law, which, if done, would show the doer of them to be the enemy of his species, – and this destruction of foxes in a hunting country may be named as one of them. The Duke might have his foxes destroyed if he pleased, but he could hardly do so and remain a popular magnate in England (II, 373–4)

– just as Phineas can vote against his party if he likes, but he can hardly do so and retain a position in the government. The individual is forever in conflict with the group, and the man's own private preferences must be weighed against his desire to move in public. Plantagenet Palliser, new Duke of Omnium, does manage to achieve something like a compromise: "He did not hunt himself. ... He recreated himself with Blue Books, and speculations on Adam Smith had been his distraction; – but he knew that he was himself peculiar, and he respected the habits of others" (II, 375). And so the Trumpeton Wood affair is finally settled (for this novel at least) – but not without much wailing and gnashing of teeth.

To move (by the way of the hunting) from the political theme to the domestic, from the public life to the private. The hunting analogy is developed here too, in the story of Mr. Spooner's pursuit of Adelaide Palliser and the progress of his desire for her, first as a "clean-made little mare" (I, 197), and finally, after she has demonstrated her recalcitrance, as "the d – t vixen" (II, 147). But Trollope had developed the imagery of matrimonial hunting with grimmer suggestiveness in the story of the Sir Griffin Tewett and Lucinda Roanoke in *The Eustace Diamonds*.

We saw in *Phineas Finn* how Trollope, in pursuing the history of his romantic young politician, explored the interrelation of love and power. For young Phineas his political and matrimonial aspirations were both vigorous and healthy growths that intertwined and reinforced one another. But in *Phineas Redux* it comes about that the public and private lives are in agonizing conflict. The public gossip about his duel and his women and his good looks had been so much grist to the young Phineas's political mill, but in *Redux* the publicity of his private life – and it is usually false publicity – does him grave professional damage.

The large part of the novel concerned with Phineas's place as an unwilling member of an eternal triangle with the Kennedys is simply splendid story-telling. The episodes of his visit to Kennedy at Loughlinter, to Lady Laura in Dresden, Kennedy's attempt at murder (on a Sunday, moreover)[5] in the stuffy little hotel room, Slide's unctuous gloating over his scandal for his self-righteous little rag of a paper, and Phineas's management of his attempt at blackmail – all these are telling and memorable. The events themselves are close to being melodramatic, and yet they are saved from being *merely* melodramatic by Trollope's delicate evocation of the psychology of the decent citizen's reaction to passion and violence. We are told, after Phineas has bounded out of the room where Kennedy has fired a pistol at his head, that "His first difficulty consisted in this, – that his hat was still in Mr. Kennedy's room, and that Mrs. Macpherson [the proprietress] altogether refused to go and fetch it" (I, 251).[6] And as Phineas frets a little under the wife's passion that he cannot return, he has his similar embarrassments: "He was still standing with his arm round [Lady Laura's] waist, and he did not like to mention the name of Madame Goesler" (I, 417).

By means of Quintus Slide, the editor of *The People's Banner* (a character as odious as Mr. Slope in *Barchester Towers*, and made repellent by the same ugly sexual overtones) Phineas's private embarrassments become public. Slide comes to Phineas with Kennedy's libellous letter, and with a spiel about how "We go in for morals and purity of life, and

we mean to do our duty by the public without fear or favour" (I, 242).
He is fairly salivating about his juicy piece of gossip. Of the letter
Phineas asks,

> 'You don't mean to say that you'll publish it.'
> 'Why shouldn't we publish it?'
> 'It's a private quarrel between a man and his wife.' (I, 241)

But of course Slide is not about to be persuaded by any such argument –
the publicity of private quarrels being his very special delight: all done
in the name of "morals and purity of life." And so, though he is
prevented from publishing the letter itself by Phineas's speedy action in
getting the injunction from the Vice-Chancellor, he has a field-day with
the information in it. The injured husband's cause is taken up by the
injured editor, and the private is made public:

> On the next morning from the columns of The People's Banner was
> hurled the first of those thunderbolts with which it was the purpose of
> Mr. Slide absolutely to destroy the political and social life of Phineas
> Finn. He would not miss his aim as Mr. Kennedy had done. (I, 297)

And indeed he does not miss his aim. Not only does he make Phineas
squirm at the time ("the dagger went right into his bosom. Every word
told upon him"), but he also succeeds in influencing the world against
his victim, so that ultimately Phineas is not offered a place in the next
government. His enemy Bonteen puts in decisive words against him:
officially their quarrel is on the political issue of Phineas's vote against
his party, but Bonteen stabs him in the back by unprofessional allusion
to Phineas's part in the collapse of the Kennedy marriage (I, 410; II, 24).

The quarrel with Bonteen is also an issue given undue proportions by
publicity. Their rivalry is initially a personal matter – the two men
simply don't like each other. And, as with many antagonists in fiction
(Pip and Orlick spring to mind[7]), there are certain parallels in their personal lives that give an edge to their enmity: Bonteen is involved with
Lizzie Eustace, another married woman who is looking for a way to un-
load her husband, as Phineas is involved with Lady Laura. But then the
two become also rival candidates for office; and the quarrel between
them becomes a quarrel between factions, as Lady Glencora and her
forces band together to promote the reluctant Phineas, and Bonteen
gathers his allies.

Bonteen's ministerial appointment is matter for debate in the house,
and finally there is a public quarrel before the assembled company at
the "Universe" Club. What began as a temperamental dislike becomes a
public battle and at last ends as a clandestine clubbing in a dark alley, of
which the public at once assumes Phineas to be guilty. The public knows

at once too much and too little about Phineas. They know too much about the external actions – about his shaking his life-perserver in the direction of Bonteen's retreating figure – and not enough about the private internal principle, which would make it unthinkable that such a man as Phineas would do such a deed.[8] Trollope's vision is of the self that alternately withers under the glare of undue publicity and shrinks in the darkness of the public's ignorance of the private truth.

Bradford Booth suspected that the murder and trial were not part of an original plan, but that Trollope threw them in late in the novel's development to regenerate the reader's flagging interest.[9] Trollope admitted that the incidents of his stories "were created for the most part as they were described" (*A*, 274). But however unpremeditated this set of events was, the trial is thematically integral. Here we see the individual in his personal agony put on public display, and Phineas subject to the "spurns That patient merit of the unworthy takes." The two themes of injustice and the sacrifice of the private life of the public here converge in a trial that is as thematically central as the trial of Magwitch in *Great Expectations*, or the mock trial of Goneril and Regan in *Lear*.

If Trollope introduced the trial for suspense and excitement, he certainly succeeded. The business of the grey coat, Chaffanbrass's ingenious defence, Marie Goesler's romantic search for evidence in remote corners of Europe, and the dramatic arrival of the information about the latch-key: so much should certainly goad the most jaded reader to be anxious for the next page. But Trollope has the skill to manage all those matters without much effort. Where he *has* expended effort is in those passages where the suspense-hungry reader will tend to be impatient: in the psychology of the defendant. What goes on in the mind of a man who is on trial for his life for a crime he did not commit? What happens to a man who has been through such an ordeal?

We have seen how the young Phineas was gifted with a happy lack of self-consciousness, a natural facility for feeling and saying and doing the right thing without much thinking about it. His interest went out toward the world, and was not turned inward. But now in prison he finds he is obsessively concerned with himself:

> The paper and pens he could use because he could write about himself. From day to day he composed a diary in which he never tired of expatiating on the terrible injustice of his position. But he could not read. He found it to be impossible to fix his attention on matters outside himself. (II, 215).

Phineas was changed from his younger self at the outset of this novel, but this event, as indeed might be expected, changes him still further. It is a trauma. The reader who enjoys the excitement of the trial and the last-minute revelations is apt to expect the hero and his friends to go out for a jubilant celebration after the successful outcome, and he, like some of the hero's friends, is rather impatient with Phineas's apparent spinelessness in having something like a nervous breakdown instead. But Trollope is surely right in insisting that a man of any sensitivity cannot go through such an experience and be the same afterwards. Again he insists on the process of change. His description of Phineas's behaviour after the trial, his agonizing sensitivity and fear of meeting people, his secret visit to the scene of the murder he was supposed to have committed, his conscious self-absorption – this springs out of the same deep knowledge of human psychology that made Trollope able to create the more obviously and permanently unbalanced characters in his novels – people like Kennedy and Trevelyan, who have received a good deal more critical admiration than Phineas. Phineas is a delicate mechanism, as Trollope suggests through the clock metaphor I quoted in the last chapter (II, 301), and his works have been severely jolted. Self-absorption, the disease from which he had been so singularly immune, is the result. He confides to Lady Laura, "I am conscious of a certain incapability of getting rid of myself." And he dares not return to the House because of a nightmarish fear: "I shall be afraid to get upon my legs, lest I should find myself talking of the time in which I stood before the judge with a halter round my neck" (II, 331–2).

It was not the fear of death, even death by hanging, that most shook him. It was the thought that people who knew him – in fact that anyone – should have believed him capable of the deed. It is in Phineas's character to seek the public life, because the estimation of other people is what he most cares about. He is no romantic hero, content to be at odds with the world if he is at peace with himself. He cannot bear to be believed guilty of the ultimately unsociable act of murder. Chaffanbrass, as lawyer for his defence, sets before himself the task of getting "a verdict of acquittal if he can" (II, 217); but Phineas says he cares relatively little for a simple legal acquittal: "I have known men to be so acquitted that every man in court believed them to be guilty." He wants to be fully justified as innocent in the eyes of all the world. This is where Trollope differentiates between the two women who love Phineas. Lady Laura secretly hopes that he will be acquitted, but acquitted on those terms that Phineas himself finds unacceptable – because if all the world rejects him then he will be hers: "Should he escape, but escape ingloriously; – ah, then he should know what the devotion of a woman could do for a man! But if he should leave his prison with flying colours, and come forth a hero to the world, how would it be with her then?" (II, 268). Secretly she longs to have him to herself, to demonstrate the force of her passion against the whole world. She even has a romantic fantasy of marrying him at the foot of the gallows (II, 119).

Marie Goesler, on the other hand, is determined there shall be no transaction with the gallows whatever. Her wishes coincide with

6. Marie Goesler: Holl's illustration for *Phineas Redux*, chapter 15

Phineas's in that she is determined he shall be acquitted not merely on a
technicality, but in such a way as to convince the world he is innocent.
"It would not be sufficient for her that Phineas Finn should be
acquitted. She desired that the real murderer should be hung for the
murder, so that all the world might be sure, – as she was sure, – that her
hero had been wrongfully accused" (II, 180). And, enterprising and
resourceful woman as she is, she takes steps to bring this about.
Through her exertions over the grey coat and the latch-key, and with the
able help of Chaffanbrass, Phineas gets the acquittal on the terms that
are acceptable to him.

Phineas does recover from his experience, though. He is, after all,
Phineas Finn still, and though he has lost much of the elasticity and optimism of his earlier days, he still has the resilient health to enable his
injuries to heal. We remember how well he managed to hobble, and
soon even to gallop, after the news of Violet's engagement by which he
thought "his back was broken." This time the metaphor changes to one
taken from Elizabeth Barrett Browning's "A Musical Instrument":[10]

> He had been so hacked and hewed about, so exposed to the gaze of
> the vulgar, so mauled by the public, that he could never more be
> anything but the wretched being who had been tried for the murder
> of his enemy. The pith had been taken out of him, and he was no
> longer a man fit'for use. He could never more enjoy that freedom
> from self-consciousness, that inner tranquillity of spirit, which are
> essential to public utility. (II, 293).

This self-consciousness is not a healthy self-awareness, but a morbid
and paralysing self-absorption. Phineas's sensibility has inevitably
expanded, but for the moment he is crippled and incapacitated, and,
like Hamlet, simply sickened by himself and the world. Nevertheless, as
he did from his "broken back," he begins to rally: "Though at this
moment he was low in heart, disgusted with the world, and sick of
humanity, – though every joint in his body was still sore from the rack
on which he had been stretched, yet he knew that it would not be so with
him always" (II, 340). And when he goes to Matching he displays his old
uncalculated grace in his unpremeditated kissing of his saviour Marie.
But the change has in some senses been more permanent than his rapid
recovery at Matching would suggest. Everything has gone sour, and the
zest has been taken out of the old pursuits: "during the last few months
a change had crept across his dream, – which he recognised but could
hardly analyse. He had seen a man whom he despised promoted, and
the place to which the man had been exalted had at once become contemptible in his eyes. And there had been quarrels and jangling, and the
speaking of evil words between men who should have been quiet and
dignified" (II, 401). And this is no mere cynical disguise for sour grapes.

When at last he is offered the place for which he had been hungering, he turns it down, even though in doing so he takes a risk of ending his political career entirely (Marie's fortune is to save him; but he refuses the place before he knows this).

This sense of disillusion and disgust with the operation of the world pervades not only Phineas's own development, but the novel as a whole. Plot and subplot, action and incident and character are arranged to reiterate the proposition that the time is out of joint, that virtue is not rewarded, that there are no just deserts. Truth and justice do not pertain, but lies and faction. We have here the vision of Ecclesiastes, which coincides with Hamlet's: "The race is not to the swift, nor the battle to the strong, neither yet bread to the wise, nor yet riches to men of understanding, nor yet favour to men of skill. But time and chance happeneth to them all."

Consider the subplot. Bradford Booth, who has much to say on the structural weaknesses of Trollope's novels, points out that the story of Adelaide Palliser and Gerard Maule "has no slightest bearing on Phineas Finn,"[11] and certainly the links through the action are of the lightest. But again the unity is thematic. It was quite Trollope's plan to make this little love story (not that it deserves the name) unsatisfying. There is simply no rhyme or reason for it, and that is the point. Adelaide Palliser is a fine and intelligent young girl, and yet she gives herself to the worthless Gerard Maule, who is virtually a negative quantity. He is completely lacking in determination or energy or social position or money. "I'm a poor creature," he says of himself, and he is right (I, 78). The well-heeled Mr. Spooner, Adelaide's other suitor, who though he may not be lovable at least has the right to propose to her and receive a courteous answer, she utterly and unreasonably scorns. On finding Maule preferred to himself, Spooner indignantly concludes, "Because a man greases his whiskers, and colours his hair, and paints his eyebrows, and wears kid gloves, by George, they'll go through fire and water after him" (I, 318). And that's about the size of it. Worth has nothing to do with the matter. Gerard Maule and Adelaide are the "young lovers" of the novel (at least one of Trollope's reviewers felt it necessary to apologize for him that the other lovers are "on the shady side of thirty"[12]), and Trollope as a matter of course gives them a happy ending. But he is careful to make the sentimental reader feel uncomfortable about the matter. There is simply no consonance between the deserts of the couple and the comfortable legacy that descends on them out of the blue. Lady Glencora, who has never shown any interest in her husband's cousin before, takes it into her head to play fairy godmother to the couple and hand over an awkward rejected legacy. But she admits, "She is nothing to me, – and as for him, I shouldn't know him again if I were to meet him in the street" (II, 388). The matter is settled quite arbitrarily, and the seeker after virtue rewarded is balked of his expectations.

If there is no alignment between virtue and reward, so there is little between vice and just deserts. Trollope knows very well how to create a properly offensive antagonist when he wants to – there is some spirit in the flashy self-satisfaction of a Crosbie or the wily calculations of a Mr. Scarborough. But Bonteen! – he scarcely deserves the name of villain, and Phineas is almost ashamed of disliking such a totally undistinguished and pettifogging little official. He is "a hack among the hacks" (I, 344). And yet he succeeds, through no will or skill of his own, in getting the ultimate last word: your enemy's last unanswerable insult is to die on you. And in this case Phineas is even held guilty of the murder.

Phineas is often led to reflect on the injustice of the world's dispositions. Through the whole novel he is constantly reminded of the lack of correspondence between emotion and its stimulus. Whatever he does, he knows that Lady Laura's love will remain constant, and apart from a cause: "Why should this woman love him so dearly? She was nothing to him." And when she seeks the comfort of supposing her unhappiness is a just result of her guilt, he corrects her.

'If I had not been very wrong all this evil could not have come upon me.'

'Misfortune has not always been deserved.' (I, 116).

And nor has good fortune, either.

It is the same in the political world: and Phineas's constituency, Tankerville, is an index of the illogical operation of public opinion. For years the constitutents have been satisfied with their completely undistinguished member Mr. Browborough, who is equivalent as a politician to Gerard Maule as a lover: "– a man who could not say ten words, of no family, . . . distinguished by no zeal in politics, entertaining no special convictions of his own" (II, 33). He loses the seat to Phineas because bribery is proved against him. Here old Browborough has his own reflections on injustice: "He had spent his money like a gentleman, and hated these mean ways" (I, 140). But when he is tried for the offence, the Tankervillians fold him to their hearts as a persecuted martyr, and Phineas is considered the villain of the piece. "Everybody knows that he bribed and that you did not," his friends console him. "Yes; – and everybody despises me and pats him on the back," is Phineas's bitter rejoinder (II, 44–5). Here Phineas's antagonist has been tried and found guilty, but Phineas is felt to be the culprit. Later Phineas himself is to be tried and found innocent, but the guilt attaches to him none the less. You can't win – these are more of the spurns that patient merit of the unworthy takes. Phineas's hour of glory in the eyes of his constituents is to come when he has been through his ordeal of the trial – as though that had anything to do with his quality as a politician. He applies for the Chiltern Hundreds, but his enthusiastic constituents positively refuse not to return him again. "I am told that I am to be re-elected triumphantly at Tankerville without a penny of cost or the trouble of asking for a vote, simply because I didn't knock poor Mr. Bonteen on the head," Phineas reflects disgustedly (II, 333).

The fickle mob is always shown as fastening on this man at that for the wrong reasons. Trollope is in his element in discussing the crowd psychology on the news of the murder. A great deal of prestige is attached to the deed of violence, and people who know Phineas immediately believe him to be guilty, and almost think the more of him for it, taking to themselves some share of reflected glory: "To have known a murdered man is something, but to have been intimate with a murderer is certainly much more" (II, 101). There is even a certain amount of jealousy about the candidates for guilt: Lizzie Eustace rather hopes her own husband is the murderer, for "There was a dash of adventure about it which was almost gratifying. . . . [She felt] certain that it was the bold hand of her own Emilius who had struck the blow" (II, 198).

Society grants its adulation to people who have done nothing to deserve it. We hear much of the old Duke of Omnium, who dies in the course of this novel. The bulletins about his condition are received and reverently discussed in the clubs as though he were a national benefactor. "And yet, perhaps, no man who had lived during the same period, or any portion of the period, had done less, or had devoted himself more entirely to the consumption of good things without the slightest idea of producing anything in return!" (I, 260). On a smaller scale, there are others, like the vapid and morally bankrupt Mr. Maule, Senior, who manage to be social successes without any manifest reason. "He was known as a good diner out, though in what his excellence consisted they who entertained him might find it difficult to say. He was not witty, nor did he deal in anecdotes . . ." and nor does he have any other quality that should earn him such a reputation (I, 224). The race is not to the swift. And so with the institutions, like the allegorically named Universe Club:

> Its attractions were not numerous, consisting chiefly of tobacco and tea. The conversation was generally listless and often desultory; and occasionally there would arise the great and terrible evil of a punster whom everyone hated but no one had life enough to put down. But the thing had been a success, and men liked to be members of the Universe. (I. 372–3.

And so too with the major event of the novel, the trial. An innocent man is put on trial for his life. The superficially clumsy set of coincidences that incriminate Phineas is again part of Trollope's plan – he *means* the affair to be accidental, wild, unlikely, arbitrary. The theory is that a suspect is innocent until proved guilty, but the *practice* is of course that the mere fact of Phineas's arrest makes the public automatically believe him to be guilty. When Phineas faces the likelihood of being hanged, and Mr. Low says comfortingly "May God, in His mercy, forbid," Phineas replies indignantly, "No; – not in his mercy; in His justice. There can be no need for mercy here" (II, 162). He wants only justice, but he does want that. And of course he finds that the law and justice do not coincide. Phineas is aware that his attorney, Mr. Wickerby, though conscientious in his work for the defence, believes him to be guilty. The law is not in pursuit of the truth. This is an old theme of Trollope's, familiar especially from *Orley Farm*, but here it is part of a total pattern. Mr. Chaffanbrass, heroic and effective though his defence is, is concerned not with the facts, but the evidence; his object is not to demonstrate innocence, but to attain a *verdict* of not guilty. And he does his work on Phineas's behalf while privately believing him to have committed the murder. When Phineas wants to speak to him before the trial, he goes reluctantly, believing he will hear more than he wants to know. He unblushingly acknowledges, "I do not in the least want to know the truth about the murder" (II, 213). Such an attitude is torture to Phineas, who in his conscious innocence feels that to be condemned in men's minds is simply the equivalent of being physically strung up on the gallows.

The lawyers are rather proud of the process by which Phineas is eventually acquitted; it demonstrates to their satisfaction that justice has been done. The judge spends four hours, in front of an impatient jury that has already made up its mind, in convincing himself and his audience that even without the fresh evidence they would not have been in danger of convicting an innocent man, and congratulating the law for its virtual infallibility in this matter; and indeed the jury produce their verdict of Not Guilty "without half a minute's delay" (II, 287). This, in the usual story constructed around a trial, is the moment of triumph. But it is not so with Phineas.

> Thus Phineas Finn was acquitted, and the judges, collecting up their robes, trooped off from the bench. . . . Mr. Chaffanbrass collected his papers, . . . and the Attorney and Solicitor-General congratulated each other on the successful termination of a very disagreeable piece of business.
> And Phineas was discharged. (II, 288–9).

All the pomp and paraphernalia of the law leaves the client not triumphant and vindicated, but utterly disillusioned and broken. The injustice for Phineas is not in the verdict, but in the fact that he had been put on trial at all. The accurate verdict has not proved that the law is just, because so far as Phineas is concerned the punishment of the innocent has already occurred by the very suspicion of murder and the ordeal of the trial. He cannot rejoice in being declared innocent, when he has for so many days been shown that the nation believed him guilty. As well expect a man to rejoice in being told he hasn't got cancer, when he has been dismembered in the process of diagnosis.

This is the way Trollope defeats the expectations of the sensation-hungry readers; he has used the trial for purposes of suspense, but he has made it conduce to his dominent themes of the novel, and further our knowledge of human psychology. The reader who looks for the triumphant vindication after the trial ordeal is left instead with the same kind of distaste and disillusion that he has in reading other tales with bitterly qualified happy endings: *Job*, or Chaucer's *Clerk's Tale*, or *Measure for Measure* or *The Winter's Tale*. At the end of *Job* we are told "So the Lord blessed the latter end of Job more than his beginning." And at the end of *Phineas Redux*, "Of Phineas every one says that of all living men he has been the most fortunate" (II, 433). It all comes right in the end. But we remain appalled that it should ever have gone so wrong.

5   *The Eustace Diamonds*: "What is Truth?" Said Jesting Pilate

The Eustace Diamonds is generally admired by Trollope's critics, Bradford Booth excepted; but considering its accepted status it has attracted little close analysis of theme or technique, and has suffered from the general tendency to treat Trollope's work as all of a piece. Booth acknowledges the plot is unusually good for Trollope, but is unimpressed, "(Trollope's particular charm having nothing to do with plot anyway)."[1] Ruth ap Roberts refers to it in the context of Aitken's contention that imagery is "rather unimportant in the general scheme of [Trollope's] art."[2] Others have lumped it in with Trollope's notorious tactlessness in naming his characters, or with his carelessness in any systematic pursuit of an idea. Though I am far from being ready to dismiss the rest of Trollope's novels as ill-plotted unintellectual stories, bare of significant imagery and cluttered with implausibly named personages, it seems to me that in the case of *The Eustace Diamonds* we are dealing with a work that has been more than usually wrought round a central theme, and one in which imagery, action and character, even to the naming of characters, interact and support that central theme.

   Trollope's subject is the same as Bacon's in his essay "Of Truth,"[3] and Spenser's in the first book of *The Faerie Queene*; and the novelist is consciously going over the same ground as the philosopher and the moral allegorist. Like Bacon, he finds that the investigation of truth involves a very thorough investigation of lies too, and they both speculate on the unlikely but demonstrable attractions of truth's antagonist. "It is not only the difficulty and labour which men take in finding out of truth; nor again, that when it is found, it imposeth upon men's thoughts, that doth bring lies in favour; but a natural though corrupt love of the lie

78

itself." In Lizzie Eustace we see embodied that natural though corrupt love of the lie itself. She loves lies, and makes men love the lies she tells. Plain, unadorned little Lucy Morris – she is not so successful a creation as Lizzie, but still, she is no failure – is humdrum, ordinary, light-of-day truth: "This same truth is a naked and open daylight, that doth not show the masks and mummeries and triumphs of the world, half so stately and daintily as candle-lights. Truth may perhaps come to the price of a pearl, that showeth best by day, but it will not rise to the price of a diamond or carbuncle, that showeth best in varied lights." Lucy's name associates her with light. Lizzie is identified with her diamonds; and her chosen associate is Mrs. "Carbuncle."[4]

There is a simple allegorical meaning in the opposition of Lucy to Lizzie, although the novelist works out his theme in a fine and realistic complication of character and incident. The people and the action and the imagery are all arranged with a view to the investigation of truth.[5] That characteristic phrase of Trollope's, "in truth" – which he uses in preference to the less emphatic "indeed", and so ubiquitously that it becomes sometimes almost invisible, like the air – in this novel has a special resonance. Simply the number of times "the truth" is mentioned, both by narrator and characters, is amazing once you start looking for it. But unless you look for it it is not obtrusive – the truth, like Lucy, being undemonstrative and often obscure.

Bradford Booth calls Lizzie "the poor man's Becky Sharp," and actually takes Trollope to task for failing to make Lizzie as likable as Becky.[6] Other critics, including the original reviewers, picked on the same analogy, which Trollope himself acknowledged in referring to her early in the novel as "that opulent and aristocratic Becky Sharp" (18). But not only has her likeness or unlikeness to Becky little to do with her quality as an independent creation: the analogy is for the most part the wrong one. Becky, although she constantly deceives others, seldom deceives herself: she retains a grasp on reality, and has shrewd and acute moral perception even if she is herself immoral. She can accurately assess the worth of George Osborne and Dobbin, for instance, where Amelia is completely blind. But Lizzie constantly and wilfully fools herself as well as others, and believes in her own phoney poses. And as Trollope explains when she entertains the suit of the greasy humbug Emilius, she is "altogether deficient in what may perhaps be called good taste in reference to men" (595).

A more appropriate analogy from Thackeray is Blanche Amory in *Pendennis*.[7] She goes in for "poetry" in the same way as Lizzie; she tries to live her life as romance; and she has no centre of identity, but is simply an encrustation of super-imposed poses with no real self inside. "This young lady was not able to carry out any emotion to the full; but had a sham enthusiasm, a sham hatred, a sham love, a sham taste, a sham grief, each of which flared and shone very vehemently for an instant, but subsided and gave place to the next sham emotion" (*Pendennis*, ch. 73). (Trollope quoted from this passage in his book on Thackeray.) Similarly we hear of Lizzie, "She was always shamming love and friendship and benevolence and tenderness. . . . Yet she knew that she herself was ever shamming, and she satisfied herself with shams" (125). There are certain close echoes of *Pendennis* that occasionally suggest a direct influence: for instance we hear of Blanche that "her hostilities [were] never very long or durable," and of Lizzie, "she was almost incapable of real anger" (17). But the parallel seems to me most interesting not as a study in influence, but as a suggestion of affinity in theme. Thackeray's central concern in *Pendennis*, like Trollope's in *The Eustace Diamonds*, is the pursuit of truth and honesty, which the heroes can approach only after prolonged encounters with falsehood.[8]

"Poor Lizzie Eustace!" the narrator exclaims in *Phineas Redux*, at the end of our acquaintance with her. "Was it nature or education which had made it impossible to her to tell the truth, when a lie came to her hand? Lizzie, the liar!" (II, 351). Lizzie is not just another scheming, deceitful self-seeker, like Blifil or Pecksniff or Becky, who lie with a definite end in view, to gain something for themselves; nor is she a self-deceiving hypocrite like Bulstrode, who believes in the virtue of his own acquisitiveness. But she is closer to being falsehood itself, like Spenser's Duessa, because she loves lies for their own sake, and not just for what she can get by them. Her complex commitment to falsehood is not only frequently stated in *The Eustace Diamonds*, but abundantly and delightfully dramatized. "The guiding motive of her conduct," we hear, "was the desire to make things seem to be other than they were. To be always acting a part rather than living her own life was to her everything" (175).

Her lies are pointless and often transparent. She recalls Bacon's wonder that men should love lies "where neither they make for pleasure, as with poets; nor for advantage, as with the merchant, but for the lie's sake." So though Lard Fawn carefully explains his position and circumstances to her when he proposes to her, she deliberately misinforms her relatives about him, and gushes about how her son loves him, although in fact they have not met.

But, true to her guiding motive of making things seem to be other than they are, she is always invoking the truth, and suggesting that the traitors and hypocrites are the people who surround her. Duessa's alias, after all, is Fidessa. The promise she extorts from her men is that they should be true to her. To Frank down among the rocks of Portray she insists,

'Frank, you'll be true to me?'
'I will be true to you.'
'Then go now,' she said. (240)

And she maintains the pose with him of one so essentially honest that
the truth must burst from her, even though her overmastering passion
should in delicacy remain concealed:

'I did not mean to say all this, but it has been said, and you must leave
me. I, at any rate, cannot play the hypocrite; – I wish I could.' He rose
and came to her, and attempted to take her hand, but she flung away
from him. 'No!' she said, – 'never again; never, unless you will tell me
that the promise you made me when we were down on the sea-shore
was a true promise. Was that truth, sir, or was it a – lie?'
      'Lizzie, do not use such a word as that to me.'
      'I cannot stand picking my words when the whole world is going
round with me, and my very brain is on fire. . . . You know my secret,
and I care not who else knows it.' (286–7)

Never was such passionate and imprudent honesty! One must allow that
Lizzie is good at a scene.

At her next determined pitch for Frank, she pursues the same line.
"Frank, you are false to me! . . . You know, better almost than I can
know myself, how my heart stands. [Yes, one is inclined to acknowledge;
but that's not saying much.] There has, at any rate, been no hypocrisy
with me in regard to you. Everything has been told to you; – at what cost
I will not now say. . . . Honesty in a woman the world never forgives"
(481). She is regularly a martyr to the truth.

Among her other exclusive and unalterable passions is her love for
Lord George, and it is satisfying to recognize the old refrain. This scene
takes place in between the two with Frank, quoted above. " 'You will be
true to me; – will you not?' she said, still clinging to his arm. He
promised her that he would. 'Oh, George,' she said, 'I have no friend
now but you. You will care for me?' He took her in his arms and kissed
her, and promised her that he would care for her. How was he to save
himself from doing so?" (462).

This substitution of lies for truth makes a splendid tangle of Lizzie's
love life, as she scoops towards herself all the credit for truth and hands
out the lie to other people. "The truth is," she says with the authority of
one who has long studied the subject, and has at last grasped the
ultimate reality, "Lucinda Roanoke did not understand what real love
means" (638). She uses her tags boldly, but they no longer have any distinction, and she is quite unable to know anything about the state of her
own heart, apart from the lying and irreconcilable statements she makes
about it. She is heartless, but "she would have described herself, – and
would have meant to do so with truth, – as being all heart" (238). In the
second half of the novel we see her frantically trying to make sure of her
men, working on Frank, Lord George and Lord Fawn in turn. "She
would sometimes tell herself that she was violently in love; but she hard-

ly knew with which" (474). And we see her in moods of pathetic self-righteousness, counting her grievances: "Had she not loved her Corsair truly, – and how had he treated her? Had she not been true, disinterested, and most affectionate to Frank Greystock; and what had she got from him?" (609). In her self-pity, she apparently feels that the more men she has been trying for at the same time, the more pathetic and love-lorn she must be in her disappointment.

In her last man, Emilius, she finds her soulmate. Here Trollope perhaps has some difficulty in reconciling his allegory of truth and falsehood with the demands of realistic fiction.[9] On the face of it it is not likely that Lizzie, who does have her wits about her so far as social prestige goes, should throw away herself and her fortune on so manifest a charlatan. We can believe she is dificient in taste in men, but then she has in her way been able to recognize certain reliable qualities in Lord Fawn, Frank and Lord George. Would she sink this low? But Trollope is constant to his allegory, and unites falsehood with falsehood at the end.

And he does succeed in making the match plausible. He shows how Emilius is clever enough to come courting when Lizzie is most in need of a husband, and how he can talk the "poetry" Lizzie longs for:

> 'Darling of my heart, queen of my soul, empress presiding over the very spirit of my being, say, – shall I overcome? . . .'
> She had never been made love to after this fashion before. She knew, or half knew, that the man was a scheming hypocrite, craving her money, and following her in the hour of her troubles, because he might then have the best chance of success. She had no belief whatever in his love. And yet she liked it, and approved his proceedings. She liked lies, thinking them to be more beautiful than truth. (718–9)

And so Lizzie Eustace, the carefully characterized inhabitant of a realistically conceived world, coexists with the allegorical conception Lizzie the liar; and Duessa finds refuge with her Archimago.

If Lizzie is Frank Greystock's Duessa, Lucy is his Una. She is insistently indentified with the truth – in fact Frank writes to her in so many words, "You are truth itself" (120). Lucy and Lizzie are paired and contrasted from the first. They are both orphans left penniless on the world. Lizzie schemes and entraps a rich husband, but Lucy works for her living as a governess. She has an instinct for discovering falshoold, and is early on her guard against Lizzie: "when Lizzie talked to her of their old childish days, and quoted poetry, and spoke of things romantic, – as she was much given to do, – Lucy felt that the metal did not ring true" (20). Lizzie has no centre of identity and is all sham, through and through; but Lucy is "one who had a well-formed idea of her own identity" (25).[10]

"She was a proud, stout, self-confident, but still modest, little woman, too fond of truth to tell lies of herself even to herself" (59–60). She does not go in for rhapsodies of expression, like Lizzie, but on the other hand her tone and her few simple non-committal words convey the fact of her love and her lasting fidelity to Frank more than all Lizzie's passionate outbursts. "It was not in her to tell a lie to him, even by a tone. She had intended to say nothing of her love, but he knew that it had all been told. ... Certainly there never was a voice that brought home to the hearer so strong a sense of its own truth!" (114).

It is Lucy's part to be unassertive and retiring; and Trollope knows and acknowledges that the story of the Eustace Diamonds is really Lizzie's story, not Lucy's. Lucy's role is to endure and to be quiet, and she can't have much of the drama in a story where Lizzie's histrionic posturings are to be so exposed. Nevertheless, she is one of the more spirited and sympathetic of Trollope's good girls. The heroically self-abnegating heroines of the Barset novels, like Mary Thorne, Lucy Robarts and Grace Crawley, who refuse their suitors for their suitors' own good and so take on a moral burden for two, do not set the pattern for Lucy Morris. She is not one to conceal her own love, even for her lover's sake. "She threw from her, at once, as vain and wicked and false, all idea of coying her love. She would leap at his neck if he were there" (135). The idea of her possible moral duty to refuse him for his own good does occur to her, but she rejects it: "I couldn't give you up. I almost thought that I ought to refuse you because I can do nothing, – nothing to help you. But there will always come a limit to self-denial. I couldn't do that!" (169). Among the ranks of Trollope's good girls, Lucy is rather bold in thus clinging to her own interests instead of her lover's. But Jane Austen, at least, would hardly have sympathized with the heroic self-abnegation of the Barset girls, having treated the notion of self-sacrifice in such a context with some irony. When Emma finds that Mr. Knightley loves her, after all, and not Harriet, she accepts him joyfully: "for as to any of that heroism of sentiment which might have prompted her to entreat him to transfer his affection from herself to Harriet, as infinitely the most worthy of the two – ... Emma had it not." One suspects that Jane Austen might have called Mary Thorne's grand gesture of refusing Frank Gresham a "flight of generosity run mad" (*Emma*, III, ch. 13).

Lucy's resolution not to give up Frank Greystock is put to the test later on, when Frank has humiliatingly neglected her, and she is told from all sides that it would be against his best interests to keep his engagement to her. She does write him a letter in which she tells him, "I certainly do not wish to be the cause of injury to you. All I ask is that you should tell me the truth" (528). The words are literally true; but she recognizes that the implication of her letter is that she absolves him from his promise, and that she knows would be false. So she doesn't send the letter. Lucy broods on these matters, and is determined to be exactly honest.

Like Una, Lucy must suffer, while her Frank goes dangling after his Duessa. And Trollope succeeds in investing her situation with a real pathos, as, deserted by her love, she tries to maintain her faith to him among his enemies, while she keeps getting fresh evidence of his derogation. She recalls the neglected Una's address to her tardy knight:

> Ah my long lacked Lord,
> Where have ye been thus long out of my sight?
> Much feared I to have bene quite abhord.
>
> (*Faerie Queene*, I, iii, 27)

But there is a certain active quality about Lucy's passive endurance. Having a reality and a centre of self, Lucy can be fully happy, as she is when Frank declares his love, but she can also suffer fully. When she believes Frank has deserted her, she is utterly desolate: "How bitter to her was that possession of herself, as she felt that there was nothing good to be done with the thing so possessed!" (544). Lizzie, on the other hand, is simply not accessible to any real emotion, and can be neither genuinely glad nor genuinely sad. Scruple she has none, and shame she has none. "I ain't a bit ashamed of anything," she declares brassily, when she has been through her ritual confession of what Camperdown takes to be her iniquities (655). Experience simply cannot touch her, though she puts up a great show of falling upon the thorns of life and bleeding.

In the few encounters between Lizzie and Lucy, Lucy decidedly comes out best, though Lizzie has nearly all the cards in her hand. Lizzie, as she thinks discreetly, once offers Lucy a bribe: "If you'll be true to me, Lucy, in this business, I'll make you the handsomest present you ever saw in your life." But Lucy, unlike Lizzie's men, understands exactly what being "true" to Lizzie means, and replies roundly, "You mean thing!" (140). And in their final interview, when Lizzie comes the compassionate bosom friend who must tell Lucy her fiancé loves another (that other being herself), Lucy knows how to slice right through the falsehood.

> 'You can't make me angry, Lucy, because my heart bleeds for you.'
> 'Nonsense! trash! I don't want your heart to bleed. I don't believe you've got a heart. You've got money; I know that.' (580)

And though Lizzie is the one who makes most play with the tactic of giving the lie to people, Lucy is the one who most effectively gives Lizzie the lie. On the same occasion, she tells Lizzie, "if you tell him I do not love him better than all the world, you will lie to him. And if you say that he loves you better than he does me, that also will be a lie. I know his heart" (581). Lizzie is powerless against this kind of steadfastness.

Frank Greystock may be a rather feckless Redcrosse Knight, but perhaps the choice of his name, "Frank," does among other things carry on the allegory, and suggest his quest for honesty in a world where falsehood has most of the power and glamour. Placed between Lizzie and Lucy, "He knew that the difference was that between truth and falsehood; – and yet he partly believed the falsehood!" (174). Like Redcrosse, he makes an initial commitment to truth, and is then for a long time seduced away from his Una by the wiles of Duessa. And although his moral struggle is not the most interesting part of the book, and is, indeed, a repetition of many another man-between-two-women situation in the novels, Trollope has expended some care on it, and has concentrated here on showing the seductive and corrupting force of falsehood.

We are expected to believe in his love for Lucy, as in hers for him, as an undebatable fact, part of the donné of the story. But like so many of Trollope's central male characters, he is lacking in decision and steadiness, and simply allows himself to be swayed this way and that by the action of persuasion and circumstance. Early we see him about to propose to Lizzie, simply because time and occasion and the course of the conversation lead him that way; it is only the accidental entry of Lady Linlithgow that prevents him. Next, only on the impulse of the moment, he declares his love to Lucy, and then he backs his declaration with a written proposal which he almost does not send. But having bound himself so far to Lucy, he responds to the more importunate demands of Lizzie for most of the main action of the novel; and in the course of his attendance on her, he is in a fair way to becoming a false knight.

Trollope shows his gradual concessions to falsehood in his attendance on Lizzie. First, like Pen with Blanche Amory, he makes love to her "as your brother," so that they are "acting their little play together" (176). Soon he is lying by omission to Lizzie in not telling her of his engagement to Lucy. And when Lizzie taxes him with wanting Lucy and what she calls "repose," he replies evasively,

> 'We seldom know what we want, I fancy. We take what the gods send us.' Frank's words were perhaps more true than wise. At the present moment the gods had clearly sent Lizzie Eustace to him, and unless he could call up some increased strength of his own, quite independent of the gods, – or of what we may perhaps call chance, – he would have to put up with the article sent. (237–8)

Soon we find him equivocating in the face of direct questions. When Lizzie asks him, "When is Lucy to be made blessed?" the artificiality of her question gives him occasion for an evasive reply, and he uses it. "I don't know that Lucy will ever be made blessed, . . . but I am sure I hope she will" (382). We see the process by which Lizzie can infect people, and make them false like herself. Next Frank is even producing for Lizzie's enlightenment a whole philosophy and ethics of dishonesty which sounds like the basis for *The Way We Live Now*. He admires "the courage, the ingenuity, and the self-confidence" of the large-scale embezzler, and goes on,

> 'And then there is a cringing and almost contemptible littleness about honesty, which hardly allows it to assert itself. . . . Honesty goes about with a hang-dog look about him, as though knowing that he cannot be trusted till he be proved. Dishonesty carries his eyes high, and assumes that any question respecting him must be considered to be unnecessary.'
> 'Oh, Frank, what a philosopher you are.'
> 'Well, yes; meditating about your diamonds has brought my philosophy out." (480–1)

He really exceeds himself when as the champion of injured innocence he lectures Lord Fawn on his dilatory conduct to his fiancée, and insists that Lizzie's conduct in the engagement has been "without reproach" (500) – when he knows only too much of her seductive blandishments among the rocks at Portray. Frank's plausibly motivated and vividly dramatized entanglement with Lizzie is the realistic novelist's version of Redcrosse's sojourn with Duessa. What Frank's behaviour demonstrates at length is that "young or old, men are apt to become Merlins when they encounter Viviens" (584). Lizzie has the power to transform the truth into her own likeness.

When events and revelations make Frank forcibly aware of the extent of Lizzie's lies, and of his own in supporting her, he does regain some power of judgment, both of her and of himself. "I have been led to make so many statements to other people, which now seem to have been – incorrect!" he admits ruefully (642). He goes through no such penance as does Redcrosse for his association with Duessa; but still we are carefully led to the moment of his ability at last to see Lizzie as in herself she is. It is when she makes her last-ditch attempt to catch him, on the train journey back to Scotland.

> In real truth Frank was becoming very sick of her. It seemed to him now to have been almost impossible that he should ever soberly have thought of making her his wife. The charm was all gone, and even her prettiness had in his eyes lost its value. He looked at her, asking himself whether in truth she was pretty. She had been travelling all day, and perhaps the scrutiny was not fair. But he thought that even

after the longest day's journey Lucy would not have been soiled, haggard, dishevelled, and unclean, as was this woman. (688–9)

This is the moment of revelation, and it has its place in the allegory. In the same way Duessa was revealed in her true form:

> Such as she was, their eyes might her behold,
> That her misshaped parts did them appall,
> A loathly, wrinckled hag, ill favoured, old,
> Whose secret filth good manners biddeth not be told.
>
> (*Faerie Queene*, I, viii, 46)

Spenser goes on to describe the stripped Duessa in memorable detail, whereas Trollope certainly stops within the bounds of those "good manners," and for the most part accounts for the change in realistic terms. But Frank has had his revelation, and the final, biblical term, "unclean," reminds us that this is moral allegory as well as realistic narrative.

Incidentally, Lizzie once starts reading *The Faerie Queene*, but understandably gives it up early (199). Probably Duessa wouldn't have found it congenial reading either.

Trollope's investigation of truth and falsehood includes a consistent patterning in the creation of the minor characters as well as the major ones. Although they exist, as Trollope ensures all his characters seem to do, in their own right, we always see them presented in the context of their relation to truth and lies. It is only Lucy who is "truth itself," and we see in her drab grey dress and rather Spartan nature something of the reason why truth does not have the glitter and attraction of lies. Una too wore a veil. In other characters we see more of the somewhat forbidding aspects of truth.

Lady Linlithgow specializes in announcing the uncomfortable truth. She is one of the most vividly individualized of Trollope's many fearsome aristocratic duennas. And she is particularly dreadful to Lizzie because of her definitively announced intention. "I shall say just what I think, Lizzie" (52). She is presented as the proper antagonist to sham and deceit: "Her appearance on the whole was not prepossessing, but it gave one an idea of honest, real strength. What one saw was not buckram, whalebone, paint, and false hair. It was all human, – ... a human body, and not a thing of pads and patches" (51). Bunyan could hardly have described Mr. Valiant-for-Truth more tellingly. It is appropriately Lady Linlithgow's interruption that prevents Frank's proposal to Lizzie at the outset. And again she has an allegorical function in providing a refuge for the forsaken Lucy. She is in fact rather like Una's Lion, though she is very far from gentle, even to Lucy. She wants to rub her nose too in disagreeable truths: "And dame Greystock, from

Bobsborough, has sent you here to keep you out of her son's way. I see it all. And that old frump at Richmond [that is, Lady Fawn] has passed you over to me because she did not choose to have such goings on under her own eye" (312). She does indeed see it all, and she takes grim pleasure in announcing what she sees. "What is the use, Miss Morris, of not looking the truth in the face? Mr. Greystock is neglecting you," she persists (526). The seasoning of spite to her home truths makes them not altogether true, however, and she is fortunately proved wrong in the case of Lucy and Frank.

Lady Linlithgow with her aristocratic pitilessness has her lower-class equivalent in Miss Macnulty, who embodies the pathetic ineffectuality of unadorned honesty. Being utterly a dependent, she is "obliged to be a poor creature" (56), and she reminds us of Frank's philosophizing about the cringing littleness of honesty, "which hardly allows it to assert itself" (480). But in the absence of Lucy and Lady Linlithgow, she is the humble representative of truth in Lizzie's household. "Miss Macnulty was humble, cowardly, and subservient; but she was not a fool, and she understood the difference between truth and falsehood" (54). There are several funny scenes in which Lizzie tries to extract some sympathetic posturings from her companion, and fails utterly. For if Macnulty can't luxuriate in frankness like Lady Linlithgow, neither can she get up a display of partisanship for her new employer, – not perhaps from any special merit but from a constitutional incapability: "Miss Macnulty did not believe in Lady Eustace and was not sufficiently gifted to act up to a belief which she did not entertain" (189). Again we hear, "It was hardly conscience or a grand spirit of truth that actuated her, as much as a want of the courage needed for lying" (196–7). In the episode in which Lizzie spouts her newly-memorized passage from *Queen Mab*, and longs for a gush of sympathetic sensibility, Macnulty responds doggedly, "To tell the truth, . . . I never understand poetry when it is quoted" (198). She hardly realizes that "to tell the truth" is the last thing Lizzie wants of her paid employee. Lady Linlithgow sums up this poor dependent with characteristic succinctness: "She's a stupid, dull, pig-headed creature; but one can believe what she says" (420).

In Mrs. Hittaway Trollope presents the over-zealous antagonist to falsehood which itself is false. From the outset she announces Lizzie is a liar and takes it on herself to demonstrate her falsity. But she wants to select her truths and exaggerate them for her own ends. So she employs tale-bearers like Andy Gowran, and succeeds in finding out even "more than was quite true as to poor Lizzie's former sins" (160). Her fanatical partisanship takes her to ridiculous lengths in her confident assertions against Lizzie: "Of course she stole [the diamonds] herself, . . . and I don't doubt but she stole her own money afterwards. There's nothing she wouldn't do" (504).

In the midst of these extremes, and all the false claims to truth, it is not surprising that some folk should be, with the best intentions in the world, bewildered and astray. Lady Fawn and her son are the representatives of decent human beings who would be truthful if they could, but get into helpless muddles. "Lady Fawn was not clear-headed; she was not clever; nor was she even always rational. But she was essentially honest" (265). And so we see her at last wanting her son to break his engagement to Lizzie, wanting Lucy to keep Frank, wanting Frank to take Lizzie, and wanting promises never to be broken; and trying to act and advise accordingly.

Lord Fawn, with his perilous insecurity about "lies" and "untruths," is no better off than his mother. He has honesty without judgment, and a fine mess it gets him into. "Lord Fawn was certainly an honest man. . . . But then it is so hard to decide what is fair" (75). He takes pains to tell Lizzie "the exact truth" about his own circumstances, but he has no ability to discover the truth about her, until it is unpleasantly forced on him. Then indeed he has a certain dogged grasp on the facts. "He could not unravel truth quickly, but he could grasp it when it came to him" (101). Even his enemy Frank has to admit of him that he is "a very obstinate, pig-headed, but nevertheless honest and truth-speaking gentleman" (209). I have been multiplying quotations to show how explicit and insistent Trollope is in the reiteration of his central theme.

Lizzie's other Lord, Lord George de Bruce Carruthers, emerges, perhaps against Trollope's original intention, as something of a hero.[11] He makes no mystique of the truth, and is unlike Frank and Fawn in being quite relaxed and even cynical about his word and other people's. He promises to be true to Lizzie, when she extracts the promise, as a matter of course, knowing how little such avowals to her mean. And he promises not to give her away when she confides in him about the non-theft at Carlisle. But when the police are on to her and she expects him to lie for her he retorts contemptuously, "Psha; – promised! If they put me in the witness-box of course I must tell. When you come to this kind of work, promises don't go for much. I don't know that they ever do" (573). He is not particularly truth-telling – though at times, we hear, "Lord George had spoken out, and had made himself very disagreeable" (639), like Lady Linlithgow – but he is truth-seeing, and can judge a thing and a person for what they are. His own life is mysterious – he is probably the adulterous lover of Mrs. Carbuncle and possibly the illegitimate father of Lucinda Roanoke, as well as being a suspect in the theft of the diamonds; but his intimate acquaintance with falsehood has made him able to recognize it. That is the point of his otherwise rather surprising relationship with Mrs. Carbuncle. When Lizzie reproaches him with caring more for "that odious vulgar woman" than for herself he replies, "Ah dear! I have known her for many years, Lizzie, and that both covers and discovers many faults. One learns to know how bad one's old friends are, but then one forgives them, because they are old friends" (680). He can early assess Lizzie as an "infernal little liar" (393), but considers marrying her nonetheless, coolly and accurately balancing the pros and cons, and realistically acknowledging to himself that "Had there not been something crooked about Lizzie, – a screw loose, as people say, – she would never have been within his reach" (571). In a fine scene we see him in a moment of detached evaluation, looking at Lizzie and deciding whether to take her or leave her. He decides that she is "a mess of deceit," and he leaves her (575). He is the one, too, whom Trollope allows to sum up Lizzie's story and state the moral, such as it is, of all her pointless deceit. "The end of it seems to be that you have lost your property, and sworn ever so many false oaths, and have brought all your friends into trouble, and have got nothing by it. What was the good of being so clever?" (679).

Character after character is revealed in the light of his allegiance to truth and falsehood. Lucinda Roanoke, though brought up in a world where getting on in society is everything, is constitutionally unable to talk polite hyperboles and white lies. To her aunt's appeal as to whether she has ever seen such poor luck in the hunt, she responds: " 'I've been out all day without finding at all,' said Lucinda, who loved the truth" (341). That is her first speech in the novel. Her inability to accommodate to the deception that surrounds her makes hers a tragic story ending in madness. Major Mackintosh, on his single appearance, announces to Lizzie the unwelcome news, "I think, Lady Eustace, we have found out the whole truth" (615). Even Nina Fawn, the youngest of that endless brood of girls, is defined in the same context: "She is the dearest little friend in all the world, . . . and always tells the exact truth" (296). And Lady Glencora's power of persuasion over Lord Fawn is backed by her invocation of the same ubiquitous term: 'I am sure there is nothing you would wish so much as to get at the truth" (497).

Lady Glencora brings us the public aspect of Trollope's theme.[12] For he presents a whole world which is the proper habitat of Lizzie the liar, where Society pants for gossip about the latest move in the diamond controversy, where the political parties align themselves as Lizzieites and anti-Lizzieites, and the Duke of Omnium gets his senile titillation from the rumours of Lizzie's love-life.

As the public latches on to the stories of Lizzie and her diamonds, it is identified with her deceit, and we see demonstrated Bacon's dictum about the attractiveness of lies. "The general belief which often seizes upon the world in regard to some special falsehood is very surprising," the narrator comments on the growing interest in Lizzie and her fortunes. ". . . The lie had been set on foot and had thriven" (151).

As he has presented his characters and their relationships consistently in the context of his main theme, so Trollope has also organized the action and incidents to fit in with the same pattern. The two major narrative strands concern, firstly, the diamonds and what happens to them, and the way in which they become occasion and food for lies and speculation; and secondly, three engagements, which test honesty and fidelity in human relations.

In that splendid complication of incident which is the history of the Eustace diamonds, we have the lie considered legally. Here Lizzie's lie amounts actually to theft, for in lying about the place and the manner in which Sir Florian put the diamonds around her neck, she lays false claim to property that is not her own, and so steals the diamonds, as Mr. Camperdown knows, as a pickpocket steals a purse. That lie and theft Mr. Camperdown cannot prove; but in her statement to the magistrate at Carlisle, and again after the theft in London, Lizzie becomes provably guilty of perjury. That is appropriately the crime for which the law can at last punish her, and the term looms large in her consciousness from the moment Lord George uses it.

> 'I don't suppose they'd prosecute you.'
> 'Prosecute me!' ejaculated Lizzie.
> 'For perjury, I mean.'
> 'And what could they do to me?'
> 'Oh, I don't know. Lock you up for five years, perhaps.' (460)

After this, Lizzie is in a tremor about perjury, a word of which she appreciates the legal signification without having any inkling of its moral force. And once the kindly Major Mackintosh gives her the less objectionable term, "incorrect version" (617), she latches on to it gratefully. It allows her to still her fears and continue to brazen the matter out: "People, after all, did not think so very much of perjury, – of perjury such as hers, committed in regard to one's own property" (646) – so she adds up her lie of theft with her perjury, and comes up with a moral credit. However, Mrs. Carbuncle can still conjure with the term, and make herself very unpleasant:

> 'When a woman has committed perjury,' said Mrs. Carbuncle, holding up both her hands in awe and grief, 'nothing too bad can possibly be said to her. You are amenable to the outraged laws of the country, and it is my belief that they can keep you upon the treadmill and bread and water for months and months, – if not for years.' (647–8)

That is her parting shot at Lizzie.

In the other main strand of the narrative, the three love stories – or rather the three engagement stories – we have the prolonged consideration, as in *Can You Forgive Her?*, of the broken pledge. Trollope makes sure we consider the parallel cases he offers us by echoes from one name to another. In turn Lizzie, Lucy and Lucinda become engaged, for their different motives, to their three suitors; and all three matches are almost instantly in danger of being broken off. Lord Fawn hears about the diamonds and tries to wriggle out, while Lizzie has no intention of allowing him to do so; Frank Greystock has his money worries about marrying the penniless Lucy, and also allows Lizzie to involve him in a prolonged flirtation, while everyone tells Lucy she mustn't expect him to keep faith with her; and Sir Griffin Tewett proceeds from one stormy quarrel with Lucinda to another, while the friends around go through incredible exertions, right up to the morning of the abrupted wedding, to bring off the marriage.

In this exploration of the nature of the pledge between lovers we are given, of course, a fine variety of motives and modes of behaviour. Lizzie, as she juggles with her alternative prospects at the same time as keeping Fawn on the hook, has her eye as usual to the main chance. She will take the best she can get, and meanwhile will extract her promises of "being true" from as many men as possible. When Lord Fawn comes courting, she quite calmly assesses his worth as a husband. "Lord Fawn was at any rate a peer. She had heard that he was a poor peer, – but a peer, she thought, can't be altogether poor. And though he was a stupid owl, – she did not hesitate to acknowledge to herself that he was as stupid as an owl, – he had a position" (69–70). And so for these not quite overwhelming reasons she accepts him. And when he tries to withdraw she sends her other man to keep him to his word. "You can hardly mean to assert, my lord," says Frank severely, "that you intend to be untrue to your promise, and to throw over your own engagement" (145). Frank, engaged to Lucy but already involved with Lizzie, is a fine one to talk. It is presently settled that "The engagement was to remain in force. Counsel were to be employed. The two lovers were not to see each other just at present" (146). That pledge between "the two lovers" is certainly in a perilous state, and remains so for most of the rest of the novel. One can understand Lord Fawn's state of bewilderment: "Whether he was, or was not, to regard himself as being at this moment engaged to marry Lady Eustace was a matter to him of much doubt" (178).

Lucy's engagement to Frank also goes into a state of suspended animation for the main duration of the novel. Frank, in the toils of Lizzie's intrigues, sturdily reminds himself, "He was engaged to marry Lucy Morris, and to that engagement he must be true" (287) – but then he has also promised to "be true" to Lizzie, and he is not sure of the implications of that promise, nor whether it is compatible with being true to Lucy. Lizzie does all she can to make him break his engagement, and is skilful in devaluing the force of his pledge.

'That little girl has cozened you out of a promise' [she tells him].
'If it be so, you would not have me break it.'

'Yes, I would, if you think she is not fit to be your wife. Is a man, such as you are, to be tied by the leg for life, have all his ambition clipped, and his high hopes shipwrecked, because a girl has been clever enough to extract a word from him?' (483)

And this from the woman who will not by any means allow Lord Fawn to withdraw from *his* promise. As for Lucy, she knows Frank would be a "traitor" if he deserted her, but she is subject to the persuasion of Lady Fawn, who though morally exacting with her girls, is inclined to be lenient in her views of masculine accountability: "According to her view of things, a man out in the world had so many things to think of, and was so very important, that he could hardly be expected to act at all times with truth and sincerity" (415). And then, shocking as it would be, Lady Fawn would find it rather convenient if Frank broke faith with Lucy, because then he would take Lizzie off her son's hands.

Sir Griffin Tewett woos Lucinda while out hunting, and is actuated by a sadistic determination to control her and break her in, the more she demonstrates her disgust for him.[13] "He'd have her, by George! There are men in whose love a good deal of hatred is mixed; – who love as the huntsman loves the fox, towards the killing of which he intends to use all his energies and intellects" (369). As soon as they are engaged, Lucinda announces to her aunt that of all people in the world, she hates Sir Griffin the worst. And Trollope includes some fine dramatization of her sexual revulsion from him. At one point they actually come to blows. Nevertheless, the marriage is to go on, for girls have "got to be married, and they make the best of it" (376). However, Lucinda doesn't submit tamely to this necessity, and continues to be recalcitrant and to plot escape. She even goes to the play, *The Noble Jilt*, with the motive of doing some research on how the job of jilting can be done nobly. And at the very last minute she baulks at the fence.

Amidst all these broken promises, it is not surprising that people become cynical about the matter of engagements. The worldy-wise Mrs. Hittaway lectures her mother about Frank's ruptured engagement to Lucy:

'No doubt; – men do propose. We all know that. I'm sure I don't know what they get by it, but I suppose it amuses them. There used to be a sort of feeling that if a man behaved badly something would be done to him; but that's all over now. [Not much more than a year previously, Phineas and Lord Chiltern met on the field of honour over a lady.] A man may propose to whom he likes, and if he chooses to say afterwards that it doesn't mean anything, there's nothing in the world to bring him to book.' (537)

That is the Way We Live Now, according to Mrs. Hittaway.

As a parody of this upper-class cynicism about proposals, Trollope introduces the tiny subplot of Mr. Gager and Patience Crabstick. This is another engagement of interest, though in lower-class circles – Gager is a policeman who wants evidence, and Patience is a malefactor who, like Lizzie, would be very glad of "a rock" to depend on in her extremity. "You aren't a perjuring of yourself?" she asks him doubtfully in the course of their negotiations. "What; – about making you my wife? That I ain't. I'm upright, and always was. There's no mistake about me, when you've got my word. As soon as this work is off my mind, you shall be Mrs. Gager, my dear" (523). And unlike his more aristocratic counterparts, Gager is true to his word.

Besides all this discussion of truth and falsehood as they relate to pledges of marriage, there is the delightful incident at Fawn Court in which Lord Fawn is given the lie by his mother's governess, and is reduced to trembling indignation. When he calls Frank's conduct ungentlemanly, Lucy locates herself on the field of honour, and, in a faint modern echo of the days of chivalry, feels bound to tell Lord Fawn his statement is untrue; and the timid peer and the incensed governess are briefly seen as potential combatants in a duel. When he has stalked off in high dudgeon, Lucy makes up her mind to apologise; but in that memorable scene in the shrubbery, all she succeeds in doing is repeating the offence. In her prolonged consideration about the rights and wrongs of his matter, Trollope conveys a fine sense of the ritual and taboos that have come to surround words like "lie," "untruth," and "gentleman."

> She had a second time accused Lord Fawn of speaking an untruth. She did not quite understand the usages of the world in the matter; but she did know that the one offence which a gentleman is supposed never to commit is that of speaking an untruth. The offence may be one committed oftener than any other by gentlemen, – as also by all other people; but, nevertheless, it is regarded by the usages of society as being the one thing which a gentleman never does. (258)

The satire is unobtrusive, but effective. This is a further vision of that extended world of deceit and false seeming of which Lizzie is the proper representative.

When Lord George asks Lizzie, "What is a broken promise?" Lizzie's prompt answer is "It's a story" (573). Herein lies the attraction of literature to Lizzie, and the significance of the intricate pattern of literary allusion in the novel. As we have seen, Lizzie loves lies, in Bacon's phrase, "for the lie's sake"; but she also loves them when "they make for pleasure, as with poets; ... [and] for advantage, as with the merchant." She lies because she prefers lies to the truth; but as with her diamonds she certainly lies for profit, and as with her constant wallowing in "poetry", she finds literature, at least some literature, especially congenial. She finds in it not a higher imaginative reality, but food for her craving for fiction and artifice.

The novel is packed with literary references and parallels and quotations of one kind and another, and among other things provides a fairly exact picture of the contemporary reading scene. We get a precise notion both of Lady Linlithgow's taste and of public reading habits when we hear that she keeps Maria Edgeworth's novels downstairs and *Pride and Prejudice* in her bedroom, and that she refuses to subscribe to Mudie's because, she says, "when I asked for *Adam Bede*, they always sent me the *Bandit Chief*" (309). As a private joke with himself, Trollope included the account of the production and reception of his own rejected play, *The Noble Jilt*, along with criticism of it by his characters, so that we get some sense of the current taste in drama. Tennyson is respectable, and Lizzie selects a volume of his poems as one of her props when she receives Lady Glencora. On one occasion she is reading "The Holy Grail" – thus placing the action in or soon after 1869.

Of course she misreads Tennyson, and works up a phoney sympathy for the knights on their misguided quest, and prefers Lancelot to Arthur. The meaning of poetry is not her concern – she readily substitutes "primeval" for "immortal" in her passage from *Queen Mab*, and doesn't notice the difference (198) – but she wants to set her mind awash with rhythm and affected passion. So with "The Holy Grail":

> The melody of the lines had pleased her ear, and she was always able to arouse for herself a false enthusiasm on things which were utterly outside herself in life. She thought she too could have travelled in search of that holy sign, and have borne all things, and abandoned all things, and have persevered, – and of a certainty have been rewarded. But as for giving up a string of diamonds, in common honesty, – that was beyond her. (171)

Lizzie is enthusiastic about literature because she can make of it another realm for lies and artifice. If her response to literature were the norm, Plato would have been quite right to banish the poet from the Republic. For her, literature is lies, and that is why she tries to make it her element.

Trollope is faithful to his contemporary Tennyson, however, and shows Lizzie's taste as much better satisfied by the romantics, who come in for their share of criticism along with Lizzie. It is not to their credit that Emilius reads a canto of *Childe Harold* to Lizzie at her bedside, and that she finally receives him with a volume of Shelley in her hand. Shelley does not escape scatheless in that devasting piece of practical criticism on the passage from *Queen Mab*; and Byron, who is so congenial to her, sometimes seems a posturing fake like Lizzie. Trollope, like Thackeray in *Pendennis*, is exploring the complex relation between life and art, and artifice and deceit. Lizzie tries to fit her own life and the people around her into literary stereotypes – it is one more of her multiple ways of lying. So one of her men after another is tried out for the role of Corsair and promoted or demoted in her estimation according to the way he fits her preconceived requirements. Her silly habit of literary namecalling is nicely exemplified in the fragment of dialogue between her and Frank at Portray.

> 'And Lubin has gone?' [she asks.] Arthur Herriot was Lubin.
> 'Lubin has gone. Though why Lubin, I cannot guess. The normal Lubin to me is a stupid fellow always in love. Herriot is not stupid and is never in love.'
> 'Nevertheless, he is Lubin if I choose to call him so. . . .'
> 'I have had a letter from your brother-in-law.'
> 'And what is John the Just pleased to say?'
> 'John the Just, which is a better name for the man than the other, has been called up to London, much against his will, by Mr. Camperdown.'
> 'Who is Samuel the Unjust.' Mr. Camperdown's name was Samuel.
> (234)

It is her way of casting other people in roles, as she does herself. Everything and everyone must be made to seem other than they are. Poetry and posing, and quacks and geniuses can be perilously close, and in Lizzie's world they are actually equated. This is another illustration of Trollope's point from Tennyson – fiction is apt to become lies, as men are apt to become Merlins, when they encounter Viviens, as the lie transforms the truth into its own likeness.

In *The Eustace Diamonds* Trollope worked with symbol and imagery more overtly and effectively than usual. The central symbol is of course the Eustace diamonds themselves, though it suits Trollope's purpose that they do not in fact appear very often, for all the stir that is made about them: for the most part they remain, appropriately, off stage and locked up, almost an abstract principle. They are meant for beauty and display, but they are clutched at and secreted and disputed over as property. Lizzie claims them as a gift and she lies; Camperdown claims them as an heirloom, and he is wrong. Both these antagonists are tainted by their pursuit – Camperdown is of course by intention an honorable man, but he becomes irrational and obsessive like Lizzie, and longs to deposit the diamonds where they will "lie hidden and unused at any rate for the next twenty years" (705). In fact the diamonds, like Pip's great expectations, are ultimately dispersed and lost to view. They turn out to be, indeed, merely "a lot of stones hardly so useful as the flags in the street," in Mr. Dove's phrase (710).

Lizzie is identified with her diamonds, as Bacon uses diamonds as the emblem of lies. Trollope plays with this image often. When she first

wears them, he notes, "She was made to sparkle, to be bright with out-
side garniture, – to shine and glitter, and be rich in apparel. The only
doubt might be whether paste diamonds might not better suit her
character" (158). Mrs. Carbuncle's diamonds are in fact all paste. And
Lucy and Lizzie are compared as real and factitious gems. "Lucy held
her ground because she was real. You may knock about a diamond, and
not even scratch it; whereas paste in rough usage betrays itself.. Lizzie,
with all her self-assuring protestations, knew that she was paste, and
knew that Lucy was real stone" (584). The image repeats an earlier
perception of Frank's as he ponders the price and the value of the two
women: on one occasion when Lizzie dissolves into tears for his benefit
he recalls Lucy:

> How unlike she was to Lucy! . . . When Lucy was much in earnest, in
> her eye, too, a tear would sparkle, the smallest drop, a bright liquid
> diamond that never fell; . . . but how unlike were the two! He knew
> that the difference was that between truth and falsehood. (174)

The jewel imagery is extended to include not only the names, like
Garnett's and Mrs. Carbuncle's, but further figurative applications and
many actual incidents involving other gems. Lucy is opposed to Lizzie as
being "a treasure," and "good as gold," in repeated phrases; though
there is a wry opposition of the figurative to the literal applications when
Frank's mother reflects, "There was no doubt about Lucy being as good
as gold; – only that real gold, vile as it is, was the one thing that Frank so
much needed" (274).

There is further emblematic use of gems and precious stones, as they
appear in various significant situations. The story in the opening chapter
about the pawned gems that Lizzie redeems on account in order to catch
Sir Florian with them, and then charges to him afterwards, stands as a
definitive incident. Sir Florian is deeply distressed by it, as a landed fish
might be if he received a bill for the bait. And the first image we have of
her is that "when she was little more than a child, [she] went about
everywhere with jewels on her fingers, and red gems hanging round her
neck, and yellow gems pendent from her ears, and white gems shining in
her black hair" (1). Then there is the "hundred guinea brooch" with
which Lizzie tries to bribe Lucy (131); and the hilarious ado about wedding presents for Lucinda, involving the haggling between Lizzie and
Mrs. Carbuncle on the value of the silver plate, and the correspondence
with the old acquaintance about the £10 bracelet given years ago as a
wedding present. "A present so given was seed sown in the earth, – seed,
indeed, that could not be expected to give back twenty-fold, or even ten-
fold, but still seed from which a crop should be expected" (588). Such an
expectation is elevated into a principle, and when the friend responds
with only a trumpery brooch, Mrs. Carbuncle in her next letter voices

her indignation at the atrocious devaluation of the gift from one generation to the next. But she receives only the waggish reply, "I quite
acknowledge the reciprocity system, but I don't think it extends to
descendants, – certainly not to nieces. . . . At your second marriage I will
do what is needful; but I can assure you I haven't recognized nieces with
any of my friends" (589). The "reciprocity system" and the haggling
over gifts in the subplot is a comic version of what is going on in the
main plot, when the "gift" of love is the diamonds themselves, and price
and value are similarly confused.

To see how skilfully Trollope works his emblems into the dramatic
texture of the novel, it is worth considering that fine scene at Portray
where Frank, for the first time wearing Lucy's ring, is also for the first
time exposed to the full glitter of the diamonds. Lizzie as usual is dis-
coursing of her right of absolute ownership in the diamonds.

> 'They wouldn't stop you if you sold the ring you wear." The ring
> had been given to him by Lucy, after their engagement, and was the
> only present she had ever made him. It had been purchased out of her
> own earnings, and had been put on his finger by her own hand. . . .
> Lizzie was sure that it had been given by that sly little creeping thing,
> Lucy. 'Let me look at the ring,' she said. 'Nobody could stop you if
> you chose to sell this to me.'
> 'Little things are always less troublesome than big things,' he said.
> 'What is the price?' she asked.
> 'It is not in the market, Lizzie. Nor should your diamonds be
> there.' (280)

And so he brings the subject away from his engagement to Lucy, which
he has not the honesty or courage to own, and back to his cousin's present business. But there is more at stake here than her diamonds, and
she deliberately harks back to the ring, with further persistent imputations: "I'll wear [the diamonds] as commonly as you do that gage
d'amour which you carry on your finger. . . . I don't see why I should
lock them up in a musty old bank. Why don't you send your ring to the
bank?" – and so on (281). Presently she actually fetches the diamonds,
after making a fine playful scene about how they are locked in a seven-
fold box that no one but herself could open.

> 'There,' she said, chucking the necklace across the table at Frank, so
> that he was barely able to catch it. 'There it is. Ten thousand pounds'
> worth as they tell me. . . .'[14]
> 'And your husband gave it you just as another man gives a trinket
> that costs ten shillings!'
> 'Just as Lucy Morris gave you that ring.'
> He smiled, but took no other notice of the accusation. 'I am so

poor a man,' said he, 'that this string of stones, which you throw about the room like a child's toy, would be the making of me.'

'Take it and be made,' said Lizzie. . . . 'Take it with all its encumbrances, and weight of cares. Take it with all the burthen of Messrs. Camperdowns' lawsuits upon it. You shall be as welcome to it as flowers were ever welcomed in May.'

'The encumbrances are too heavy,' said Frank.

'You prefer a little ring.'

'Very much.'

'I don't doubt but you're right,' said Lizzie. 'Who fears to rise will hardly get a fall.' (282–3)

Here is Lizzie covertly after Frank again, and using the language of implication and indirection that she is so skilled at. She throws herself at him as she throws the diamonds, and the diamonds and their value are the bribe. And she plays very well with the ring too. As long as Frank equivocates about his engagement, he is, as Lizzie is aware, breaking faith with Lucy; and so it suits her to proceed by imputations rather than outright questions and answers, which might put an end to the atmosphere of half-truths and equivocation that is her element. Frank too understands fairly well what is going on, though he is not in control of the language of indirection as Lizzie is. He is visibly and consciously tempted by the thought of Lizzie and the necklace as being the possible making of him. But the proposal – and a "proposal" it certainly is – that he should take it and be made at last puts the proposition quite clearly before his eyes, and the wording of his refusal of Lizzie's covert offer of marriage – "the encumbrances are too heavy" – is perhaps a little churlish. However, he can now say courageously that he prefers the ring to the necklace – Lucy to Lizzie –, so that we can understand the note of pique in her retort: "Who fears to rise will hardly get a fall." Those were the words which were scratched on a windowpane with a diamond, in the legendary exchange between Queen Elizabeth and Leicester. It is a delightful scene, in the manner of Jane Austen, where seemingly trivial gestures and phrases are invested with a special weight of significance. The emblematic value of Frank's ring and the proffered necklace recalls Fanny Price's dilemma between Edmund's chain and the Crawford necklace in *Mansfield Park*.

Another recurring pattern that has thematic-import is the imagery of hands. Lizzie, we learn, has a standard reflex action: once having closed her fingers on something, she automatically holds it the tighter as she feels it being withdrawn. This is certainly the case with the diamonds. We do believe in the extent to which they become a burden to her, and that she would like to throw them into the sea, as she so often talks of doing, though we know she could never do it. She is close to inspiring compassion when the diamonds cause her quite genuine pain: "They

were like a load upon her chest, a load as heavy as though she were compelled to sit with the iron box on her lap day and night" (185). Even so
the monkey may hate the handful of nuts in the chained coconut trap by
which it is caught, but it cannot bring itself to let them go. We keep
hearing of this conflict in Lizzie. If Lizzie's first guiding motive is to
make things seem other than they are, the next is to hold on tight to
what she has, especially if there is any pressure in the other direction.
She is early described as "this selfish, hard-fisted little woman, who
could not bring herself to abandon the plunder on which she had laid
her hand" (43). We hear much less of the visual attraction of the stones
for her than of their tactual magnetism. John Eustace decides "it was
manifest enough that she meant 'to hang on to them'" (150); she
despises Lord Fawn "because he would not clutch the jewels" (94), and
hates Camperdown and Son because she is convinced they *do* mean "to
clutch them" (281). Characteristically, "She once thought of asking her
cousin to take the charge of them, but she could not bring herself to let
them out of her own hands" (183). Frank, pondering that possession is
nine points of the law, admits at the same time "that possession in the
hands of Lizzie Eustace included certainly every one of those nine
points" (170). The image suggests again the talons of a harpy. As with
the diamonds, so with other property. "She is dying to handle her
money," comments the bishop's lady. "She is only like the rest of the
world in that," says the bishop (12). Lizzie expects other people to be as
grasping as she is herself, and, insofar as she is the representative of a
rapacious and deceitful society, she is right – the Mrs. Carbuncles of the
world are as grasping as she. But Frank she finally despises as she
despised Lord Fawn, because "he would not open his hand to take it"
(690).

Lizzie's grasping rapacity about the diamonds extends to her
matrimonial life, which is as intricately involved with the diamonds as
are Phineas's loves with his politics. Lord Fawn she decides to accept,
though with no enthusiasm, and with the conviction that he is as stupid
as an owl. But when he begins to wriggle in her grasp, she is far from
indifferent.

> Then Lizzie looked at him, – and her look, which was very eloquent,
> called him a poltroon as plain as a look could speak. Then they
> parted, and the signs of affection between them were not satisfactory.
>   The door was hardly closed behind him before Lizzie began to
> declare to herself that he shouldn't escape her. (94)

It is her old reflex, to hang on to anything that is about to be withdrawn.
But here, with her right and physical hand she has hold of the
diamonds, while with her left and emotional hand she has hold of the

peer; and the peer does not want the connection with the diamonds. Hence arises the delightfully dramatic conflict:

> Lizzie in her excitement had forgotten ... everything except the battle which it was necessary that she should fight for herself. She did not mean to allow the marriage to be broken off, – but she meant to retain the necklace. The manner in which Lord Fawn had demanded its restitution ... had made her, at any rate for the moment, as firm as steel on this point. It was inconceivable to her that he should think himself at liberty to go back from his promise, because she would not render up property that was in her possession. ... She walked on full of fierce courage, – despising him, but determined that she would marry him. (128–9)

In the same way, she hates the diamonds, but will not let go of them.

Mr. Camperdown's favourite term of abuse for Lizzie is "harpy" – to which as the mood strikes him he adds the epithets dishonest, lying, evil-minded, greedy and bloodsucking (100, 252). The name harpy, appropriately enough, is etymologically derived from the word for snatching, grabbing, rending. And Lizzie as harpy is again symbolically suggestive of a whole society of greedy raptors and carnivores and their victims. The beast imagery is the last thematic pattern I want to discuss, and again it is consistent enough to suggest a deliberate strategy.

Lizzie herself is again the central focus. Besides being a harpy, Lizzie is referred to as "snake-like" (16), "vixen" (80), "a beautiful animal" with sharp white teeth (109), a "little purring cat" (429), and so on. The people around her include a Sir Griffin, a Mr. Dove (familiarly called Turtle Dove), and a whole family of Fawns. (The name does double duty here, suggesting as noun the timidity of the wild creature in the unworldly ladies at Fawn Court, and as verb Lord Fawn's rather cringing demeanour in society, as he throws himself at the feet of one rich lady after another.) The hunting metaphor, as I have said, is used with powerful suggestiveness, not only with Lucinda and Sir Griffin, but also with Lord George, who, when asked if his mistress would object to his taking a wife, replies coolly, "As to Mrs. C[arbuncle], she wouldn't object in the least. I generally have my horses so bitted that they can't very well object" (366). Lucinda in her engagement, an untamed shrew, we hear is "as savage as ever, and would snap and snarl, and almost bite. Sir Griffin would snarl too, and say very bearish things" (390). Mrs. Carbuncle even elevates the savagery of this pair of lovers into a general principle, and cheerfully quotes the song, "The rabbits and hares All go in pairs; And likewise the bears In couples agree" (373). Besides all this, there is the usual amount of fairly automatic analogy with animals – Lord Fawn is "as stupid as an owl," and the police before they have found the thieves are denounced in the press as "drones and moles and ostriches" (509). My list is far from exhaustive, but I want to suggest the frequency and suggestiveness of the beast metaphor, as of other consistently developed image patterns in the book.

The Eustace Diamonds is a fine novel for obvious reasons – for its wily and unscrupulous heroine and her adventures with suitors and thieves, for the skilfully managed plot, for the delightful dramas in which she is progressively involved, and for the sustained wit in the narration of all this. And it is also a beautifully organized novel, with a central idea which is supported by character, action and imagery. Lizzie Eustace, as liar, poetry-lover and harpy, is the proper heroine of a novel that is an exploration of truth and falsehood, and an exposure of a society that is, not entirely but too often, in irrational pursuit of artifice, rumour, and other people's property.

6 *The Prime Minister*: Judgment, Pride and Prejudice

In a letter to Mary Holmes in 1876, before *The Prime Minister* had completed its run of eight parts, Trollope wrote, "remember, when you read it, – if you do read it, – that though I myself am prepared to stand up for the character of the Prime Minister, and for all his surroundings, I acknowledge the story of the soi-disant hero, Lopez, and all that has to do with him, to be bad" (*Letters*, 353). The critics, both in his own day and ours, have for the most part agreed. The *Spectator* review, which gave Trollope particular pain, announced, "Lopez, the hero, is simply intolerable"[1]; "That the Wharton-Lopez story is 'unconvincing' nobody ever denied," says Booth.[2] Most commentators,[3] following Trollope's lead, have been content to jettison the Lopez plot, and have concentrated on what was dear to Trollope himself, the half of the work concerned with the Duke and Duchess of Omnium – the two characters who, along with Josiah Crawley, he believed were his greatest creations (*A*, 310).

It is understandable enough that Trollope should have loved best those creations that he had been building and perfecting, adding touch to meticulous touch, through six long novels since *The Small House at Allington*. There was no doubt from the outset a consciousness that the love and marriage of Lopez and Emily Wharton was only "an adjunct necessary, because there must be love in a novel" (*A*, 123). But as with Lucy Robarts, who was initially only that necessary adjunct in *Framley Parsonage* but became the major interest of the book, the Lopez story gathers momentum, and, Trollope's depreciatory comments notwithstanding, it is informed by considerable creative energy. Lopez the man may be intolerable, but his story need not be condemned for his iniquities. It seems to me misguided to read the novel only for the Palliser story, particularly as the two plots are carefully unfolded together with parallel episodes and moral issues, so that each forms a commentary on the other. In space the Lopez-Wharton plot occupies nearly fifty of the book's eighty chapters, so that to ignore it is to ignore the ostensible main plot of the novel. I want to look at the book whole, and to consider the ways in which the two parts relate and the light that this relation throws on the overall themes of the novel.[4]

In the action there is some connection between the stories – as much as Trollope usually gives in his bifurcated novels, and a good deal more than in some. Lopez becomes the Duchess's black swan in the days of her ostentatious hospitality at Gatherum, and her candidate for Silverbridge, the borough that the Duke is conscientiously trying to get out of his pocket. But besides the Silverbridge issue that links these lives, the connection in action is slight, and consists mainly in a visit by the newly-wed Lopezes to the Duchess's garden party at Richmond, and one well-intentioned call by the Duchess on Emily Lopez at her home.

But Trollope is careful in the mechanics of the connection between his two stories, constructing a running set of links, including some verbal echoes from one to another, as different characters react to similar situations. The novel originally ran in eight monthly parts, from November 1875 to June 1876, and each part was divided into an even ten chapters.[5] Of these the majority was usually devoted principally to the doings of Lopez and the Whartons, with three or four reserved for Palliser business. Only in the final part were the Pallisers allowed as many as six of the ten chapters. But the changes from one story to another show Trollope careful to manage an easy transition: for instance, the eighth chapter ends with the news that "all the world had begun to talk of the Prime Minister's dinners" (I, 87), and the title of the ninth takes us, for deliberate contrast, to "Mrs. Dick's Dinner Party." And we get echoes of interest as we move from the political scenes of Pallisers' life to the domestic ones at the Whartons'. The Duke, depressed at the scavenging for position that goes on among such men as Ratler and Roby, laments, "It used not to be so" (I, 78–9). And in the next chapter old Mr. Wharton, afflicted by the same melancholy nostalgia, reflects, "the world was changing around him every day" (I, 92). After a chapter has been spent showing how Glencora winces at her husband's charge of "vulgarity," we hear the same pronouncement on Emily that "She must be a girl . . . of an ingrained vulgar taste" (I, 271). (One can imagine how especially pained Trollope must have been at the *Spectator* reviewer's charge of the vulgarity of the whole novel; considering he had shown how the word smarts, it was an unkind cut.[6]) In one part, the Duke refuses to announce that it was Glencora who meddled in the Silverbridge election, insisting on taking the responsibility on himself, because "a man and his wife are one" (II, 26) and he must take responsibility for her sins; in the next we find Emily under attack for her husband's depredations on the Parkers' money: "You're one with him, ain't you?" demands Mrs. Parker (II, 173).

One could go on a long time picking out such touches. Trollope has been more than usually careful in their inclusion. But perhaps an indication of the main parallel movements in the two plots will be more useful.

At the outset we have two women, Emily and Gencora, using all their influence on their lawgivers – father in the one case and husband in the other, to get their heart's desire. Emily wants Lopez; Glencora essentially wants power, but the object of her desire is locally represented as the court position of Mistress of the Robes, her husband's acquisition of the Prime Ministership, and his permission to have a free hand in lavish entertainment – so that she may "make Buckingham Palace second-rate" (I, 66). The two men who encounter this force of desire and persuasion are reluctant to give in, yet unable to make clear their "reasons" for refusing. "But, papa – ; is there to be no reason?" Emily pleads when her father declares that her relation with Lopez must come to an end (I, 51). "Why should I be debarred from it?" Glencora demands (I, 70). The father replies that he does not know anything about Lopez, and that is "reason sufficient"; the husband likewise responds that he does "not choose" it. Nevertheless the ladies get their way, and both live to regret it.

The contrasted pairs of Emily and her father and Glencora and her husband dissolve at Emily's marriage to Lopez, and for the middle of the book we are presented with two marriages, with the two husbands trying to train their wives into their way of thinking, and the two wives, though claiming to be obedient, rebelling at every turn. "You are a child, my dear, and must allow me to dictate to you what you ought to think in such a matter as this" (I, 345); "Cora, . . . you do not quite understand it" (II, 25): – thus the husbands. And the wives make their resolutions according to their powers. "I'll obey him to the letter," says Glencora on one issue, having discovered that herein lies her present advantage (II, 13); "It is not my duty to have any purpose, as what I do must depend on your commands," says Emily, who has like Glencora learned to use obedience as a weapon (II, 225). And thus the issue of authority within marriage is kept to the fore throughout, whichever story has prominence in one chapter or another.

Lopez and Palliser are parallels as husbands, and to some extent in their careers too, as Helmut Klingler has pointed out, in that they both fail in their initial enterprises of marrying money and carrying on the Queen's government successfully. But morally of course they are strongly contrasted with one another, and the real pairs are Palliser and Emily, as the morally scrupulous partners, and Lopez and Glencora, as the erring ones. It is no wonder that Lopez for a while is Glencora's black swan: as the ambitious political and commercial climbers, they are alike in kind, though by no means in degree. The misdemeanours of these two sinners are given sufficient space in the narrative; but so too are self-inflicted pains of Emily and Palliser, who tend to be righteous over-much, and incapacitated by any breath of blame. And in the last third of the novel, the major common element in the two stories is the self-condemnation of the two upright characters: Emily imposes suffering on herself and her family by refusing to marry Arthur, although she loves him, because she considers herself defiled by her marriage to Lopez; and Palliser prolongs unnecessary hardship for himself and his country by refusing to accept office, though that is what he craves, because he considers himself unfitted by having been Prime Minister.

These it seems to me are the main movements of the novel, with each story illuminating the other as the parallel issues are faced by the different characters, in the domestic, the political and the commercial worlds. Glencora and Lopez pursue what they want with less hesitation about the world's judgment than Palliser and Emily, who are rigorous in their judgment of others and themselves. As Glencora says herself, she plays Lady Macbeth to her husband, and taunts him because what he would highly that would be holily (I, 61). Similarly Lopez has am-bitions for his wife, and intends to make sure that she learns the proper importance and power of money, however gained: "He would take a glory in seeing her well dressed and well attended, with her own carriage and her own jewels. But she must learn that the enjoyment of these things must be built upon a conviction that the most important pursuit in the world was the acquiring of money" (I, 280). He has no more scru-ple than Lady Macbeth about his means of attaining what he would highly.

In Trollope's presentation of these alignments, and the consequent examination of the issues of just and unjust authority, of proper and im-proper conduct, of the ability to choose and make decisions, and the tendency to suffer unduly from these decisions, something like an overall theme emerges. I find that judgment is the central concept, from which branch out all the subsidiary issues of misjudgment, prejudice, justice, sentence, condemnation and punishment that inform the action and outcome of the narrative. Even more than most of Trollope's novels this one is concerned with what we call, in the current jargon, the decision-making process: so we have the palava about Emily's choosing Lopez when Fletcher is so manifestly the superior suitor, or Palliser, temporarily incapacitated by the magnitude of his task, waiting for an angel from heaven to tell him whom to appoint as his Chancellor of the Exchequer (I, 74); and more than in most novels we have a following up of the mistake in judgment, the wrong decision. As in *Phineas Redux*, we find that poetic justice is not in operation; but we are especially con-cerned with the justice of the moral verdicts and moral sentences, as opposed to the legal ones, that the characters mete out on one another and on themselves, so that society's judgment on Lopez, and on the Duke for judging Lopez, is in an intimate way the subject of the story. Lopez must be brought to book, until he has nowhere to go but under the express train at Tenway Junction; and Glencora must be made to confess her sins as fast as she can. For those like Palliser and Emily, who are the harshest judges of themselves, mistakes in judgment are crimes which must be stringently punished, by internal penance and suffering if not by external force: "As a matter of course the Prime Minister in his own mind blamed himself for what he had done" (II, 295), we hear; or of Emily, "She had acted on her own judgment in marrying him, . . . and now she would bear the punishment" (II, 65). Prejudice, the decision that precedes due process of judgment, is alike part of Trollope's subject, and marvellously portrayed in the whole history of Lopez's incursion into the hallowed Wharton family.

"What," exclaims Glencora to her husband at one point, "is a man to be put in the front of everything, and then to be judged as though he could give all his time to the picking of his steps?" "Just so," replies the Duke, "and he must pick them more warily than another" (II, 122). It is a reply that Trollope applauds, and this book is devoted to the process of a Prime Minister's picking his steps, and of the judgment of others, and of his reaction to the judgment. And nor are the other characters to be exempt from the cares of picking their steps, though their mistakes and punishments are to be less public.

As a subsidiary concern we have the treatment of pride, and the question is raised again as to whether it is a deadly sin, the ambition that prompts Macbeth to regicide, or whether it is not really among the virtues. Darcy claims in *Pride and Prejudice*, "where there is a real superiority of mind, pride will always be under good regulation" (ch. 11). At this point, it will be remembered, Elizabeth turns away to hide a smile. Certainly in *The Prime Minister* it is the superior characters, morally speaking, who have the most pride, and their ability to regulate it is recurrently in question. The Duke almost withdraws his services from his country in perpetuity because he is too proud to be a subordinate in a ministry after he has been at the head: "Caesar could hardly have led a legion under Pompey" he says (II, 371). Does this in Caesar seem ambitious? Old Mrs. Fletcher says resoundingly of Emily, "It's pride. . . . She won't give way" (II, 455). The comment can equally be applied to Palliser at the same phase of the novel. Emily herself at another point admits, "I have a feeling of pride which tells me that . . . as I would judge for myself, – I am bound to put up with my choice" (II, 140). The Duke might say the same of his politically disastrous choice of Lord Earlybird as the recipient of the Garter. Here and elsewhere judgment and pride are associated.

My subtitle of Pride and Prejudice for this chapter implies a comparison of Trollope with Jane Austen. This would be a fruitful subject in itself, but I do not mean to draw any sustained parallel between *The Prime Minister* and *Pride and Prejudice*.[7] However, it does seem to me that had Trollope been addicted to thematic titles as Jane Austen was – pride and prejudice, or some variation on them, might well have figured in the title of this novel.

It is interesting, by the way, to note Trollope's preferences in titles for his works. Like Jane Austen, he often chose to define his subject by a location: Northanger Abbey, the Small House at Allington, the Belton Estate. Besides that, like other novelists, he often chooses the name of the principal character – Dr. Thorne, or Rachel Ray, or Phineas Finn. His most peculiarly characteristic titles show his tendency to view his characters, as Chaucer did, in terms of their office. As Chaucer's Oswald is most readily memorable as the Reeve, so Trollope's Mr. Harding is the Warden, Plantagenet Palliser is the Prime Minister, Gotobed is the American Senator.[8] Even where the name of the office is not the major element, the character's status, or his relation to his family or his society, often has prominence: so we have *The Duke's Children* (in Trollope's notes originally entitled *The Ex-Prime Minister*), *Doctor Whortle's School*, *The Vicar of Bullhampton*, *Editor's Tales*. The symbolic title, like James's *The Golden Bowl*, is rare, and is most memorable in *The Eustace Diamonds*. Titles that define theme, like *Persuasion* or *Great Expectations*, he does use occasionally, though his preference is not for the moral abstract but rather for the suggestive phrase or sentence: *He knew He was Right, The Way We live Now, An Eye for an Eye, Can You Forgive Her?*.

Trollope's themes, that is to say, do not announce themselves as does, say, Jane Austen's in *Sense and Sensibility*. But they are none the less there. As Jane Austen keeps her moral scheme to the fore by having her characters discuss and debate the issue – Edward Ferrars delivers a light parody on the jargon of the picturesque, or Mary Bennet expatiates homiletically on the distinction between pride and vanity – Trollope also makes his characters do the work of the novelist, by offering moral commentaries on each other's behaviour, and discussing the rights and wrongs of the major issues. His additional emphasis is to make his theme the common element in his two plots.

I have said that Trollope is concerned rather with moral than with legal judgment here; but he reinforces his themes of justice and prejudice by some of the paraphernalia of the law. He is fond of lawyers as characters, but here legal terminology and imagery become part of a general pattern. Old Mr. Wharton, whose career as a barrister has been distinguished enough that he becomes a Queen's Council, may be considered a professional in the business of justice; but his profession has hardened his prejudices and made him cantankerous. "I never knew any one so much prejudiced as you are, Mr. Wharton. . . . I suppose it comes from being in the courts," his sister-in-law tells him, with unintentional irony (I, 140). Lopez writes a lying answer to his father-in-law, rather than leaving his letter unanswered, knowing that "There is nothing that the courts hate so much as contempt; – not even perjury. And Lopez felt that Mr. Wharton was the judge before whom he was bound to plead" (II, 63). And indeed, after the suicide, when Emily and her father are rid of their incubus, the first sign that Wharton's himself again is that he sallies forth to the court, and appears "with his wig and gown, and argued a case" (II, 235). When Emily begins to realize that her husband is a bounder, we have the legal terminology again: "She tried to quench her judgment, and to silence the verdict which her intellect gave against him" (I, 446). Palliser, too, is apt to be highhanded in his judgments, at least as Glencora thinks. When he has delivered his verdict that pocket boroughs are "an old established evil," and she defends them, he replies with a dignity intended to end the argument,

> 'As to that, Glencora, I must judge for myself.'
> 'Oh yes, – you have been jury, and judge, and executioner.'
> 'I have done as I thought right to do.' (I, 364)

In fact he like Emily specializes in doing as he thinks right to do; and both, like Louis Trevelyan in the earlier novel, become obsessively determined to Know They are Right.

We have seen how reiteration is one of Trollope's ways of keeping his theme before his reader, so that in *The Eustace Diamonds*, for instance, each character in turn is labelled as truth-telling or the reverse. Here in *The Prime Minister* the matters of judgment and justice are similarly kept in the reader's mind by frequent repetition. "You must allow me to judge for myself, and I will judge" (II, 124), the Duke tells Glencora. And judge he does, until he earns both the name and the fate of Aristides the Just. He exercises himself on issues of "whether strict high-minded justice did not call upon him" to do this or that (II, 27). And in connection with him there is much play on the tag, "Ruat cœlum, fiat justitia" (I, 369; II, 252). Emily is likewise constantly at exercising her judgment, though hers is no very efficient instrument. "The girl herself might be deficient in judgment," posits the narrator (I, 171–2); when her husband does the same, she reflects angrily, "If her husband would not credit her judgment, let the matter be referred to her father" (I, 348). Lopez on the other hand insists, "I must be the judge, and not your father" (I, 430). Mr. Wharton, indeed, tends to prejudge (it is lucky he is a barrister rather than a judge). On the matter of Lopez at the outset Emily finds herself opposed to him: "she did feel that on a matter so vital to her she had a right to plead her cause before judgment should be given"; but she finds here "the sentence already pronounced" (I, 52). The legal terminology is prominent again. One could multiply examples, but I must save some for further discussion.

Mr. Wharton is a marvellous study in prejudice. And it is characteristic of Trollope's unobtrusive irony that he should be able both to lay bare the old man's bigotry and unfounded prejudice (at one point he calls Lopez "a greasy Jew adventurer out of the gutter" [I, 163]), and to confirm him ultimately as having been quite right in this instance. He is described at the outset as "a silent, far-seeing, close-fisted, just old man" (I, 26–7). He *is* just and far-seeing in his estimate of Lopez, but yet it is *per accidens*; he is right for all the wrong reasons. "Reasons" for his opposition to Emily's marriage to Lopez, as they both find, he cannot produce. Initially he rejects Lopez for what he thinks are reasons sufficient: "it was monstrous and out of the question that a daughter of the Whartons, one of the oldest families in England, should be given to a friendless Portuguese, – a probable Jew, – about whom nobody knew anything" (I, 37). Lopez argues away these reasons: he himself is English though his father was Portuguese; and he is a Christian. (On the latter point, as Trollope wryly confides, Wharton is on shaky ground anyway, for "Mr. Wharton, though he was a thorough and perhaps a bigoted member of the Church of England, was not fond of going to church" [I, 44].) But as Lopez and Emily separately persist in asking him for a reason for his continued objection, he falls back on the flimsy excuse that he knows nothing about Lopez.

'But, papa –; is there to be no reason?'
'Haven't I given reasons? I will not have my daughter encourage an adventurer, – a man of whom nobody knows anything. That is reason sufficient.'
'He has a business, and he lives with gentlemen. He is Everett's friend. He is well educated. . . . Papa, I wish you knew him better than you do.'
'I do not want to know him better.' (I, 51)

The argument has come full circle, like the old adage, "I'm glad I don't like marmelade, because if I liked it I would have to eat it, and that would be horrid." Even the respectful Emily can hesitantly ask at this point, "Is not that prejudice, papa?" But he does what he can to bully her into submission without producing a rational explanation: "You ought to feel that as I have had a long experience in the world my judgment about a young man might be trusted." It is fine scene, showing, as some of the disputes between Palliser and Glencora show, how little right reason has to do with making some of the major decisions in life. Wharton is thoroughly exposed; but then Emily really has no better "reasons" for loving Lopez than her father has for disliking him. Love, however, has long been acknowledged to be irrational. Mr. Wharton's judgment, which he says Emily must trust, is supposed to be more solidly founded.

Although he will not admit to being prejudiced to his daughter, to Lopez he almost makes a virtue of his prejudice. "Of course it's all prejudice. I won't deny that. On general subjects I can give as much lattitude as any man; but when one's own hearth is attacked . . . then a man has a right to guard even his prejudices as precious bulwarks" (I, 35).[9] The sentiment is familiar enough: I've got nothing against Portuguese Jews, but I don't want my daughter to marry one. What Trollope captures nicely is the air of self-congratulation, the sense that this shielding of the near and dear is a virtue to be cultivated. E. M. Forster, another novelist with a finely attuned ear for the nuances of prejudice, puts his finger on the same spirit in the Anglo-Indians at the club when they feel themselves threatened by the native population: "They had started speaking of 'women and children' – that phrase that exempts the male from sanity when it has been repeated a few times" (*A Passage to India*, ch. 20). The Whartons and the Fletchers are another privileged group that resists the incursion of outsiders. Their prejudices are indeed precious bulwarks to them. John Fletcher actually makes it a point of objection to Lopez that he has *no* prejudices: "He isn't of our sort. He's too clever, too cosmopolitan, – a sort of man whitewashed of all prejudices, who wouldn't mind whether he ate horseflesh or beef if horseflesh were as good as beef" (I, 183). He understands that "reasons" have nothing to do with such matters: it may be quite rational to eat horseflesh, but the right people know that it is disgusting.

In their pride of prejudice they have formidable authority behind them. Burke spoke eloquently of the uses of prejudice, and his argument, with the reiterated concern for the "reason" behind prejudice, has a special reverberation in *The Prime Minister*:

> Many of our men of speculation . . . think it more wise to continue the prejudice, with the reason involved, than to cast away the coat of prejudice, and to leave nothing but the naked reason; because prejudice, with its reason, has a motive to give action to that reason, and an affection which will give it permanence. Prejudice is of ready application in the emergency; it previously engages the mind in a steady course of wisdom and virtue, and does not leave the man hesitating in the moment of decision. . . . Prejudice renders a man's virtue his habit. . . . Through just prejudice, his duty becomes a part of his nature. (*Reflections on the Revolution in France*)

His prejudice may have been a habit of virtue in most of the emergencies of Mr. Wharton's life, but in his inability to define his reasons in this instance he reveals that he is not practising the "just" prejudice that Burke extols. His prejudice here, as Emily makes clear, is rather prejudgment. And in trusting to his prejudices and offering only perfunctory substitutes for reasons for his objection, Wharton overlooks the real and material reason. He neglects to make the necessary inquiries into Lopez's financial status, and so is unable to make the objection to Lopez that would really count. He might have managed to prove his daughter's suitor a fortune-hunter, as Dr. Sloper does in *Washington Square* – a novel that I suspect owes something to the first part of *The Prime Minister*,[10] James's rather condescending attitude to Trollope notwithsanding. As it is, being unable to justify his prejudice fully in the face of Emily's well-planned alternation of argument and submissive suffering, he wavers, and eventually gives way: "I have refused my sanction to the marriage both to him and to her, – though in truth I have been hard set to find any adequate reason for doing so. I have no right to fashion my girl's life by my prejudices" (I, 168). And so he gives in, but without surrendering his prejudice.

Lopez as the object of the wrongly-founded prejudice is, like Shylock, more sympathetic to the reader than possibly the author intended him to be. We make no mistake about his villainy, but as with Shylock we are prepared to make a few allowances. A lot of people spit upon his Jewish gabardine, so to speak, and he has trained himself into such a habit of taking insults as though he did not notice them that it is scarcely to be wondered at that he should be so steeped in duplicity. When Mr. Wharton discourteously tells him he cares nothing for his happiness, "Lopez smiled, but he put down the word in his memory and determined that he would treasure it there" (I, 158). It is one of many such uncandid smiles, which are part of the defence he puts up against a hostile society. Even Everett, who purports to be his friend and above the prejudices of the other Whartons, amiably patronizes him, telling him, "You are not quite enough of an Englishman to understand. . . . I won't say but what you may get yourself educated to it when you've been married a dozen years to an English wife . . ." (I, 243). There is a nice little touch in the naming of one of Lopez's rival candidates at Silverbridge, Mr. Du Boung. Frank Gresham of Greshamsbury (grown despressingly middleaged and reactionary since his young days chronicled in *Dr. Thorne*) says irascibly, "As for Du Boung, I'd sooner have him than a foreign cad like Lopez. . . . Du Boung used to be plain English as Bung before he got rich and made his name beautiful" (I, 381–2). There are ins and outs to prejudice that Lopez cannot master. It is apparently all right to be English and pretend you're French, but not to be English and sound Portuguese.

Lopez is shown as being so good at controlling his words and facial movements when he receives insults that it is rather difficult to credit his rowdy behaviour at Silverbridge – the pubic scenes and the brandishing of horsewhips. Trollope has tried to explain it – "he was a man, whom the feeling of injustice to himself would drive almost to frenzy, though he never measured the amount of his own injustice to others" (I, 387). But we have seen him experience plenty of injustice, and smile, at least whenever it is in his interest to do so. Here, for all his minute sensitivity to the operation of prejudice, Trollope seems a little prejudiced himself, and determined to make Lopez a villain – both the cool master of duplicity and the ruffianly bully of the Silverbridge election.

Prejudice is not the only factor that complicates the exercise of rational judgment. All the major characters, and some of the minor ones, are in one way or another engaged in making decisions, often unwise ones, and subsequently in justifying themselves, rationalizing their conduct. The initial momentum of the story derives from two mistakes in judgment, very different in their seriousness, but similar in leading to great suffering and painful self-recrimination. Emily, against the advice of all her friends and family, and against even the evidence of her own senses, marries Lopez instead of Arthur Fletcher; and Palliser, though he feels himself unfit and longs for other work, becomes Prime Minister. Mr. Wharton, Glencora and Lopez also make mistakes in judgment, but we see less of their subsequent self-condemnation.

Trollope makes much of Emily's mistake in judgment – as she does herself. As with Alice Vavasor in *Can You Forgive Her?* he makes it quite clear what is the obvious and right choice between her suitors, even to the use of the Hyperion to a satyr image. "With such an English gentleman as Arthur Fletcher on one side, and with this Portuguese Jew on the other, it was to him Hyperion to a Satyr. A darkness had fallen over his girl's eyes, and for a time her power of judgment had left her" (I, 150) – so it appears to Mr. Wharton; but Emily too can see if she chooses that Arthur is her god; but she does not choose – at least until the wrong decision has been made: "For a moment the idea of a comparison between the two men forced itself upon her, – but she drove it from her" (I, 192). There is an element of wilfulness in her misjudgment. She has "taught herself to understand," Trollope says – a familiar phrase that always reminds us of that human tendency to be activated by some individual internal mechanism that is not really reason, though clothed in reason's garb – "she . . . had taught herself to understand by some confused and perplexed lesson that she did not love [Arthur] as men and women love" (I, 191). Her relatives think her "perverse and unreasonable" for not loving Arthur, and her "greater folly and worse perverseness" is manifest to them in "her vitiated taste and dreadful partiality for the Portuguese adventurer" (I, 175–6). Their prejudices are clear enough, but they are right in calling her perverse, for she is really part of the Wharton tribe and shares their prejudices – and like Lily Dale and Alice Vavasor she enters into her suffering deliberately, as she afterwards prolongs it deliberately.

The Duke too, though at a fully conscious level, becomes Prime Minister with the full knowledge of disaster. "It is no case for exultation, Cora, for the chances are that I shall fail," he says gloomily at the outset (I, 59). And fail he does, at least in his own estimation, and also in that of Mr. Monk, a reliable authority, who feels that the withdrawal of the Duke's services consequent on the defeat of his ministry is a great loss to the country (II, 469). As Emily "soon knew that her marriage had been a mistake" (I, 451), so the Duke discovers, "Of one thing only was he sure, – that a grievous calamity had befallen him when circumstances compelled him to become the Queen's Prime Minister" (I, 367).

Glencora, too, makes her grand decision about making Buckingham Palace second-rate; flounders amidst her linen and her cooks and her guests and her unsociable husband; and finds it was all a mistake. Unlike her husband and Emily she does not hesitate at the beginning: she is the fool who rushes in where angels fear to tread, and she goes ahead with her massive arrangements at Gatherum with little doubt but that she is following the best means to a desirable end. But when things begin to go wrong and she is harrassed by such disagreeable effects as the incident with Major Pountney, even she wavers and feels the need to justify herself. "Had she not succeeded in all that she had done? Could it be right that she should be asked to abandon everything, to own herself to have been defeated, to be shown to have failed before all the world, because such a one as Major Pountney had made a fool of himself?" (I, 359). Trollope is marvellous in chronicling the mind's shifts of ground from moment to moment. At the last, of course, Glencora is to acknowledge failure like her husband, and their shared recognition of failure is to draw them closer, at least for the moment.

As for Lopez, he too has had his great expectations, and his failure is the most conspicuous of all, ending as it does in his bloody suicide at Tenway Junction. Commerce for him is a grand enterprise, almost a romantic one: "To his thinking there was something bold, grand, picturesque, and almost beautiful in the battle which such a one as himself must wage with the world" (I, 275). But after all his misjudged ventures in guano, kauri gum, and bios (he like Glencora is not very particular about keeping himself unsullied) he announces simply to his partner, "I thought I'd just look in to tell you that I'm just done for, – that I haven't a hope of a shilling now or hereafter" (II, 213). So the narrative movements of the novel depend on a series of mistaken choices.

The business of accurate judgment is made the harder by the prevalence of lies and various kinds of falsehood in the world. Trollope's concern with corruptions of the truth, the major theme in *The Eustace Diamonds* and a continuing concern in many of his novels, has some prominence here. It is quite appropriate that Lopez should gravitate towards Lizzie Eustace, though Lizzie has by now profited from her experience with Emilius. Glencora, like Lucy Morris, discovers "that the world tells lies every day, – telling on the whole much more lies than truth, – but that the world has wisely agreed that the world shall not be accused of lying" (I, 215). There is even a suggestion of an allegorical opposition, as in *The Eustace Diamonds*, between Palliser, whose "honesty is not like the honesty of other men. It is . . . more absolutely honest" (I, 323), and Lopez, who is "all a lie from head to foot" (II, 352). One of the chapters is called "Yes – a lie!", and there is much narrative comment to keep the reader informed of lies and half-truths that are being fobbed off as the truth on the unwary. "This was a lie" (I, 405); "This was a direct lie" (II, 48); "It was not absolutely untrue in words, – . . . but altogether false in spirit" (I, 459–60). Ratler and Roby, the political drones, and Major Pountney and Captain Gunner, the social drones, are two pairs of interlocutors who remind us how conversation can become simply a tissue of empty assertions: "Such assurances were common between the two friends, but were innocent, as, of course, neither believed the other" (I, 300). Lopez's dishonesty in commerce is possible because of the same cynical assumptions. In the buying and selling of shares in a commodity, he argues, it does not matter if the commodity does not actually exist (II, 37). Trollope gives a more extended account of the fictional commercial project in the history of the South Central Pacific and Mexican Railway in *The Way We Live Now*.

If the grounds of judgment are not vitiated by lies, they may be by ignorance. Here Emily is a case in point. Trollope is so busy keeping Lopez's iniquities before us that it sometimes seems Emily gets off rather lightly; but she is never finally exonerated from some responsibility in her husband's affairs, though she pleads ignorance as an excuse. "Do you understand his money matters, Emily?" her father askes her, and her stolid reply is "Not at all, papa" (II, 34; see also II, 145). Her determined ignorance is such that we have some sympathy for Lopez when he exclaims in exasperation, "By George, Emily, I think that you're a fool" (II, 82). When Mrs. Parker, whose husband Lopez ruins, reproaches her, and Emily offers her usual excuse, "I don't think I know anything about it," Mrs. Parker roundly replies, "But you ought; – oughtn't you, now?" (II, 56). Damn right, one is inclined to agree. But even when the crash comes and the Parkers are ruined, Emily still claims ignorance as her exemption from responsibility, and her father chimes in, "It is not her fault. . . . She knows less of it all than you do" (II, 175–6). There is no explicit condemnation, but the issue is fully dramatized; and Mrs. Parker, who becomes a pathetic pensioner of the Whartons, is a lasting reproach on wifely withdrawal from men's affairs.

That is a shortcoming Glencora could never be accused of. Here the issue is presented the other way – must the husband take responsibility for the wife's misdemeanours? The Duke says yes: he will never admit to the world that Glencora's interference at Silverbridge caused all the mischief, and he insists on shouldering all the blame. Glencora, to her lasting glory, argues no: she will admit to her own follies, and take the consequences unto herself. "Let me bear it. My back is broad enough," she urges (II, 120). It is another of the nicely balanced contrasts between the two plots. The issue is not resolved – Glencora is courageous and endearing, but there is a nobility in the Duke's chivalry too – but it is neatly presented and argued to and fro; and readers will take their sides according to their convictions.

Glencora's back, as she says, is broad enough to take the blame and accusations that come her way. Even the charge of vulgarity from her husband – an accusation she finds very hard to swallow – she manages to digest in the course of an evening: "Perhaps it was vulgar. But why shouldn't she be vulgar, if she could most surely get what she wanted by vulgarity?" (I, 214). And when her husband is trying to impress on her a due sense of the seriousness of her interference in the Silverbridge election, she responds cheerfully, "What's the use of going back to that now, unless you want me to put down my neck to be trodden on? I am confessing my own sins as fast as I can" (II, 123). One feels inclined to cheer. But her husband is made of finer clay – a metaphor she uses herself. In him and in Emily we have dramatized not just the mistake in judgment, but the enormous susceptibility to judgment by others, however poorly qualified the judges.

> 'I cannot endure to have my character impugned, – even by Mr. Slide and Mr. Lopez' [the Duke tells his wife in his extremity].
>   'What matter, – if you are in the right? Why blench if your conscience accuses you of no fault? I would not blench even if it did.' (II, 122)

It is a characteristic exchange between the two. Lopez and Emily never communicate with each other so fully, but the same issue is presented in their marriage. Like Glencora, Lopez can "brazen it out without a blush" (II, 138); and like Palliser, Emily is so morally fastidious that she exasperates her husband, and occasionally the reader too (one recalls her "little shudder" at the mere mention of Lady Eustace [II, 78]). Here we are dealing with the large subsidiary theme of scruple and sensitivity, a theme supported by the frequent enlarging on the time-worn image of thick and thin skins. When the Duke of St. Bungay, in a passage calculated to disappoint those with heroic notions of the qualities required of the Queen's First Minister, discusses the qualities necessary in a Prime Minister, he ends with the grand climax, "he should have a good digestion, genial manners, and, above all, a thick skin" (II, 5).

In the *Autobiography* Trollope explains again Palliser's special quality in comparison with the strong and serviceable man who is usually to the fore in politics, and who has discovered "he must harden his skin and swallow his scruples":

> But every now and again we see the attempt made by men who cannot get their skins to be hard – who after a little while generally fall out of the ranks. The statesman of whom I was thinking – of whom I had

long thought – was one who did not fall out of the ranks, even though his skin would not become hard. ... This man ... should be scrupulous, and, as being scrupulous, weak. (*A*, 308–9)

Trollope's explicit sympathies are with Palliser. He is Trollope's "perfect gentleman." But in the same passage in the *Autobiography* he goes on to say that though Glencora is by no means a perfect lady, she is "all over woman" (310). By implication, one may reverse the distinction to suggest that though Palliser may be a perfect gentleman, he is not a complete man. And Trollope's enduring admiration for him notwithstanding, how he dramatizes Palliser's weakness, his shilly-shallying, his incapacitating sensitivity! – until his ministers have to conspire in "Coddling the Prime Minister" (II, 118). We are asked to keep in mind the nobility of his high principle on the one hand, and the absurdity of his hypersensitivity on the other. So the issue is argued between him and his wife:

'You say that I am thin-skinned.'
'Certainly you are. What people call a delicate organisation, – whereas I am rough and thick and monstrously commonplace.'
'Then should you too be thin-skinned for my sake.'

It is a good argument, for Glencora's considerable energies are indeed mustered to doing things for his sake. She will not surrender this point, however, and she has her own sufficient answer: "I wish I could make you thick-skinned for your own" (II, 26–7). What Glencora recognizes and won't give in to is an assumption of superior virtue among the hyper-scrupulous. "The worst of it is," she tells Mrs. Finn, "that when [men] suffer from this weakness, which you call sensitiveness, they think that they are made of finer material than other people. [No wonder she was not about to make the effort to be thin-skinned for her husband's sake!] Men shouldn't be made of Sèvres china, but of good stone earthenware" (II, 120). But Mrs. Finn, a greater admirer of the Duke than his wife, says on the same issue, "with zeal there always goes a thin skin, – and unjustifiable expectations, and biting despair, and contempt of others, and all the elements of unhappiness" (I, 124). Mrs. Finn is actually talking of her own husband here, and in Phineas as in the Duke we have the study of sensitivity and its attendant weaknesses. It is one of the developments of the series that we move from Phineas of *Phineas Finn*, sensitive but fortunate, and able to slough off the attacks of Quintus Slide with little difficulty, through the Phineas of *Phineas Redux*, almost incapacitated in being tried for a crime he didn't commit, to Palliser here, whose peccadilloes are of the slightest, but who cannot stand even the breath of the imputation of criticism. If Phineas was the clock on whom the seconds as well as the hours are scored (*PR*, II, 301)

Palliser's dial registers the fractions and decimals of seconds.

This matter of reaction to judgment, as Trollope shows, is not a rational matter but a psychological one. Palliser blames himself even when his actions have been in accordance with the finest discriminations of justice – as with paying the Lopez electioneering expenses, or giving the garter to the meritorious Lord Earlybird. And guilt as a sort of psychological indulgence, not just in the Duke but in society at large, is plausibly dramatized in the reactions to that central event of Lopez's suicide. It is like a pebble dropped into some sensitive organism like a sea anemone – instantly all the randomly waving tentacles clutch and retract towards the same spot. People who had good cause to be glad the incubus is gone react with exaggerated grief. Emily, who had so hated him that she was glad their baby died, calls him more sinned against than sinning. The press takes up the case and calls him a martyr. Palliser as a matter of course feels responsible. Even Lizzie Eustace, who is by no means given to transports of self-condemnation, extracts a litttle *frisson* of excitement from the notion that "She was, perhaps, entitled to think that she had caused it!" (II, 246). Nearly everyone, it seems, greedily grabs for the guilt. Only Glencora is able to be rational about the matter: "Such sensitiveness is simply a disease. One can never punish any fault in the world if the sinner can revenge himself upon us by rushing into eternity. Sometimes I see him [the Duke] shiver and shudder, and then I know that he is thinking of Lopez" (II, 261).[11]

Poor Palliser, retiring to his inner sanctum with his copy of *The People's Banner* (to which he secretly subscibes) to finger his bruises over the latest vilification of himself, is both tragic and comic. Trollope has marvellously maintained this delicate balance in him, and kept the issue of scruple and sensitivity before the reader through the analytical discussions of his characters as well as through the action and the authorial commentary. For Trollope's characters here are particularly able assistants to the novelist, and go about the business of analysing character and debating merits with a zeal that engages the reader too.

If the reader becomes exasperated along with Glencora at the Duke's superior virtue, so, ultimately, does the public at large. This is the point of the repeated comparison of him with Aristides the Just (see II, 269, 294, 326). Trollope's use of allusion here is more than a passing figure of speech.[12] According to the mythologized bits of Greek history familiar to every schoolboy, Aristides was ostracised; and when one illiterate voter, not knowing him, asked him to write the name of Aristides on his oyster-shell, Aristides asked him if he had ever injured the man. "No," said the voter, "but it vexes me to hear him everywhere called 'the Just'." When the Duke gives the garter to the irreproachable Lord Earlybird, instead of to himself or to someone of comparable rank and status, the Duke of St. Bungay calls him "Quixotic" – a strong term for him – and members of the House and the public generally are exasperated: the Prime Minister has been "guilty of pretentious love of virtue." "When Aristides has been much too just the oyster-shells become numerous" comments the narrator (II, 294). The allusion goes further, I suspect. Aristides' great rival was Themistocles, who opposed Aristides' quiet and conservative policy and advocated a strong navy – he it was, according to Plutarch, who first persuaded the Athenians that they should "employe the money in making of gallyes."[13] One thinks of Sir Orlando Drought, First Lord of the Admiralty and leader of the House of Commons, with his ambition and his busy fidgeting about "a distinct policy," and his hot idea of "building four bigger ships of war than had ever been built before, – with larger guns, and more men, and thicker iron plates, and, above all, with a greater expenditure of money" (I, 360). Sir Orlando, like Themistocles, is the principal agent in destroying the Duke's ministry; and the Duke, like Aristides, is eventually defeated because he is too just. Slide, as the author of the bitter article on "Our Prime Minister's Good Works," does well as the modernized version of the illiterate bumpkin who hates Aristides for his justice.

In the other plot we see the proud determination to be right, and the agony of self-condemnation, carried to pathological extremes. Emily has the same determination as Palliser that her conduct should be irreproachable. She fiercely declares to her husband, "with open eyes and extended nostrils[,] 'Whatever may come, however wretched it may be, I shall not be ashamed of myself.'" Her husband continues for her, with more justice than she will admit, – "But of me!" (II, 39–40). She insists on her resolution to "be true to him" (II, 77); but by the time she has disobeyed him, abused him to her father, told him she doesn't love him, and allowed Arthur to kiss her, one wonders whether her declaration has much more force than Lizzie's in *The Eustace Diamonds*. Her determination not to be ashamed of herself has no more weight – in fact, of course, she is pathologically and monstrously ashamed of herself. "I am disgraced and shamed. I have lain among the pots till I am foul and blackened" (II, 402), she exclaims, when Arthur proposes yet again. The expression suggests some sin of passion, but Emily is in fact most ashamed of her sin of judgment. The sin is greater, as she feels, because she had in manner specialized in discernment in insisting on deciding for herself in the teeth of all the advice from her family: "But now, – now that it was all too late, – the veil had fallen from her eyes. . . . Ah, – that she should ever have been so blind, she who had given herself credit for seeing so much clearer than they who were her elders!" (I, 452). Emily does not have much else in common with Elizabeth Bennet, but in this moment of the falling of the veil from her eyes her experience is very close to Elizabeth's after the reading of Darcy's letter, when she acknowledges that "she had been blind, partial, prejudiced, absurd. 'How despicably have I acted!' she cried. – 'I, who have prided myself on my discernment!'" (*Pride and Prejudice*, II, ch. 13).

In a passage that connects Trollope's themes of judgment and pride, Emily tells her father, "I have a feeling of pride which tells me that as I chose to become the wife of my husband . . . – as I would judge for myself, – I am bound to put up with my choice." So she consigns herself to "perpetual prison" (II, 140). Her mistake in judgment is charitably viewed by others, who are quite ready to forgive her and welcome her back after Lopez's suicide; but Emily now pronounces judgment on herself and allots her own "punishment." By some grim interior logic, which is psychologically convincing if not rationally justifiable, she has decided that she must refuse Arthur and go on being miserable. In this new act of judgment she is quite fanatical. "She was quite clear as to the rectitude of her own judgment, clear as ever," says the narrator, with some irony (II, 356).

As with the Duke, there is plenty of discussion between the characters as well as in the authorial commentary as to the rights and wrongs of Emily's conduct, and whether her pathological sensitivity is a fault or a virtue. Arthur is more enamoured than ever, and takes an almost mystic delight even in her determination to refuse him. But his mother, like some critics of Palliser, is "almost jealous of the peculiar superiority of sentiment which her son seemed to attribute to this woman" (II, 353). Her own diagnosis is, "It's pride. . . . She won't give way" (II, 455). Emily is at last persuaded to marry Arthur by his authoritative and appropriate declaration, "You have no right to set yourself up to judge what may be best for my happiness. They who know how to judge are all united" (II, 459). (The wording of a final proposal is often of thematic import, as with Johnny Eames's in *The Last Chronicle* or Grey's in *Can You Forgive Her?*) Emily gives way to Arthur's persuasion at the end of the penultimate chapter. At the end of the last we are allowed to look forward to some time when the Duke "may again be of some humble use," and accept office. Both have worked through their mistakes in judgment, their consequent self-condemnation which their proud rectitude demands, and their self-inflicted punishments.

I feel I should admit at this point what is no doubt already plain enough – I find Emily a real pain, one of the most unpleasant characters in the novels. Her scenes with Arthur Fletcher, in which he finds her so irresistibly desirable, make me feel quite queasy because of the elevation of her language and her implied self-martyrdom and self-glorification. My personal likes and dislikes are perhaps not very interesting – no more than those of Trollope's nineteenth-century critics who condemned Lopez as bad art because they did not like his character. But there is a genuine critical issue here in the matter of Trollope's rhetoric. As Polhemus notes, in the case of the Whartons, "he presents things from their point of view and seldom criticizes them in his own voice. His indictment of them and what they stand for seems to come almost against his will, and that is why it carries such convincing force."[14] One really wonders how one is meant to respond to Emily and her kind, and I would like to examine some of the evidence.

Without trying to make an angel of Lopez, one can yet see that he gets a raw deal. Wharton we know was ready to hand over £60,000 to Arthur as Emily's dowry, but he offers Lopez nothing, and gives him £3000 only under pressure, and then refuses any other settlement. It is not only Lopez who feels that "if Mr. Wharton would only open his pockets wide enough things might still be right" (II, 134–5). Wharton's tight-fistedness is amply documented. And Lopez's sins, as seen through the eyes of his coldly evaluating wife, are not always as heinous as she thinks them. When he holds a dinner party in her father's absence, for instance, her horror is absurdly exaggerated: "It seemed to her to be sacrilege that these women should come and sit in her father's room" (II, 84). Lizzie Eustace may be a little shady, but she's not that bad! Well might Emily's aunt "laugh at her scruples."

And then what are we to make of Emily's other man, Arthur, "the very pearl of the Fletcher tribe"? (I, 162). Here so far as any explicit comment goes it is clear we are supposed to admire him. But such an upright, downright, forthright, square character is bound to be a problem to his author; and one little hint makes me wonder if Trollope himself had much sympathy for his paragon. Perhaps it is easy to be good, he suggests, if you are born with a silver spoon in your mouth:

> There was no one who in his youth had suffered fewer troubles from those causes of trouble which visit English young men, – occasional impecuniosity, sternness of parents, native shyness, fear of ridicule, inability of speech, and a general pervading sense of inferiority combined with an ardent desire to rise to a feeling of conscious superiority. (I, 162)

The passage is really a digression – these are all the things that Arthur Fletcher did *not* suffer from. But we know someone who did: Trollope himself, who was soon to write – perhaps was already writing – the autobiography where all those troubles are so intensely remembered and so painfully chronicled. Perhaps this little touch of personal reminiscence, as I suspect it is, can hardly be called part of Trollope's rhetoric. But I find in it a hint that Arthur Fletcher has not engaged any warm personal sympathy in his author. When Trollope elsewhere seems to be aligning himself and his reader with the Whartons and Fletchers – "We, who know the feeling of Englishmen generally better than Mr. Lopez did . . ." – we should be cautious of assuming that Trollope is really one of them (I, 390).

I hazard a speculation that Trollope is here setting up a case for the reader's judgment. Lopez is bad no doubt, he argues, but need he have been as bad? The Whartons and Fletchers are the backbone of England of course, but how blind are their habits of prejudice, and how morbid is their determination to be in the right? The absence of explicit authorial commentary on these issues is an invitation to assessment by the reader, an opportunity for the operation of his own judgment or prejudice. It is a process that is of course always going on in Trollope's work – "consider this but consider that" being an implied request in all he writes, and the major motive behind, say, *The Warden*, which is explicitly an attack on all fanatical and one-sided opinions whatever. But I think his presentation of Emily is deliberately ambiguous, with the intent of involving his reader in the act of judgment.

The Prime Minister is a searching account of two marriages, and without expanding further on the themes of authority and judgment that are enacted between the two husbands and the two wives, I would like to discuss Trollope's marvellous presentation of the two sets of physical, emotional and psychological relations in marriage. Here again we are to compare and contrast, to consider a range of possibilities in response to similar situations. Emily, for instance, in marrying a handsome ne'er-do-well who loves her and her money too, against the wishes of her family, is doing just what Glencora had wanted to do in her youth. We see how Emily's marriage is a romance that goes sour, as Glencora's to Burgo would undoubtedly have gone sour too; whereas Glencora's marriage to Palliser is a non-romance that turns sweet, in its quiet and unspectacular way.

Trollope does not go into the details of the bedroom, but he gives us enough information to make it a fairly good guess that the Pallisers' sex life has more or less petered out. "I can't live with him because he shuts himself up reading blue-books," Glencora mentions in passing at one point (I, 426). The context is not solemn, and one is not sure quite what she means by her phrase; but it is fairly strong language any way you take it. "He is as dry as a stick" (II, 185), she says more than once. She is vexed when he comes down to Gatherum with her. Such phrases as "they met at dinner" obliquely suggest that is the place where they are most likely to meet. And when the Duke, as he sometimes does, makes some set speech about Darby and Joan – "I am dreaming always of some day when we may go away together with the children, and rest in some pretty spot, and live as other people live," the Duchess's sotto voce comment is "It would be very stupid" (II, 125). Relations between them are sometimes governed by an exacting personal protocol, which Glencora makes explicit. On certain issues she is kept informed of her husband's wishes only through the Prime Minister's private secretary, Mr. Warburton; and Glencora is watchful that the proper channels of communication should be observed. On the delicate matter of her decision not to invite Sir Orlando to her dinners, she tells Mrs. Finn,

> 'I'm told that Sir Orlando has complained to Plantagenet that he isn't asked to the dinners.'
> 'Impossible!'
> 'Don't you mention it, but he has. Warburton has told me so.' Warburton was one of the Duke's private secretaries.
> 'What did the Duke say?'
> 'I don't quite know. Warburton is one of my familiars, but I didn't like to ask him for more than he chose to tell me. Warburton suggested I should invite Sir Orlando at once; but there I was obdurate. Of course if Plantagenet tells me I'll ask the man to come every day of the week; but it is one of those things that I shall need to be told directly.' (I, 433–4)

Such is the minute accounting and manoeuvring in communication between husband and wife.

Glencora's frequently mentioned need for a female confidante seems to be one result of her rather arid relations with her husband. Of course it is convenient for Trollope to have Alice Vavasor or Mrs. Finn as a ficelle, a medium through whom his main character's views can be communicated to the reader. But he refers to Glencora's special reliance on Mrs. Finn often enough to make it clear that it is part of Glencora's character, not just an authorial convenience. To Mrs. Finn she can speak of her marriage and other subjects frankly and intimately, and without fear that she will be lectured for her indiscretion or her racy language. She can talk of Palliser as a "god" – but with her own characteristic reservation: "He is a god, but I am not a goddess; – and then, though he is a god, he is a dry, silent, uncongenial and uncomfortable god" (II, 185). Poor Glencora, born a "talker" as she told Alice Vavasor, yet with a husband who has no ear for such talk, nor much sympathy for it! No wonder she needs some compensatory relationship. As she tells him, without intentional pathos, "She is in truth the only woman in London, to whom I can say what I think. And it is a comfort, you know, to have some one" (I, 87). The *Duke* can't be the person to whom she can say what she thinks. It seems to be often the case between them that, as she tells Mrs. Finn, "In this matter it has gone beyond speaking" (II, 186).

But yet through the apparently desiccated tissue of their marriage there is a live artery of tenderness, even of passion. In the last novel that dealt in detail with Glencora's emotional life, *Can You Forgive Her?*, we had been shown the great romance of Glencora's life, her love for Burgo Fitzgerald. In the intervening novels she is quite comfortably aware that she could never have eloped with him, and reconciled to her life with the dry stick, her husband. But at the beginning of *The Prime Minister*, and notwithstanding the continuing dull state of one level of their relation, romance blossoms for Glencora again:

> 'I have received her Majesty's orders to go down to Windsor at once. I must start within half-an-hour' [the Duke tells her].
> 'You are going to be Prime Minister!' she exclaimed. As she spoke she threw her arms up, and then rushed into his embrace. Never since their first union had she been so demonstrative either of love or admiration. [Not then either, one might note in passing.] 'Oh, Plantagenet,' she said, 'if I can only do anything I will slave for you.' As he put his arm round her waist he already felt the pleasantness of her altered way to him. She had never worshipped him yet, and therefore her worship when it did come had all the delight to him which it ordinarily has to the newly married hero. (I, 58)

His Prime Ministership, then, is their second honeymoon. And though at one level their relation continues to be incomplete and unsatisfying, their love is concurrently renewed and rejuvenated – indeed one might almost say that hers for him is actually born, since it was never a very robust entity before. And so we have the rather touchingly innocent bits of lovemaking between this middle-aged couple. "His manner to her lately had been more than urbane, more than affectionate; – it had almost been that of a lover. He had petted her and caressed her when they met, and once even said that nothing should really trouble him as long as he had her with him. Such a speech as that never is his life had he made before to her!" (I, 359–360). If in the fifteen years or so of their married life he had never made such a speech, one may well feel this marriage has been deficient in love, or at least in the expression of it. But then the tenderness has a certain special poignancy when it does come. Or again, "now he sat down by her, very close to her, and put his hand upon her shoulder, – almost round her waist" (II, 25). Big deal, one might sneer. But yet Trollope manages to suggest that the movement has the freshness and excitement of the approach of first love. And even in the midst of her exasperation that he refuses to acknowledge to the world her responsibility in the Silverbridge business, she is moved to wonder at the extent of his love for her, and to consider him as a knight of chivalric romance:

> 'Though in manner he is as dry as a stick, though all his pursuits are opposite to the very idea of romance, ... there is a dash of chivalry about him worthy of the old poets. To him a woman, particularly his own woman, is a thing so fine and so precious that the winds of heaven should hardly be allowed to blow upon her.' (II, 185)

Incongruously, he does fill the role of her knight in shining armour, as he is Trollope's "perfect gentleman." There are two romances in Glencora's life; and, sadly but probably inevitably, both of them are failures.

In a moment of disillusion Glencora once tells Mrs. Finn, "I have never really enjoyed anything since I was in love [with Burgo, she means], and I only liked that because it was wicked" (II, 366). The Burgo episode always retains its place in her memory as her own really intense experience. But by the end of the novel there is another memory that has joined it, as she recalls the day on which she threw up her arms and rushed into Palliser's embrace: "When he became Prime Minister, I gave myself up to it altogether. I shall never forget what I felt when he came to me and told me that perhaps it might be so" (II, 466). Gave herself up to *it*, she says. And there is a rather questionable element to Glencora's second love. It is the office she has loved, rather than the man. As the Duke of St. Bungay reflects shrewdly, "It now seemed to him that though she had failed to love the man, she had given her entire heart to the Prime Minister" (II, 291–2). It is in this rather cynical sense that we can consider *The Prime Minister* as a love story, even without the Lopez plot. The Duke is quite right to be jealous, as he is, of her power and success, because the more she sees herself as the Prime Ministeress, the less love she can spare for the Prime Minister. And in *The Duke's Children*, in an act of posthumous infidelity, she reverts to her first romance with Burgo as the paradigm for her daughter's life: for the Duke is by then only the Ex-Prime Minister. The inter-relatedness of love and power, as we saw in the *Phineas* novels, is one of the connecting themes of the whole Palliser series, of which Glencora is the leading lady. However, though we may accuse her of loving power rather than persons, she can take it: her back remains broad enough.

If love and power are blended in the Palliser plot, love and money are similarly involved in the Lopez plot. Lopez, like Glencora, finds romance in success, though he is unable to communicate his sense of the picturesqueness and high adventure of commerce to his wife. But in this marriage too Trollope has suggested, more obliquely but still clearly I think, some of the unsavoury constituents of love. It is not just that Lopez is a fortune hunter: but for him the lust after profit is like the lust after flesh, and is even confounded with it.

Trollope is of course much less sympathetic to the love-money identification than to the love-power one. To begin with he makes it clear that Lopez's ventures in commerce are not only shady but dirty. They usually stink in one way or another. The first commodity he deals in is guano.[15] Trollope similarly associates Lopez's money dealings with deceit, blood, and death. Kauri gum and bios are to be sold as cheap substitutes for amber and whiskey respectively. Mrs. Parker, who was happy when her husband made money as a result of his hard work, "by the very sweat of his brow," finds that once he makes money itself his business by going into commerce with Lopez, he turns into something like a ravening beast or a vampire: "Them men, when they get on at

money-making, . . . are like tigers clawing one another. They don't care
how many they kills, so that they has the least bit for themselves. . . .
Why, it's altered the looks of the man altogether. It's just as though he
was a-thirsting for blood" (II, 74). And Lopez, whose view of human
nature is that men "rob and cheat on their death-beds" (I, 338), and
who takes his main comfort in the thought that his father-in-law "can't
carry his money with him" when he dies, habitually thinks and talks of
money and death in the same breath.

Defoe shows in *Moll Flanders* a rather more explicit version of what
Trollope is dealing with in Lopez and Emily. In her affair with the elder
brother, Moll is consistently trained to associate love and sex, so that
when he kisses and tips her, or puts a purse of gold in her bosom, we
hardly know if she is moved by lechery or avidity, and nor does she.[16] In
the Lopez marriage, Emily is similarly initiated into sex and money
matters simultaneously: "She must be taught the great importance of
money" – that is to be the lesson of the honeymoon (I, 280). Lopez
makes a brief attempt to avoid the discussion of his financial desires at
the beginning, but he soon abandons it. Even in the carriage driving
away from the wedding, and with his arm around his bride's waist, he is
thinking of money. He takes time first to be a magnetic and absorbing
lover:

> This man, of whom she knew in truth so little, had certain good gifts,
> – gifts of intellect, gifts of temper, gifts of voice and manner and out-
> ward appearance, – which had hitherto satisfied her. A husband who
> is also an eager lover must be delightful to a young bride. And hither-
> to no lover could have been more tender than Lopez. Every word and
> every act, every look and every touch, had been loving. (I, 283)

Then the next paragraph begins, "But the moment for the first lesson
had come." It is a scene of connubial intimacy – Emily nestles by his side
and rubs her face on his arm. And he leads up to his subject by stating
his surprise that her father has not written to her.

> 'Do you mean about money?' she asked in a very low voice.
> 'Well; – yes, I do mean about money.' (I, 284)

The subject is an almost unmentionable one. And it seems her father has
never given her the equivalent of the talk on the birds and the bees: "He
never said a word to me about money in his life". She has been kept
more innocent of money than Victorian ladies are said to be about sex.
"And yet, my darling, money is most important" – and so the new husband continues his bride's initiation (I, 285): "It was necessary that she
should learn her lesson, and she could only do so by having the subject
of money made familiar to her ears" (I, 290). As for Lopez himself, his

sexual and financial passions flow in one channel: when the long-awaited letter from Mr. Wharton arrives, with the welcome news that the £3000 will be forthcoming, "he chucked the letter, lightly, in among the tea-cups, and coming to her took her closely in his arms and almost hurt her by the violence of his repeated kisses" (I, 292). The access of money triggers an access of physical passion. He is like Moll, who after being kissed "most violently" by the elder brother, and tipped five guineas, confesses that she "was more confounded with the money than I was before with the love." It is all an intricate package deal.

Emily, of course, is by no means like Moll, and wants to keep her husband's love and his career in quite different compartments. She has a qualm of disgust when, with his arm around her waist, he talks of his bribing presents to her aunt as "part of the price I had to pay for being allowed to approach you" (I, 339). And she is offended when he boasts that having beaten Arthur Fletcher in his suit of her, he can beat him again in the election – because "by doing so he likened the sweet fragrance of her love to the dirty turmoil of an electioneering contest" (I, 342). The history of the deterioration and ruin of their marriage is concurrent with the history of Lopez's financial deterioration and ruin, since he is unable to teach her to interest herself passionately in his money-making.

As a contrast with Emily's moral fastidiousness, Trollope offers Lizzie Eustace, who, though a creature of innumerable wiles, is a fairly simple and uncomplicated organism, and so good for allowing Trollope to underline his themes. She and Lopez understand each other very well, and operate similarly: "She had flirted with him in a very pleasant way, mixing up her prettiness and her percentages in a manner that was peculiar to herself" (II, 167). Lopez, however, is unable to produce the capital to activate Lizzie's passion, and so in that memorable scene she is able to expose his substitution of money for love:

"Lizzie Eustace, if you will say the word I will take you to that land of glorious happiness.'
    But Lizzie Eustace had £4000 a year and a balance at her banker's.
'Mr. Lopez,' she said.
    'What answer have you to make me?'
    'Mr. Lopez, I think you must be a fool.' (II, 169)

His proposal to her was perhaps the most ill-advised of all Lopez's commercial ventures.

And so, alongside the love of the Pallisers, which in the wife is activated by power and office, Trollope places the love of the Lopezes, which in the husband is activated by money. He is not making a satirical study, however, as this simplified statement would suggest. He is as always locating the complexities of the human psyche and anatomizing the precise constituents of such an amorphous quantity as we call by the untidily inclusive name of love.

The Prime Minister is a large novel, but it is all of a piece. The two plots are intricately developed as commentaries on one another, and the themes of authority in marriage, love and power, judgment and misjudgment, prejudice and proud self-condemnation, gain in depth and force as each issue is raised, with its different content of character and attendant circumstance, in each plot successively. Trollope's and the reader's sympathies are most engaged in the study of the Palliser plot, but the system of contrasts and parallels by which it is bound to the Lopez plot reminds us always to be attentive to the particular situation and not just to general rules; and that judgment is no simple business.

7 *The Duke's Children*:
Past and Present

When the young Lady Glencora Palliser was straying by moonlight in the ruins of Matching Priory, the place where she can best summon up romantic fantasies about eloping with Burgo Fitzgerald, she told Alice Vavasor that she could not imbue her husband with the same fervour for her romantic ruin, though he does show a proprietory interest:

> 'I made him come once, but he didn't seem to care about it. I told him that part of the refectory wall was falling; so he looked at that, and had a mason sent the next day. If anything is out of order he has it put to rights at once. There would have been no ruins if all the Pallisers had been like him.'
> 'So much the better for the world.'
> 'No; – I say no. Things may live too long.' (*CYFH*, I, 349–50)

It is a telling little exchange, one more of the thousand touches by which Trollope identifies and differentiates his characters. Glencora loves the Priory because it is a ruin, remote from everyday concerns, and hence a site for the accumulation of romantic association, for the entertainment of wild speculations which she will indulge but not apply. For Palliser the place is the less useful in being ruinous, and he thinks moonlit walks there in winter are silly and imprudent. But he honours the past and seeks to preserve it.

That was back in *Can You Forgive Her?* But in *The Duke's Children*, when Glencora is buried in the Priory, and their children are grown up, the Duke is still occupied in keeping the past intact, and he has a great deal to suffer and to learn in discovering that some things may indeed live too long. The past that he is preserving was recorded in that other novel, and now after fifteen years and many hundreds of pages, in which

7. Glencora and Alice in the Priory ruins: Browne's illustration for *Can You Forgive Her?*, chapter 27

Trollope has minutely depicted the character and principles of the dedicated Liberal statesman, we are to find how fully he is, by temperament rather than political conviction, a conservative, a preserver of the past.

But it is not just the Duke in this novel whose sympathies are anchored in the past. He indeed clings to it, preserves it, seeks to reconstruct it, and finally must in some sense relinquish it. But all the major characters are examined for the degree of their commitment to the past and their ability and propensity to change and adapt for the present. They are being tested for qualities of memory, fidelity, and the kind of integrity that may still be compatible with a changed mind.[1]

Can You Forgive Her? and *The Duke's Children* are the Past and Present of the Duke's world,[2] and the story of the latter novel, in which the two generations of the title are to come to accord, is the story of the accommodation of the past to the present. In so explicitly reviving *Can You Forgive Her?* in his late novel, Trollope gives a measure of structural unity to the series. He had just finished writing his autobiography, and he must have felt strongly the Wordsworthian impulse, "I could wish my days to be/Bound each to each." The Duke, like Wordsworth, seeks for stability; or, if that cannot be achieved, a repetition of the past: "So was it when my life began;/ So is it now I am a man;/ So be it when I shall grow old." So it is moving to find Trollope, at this late stage in his career, when his sympathies are so manifestly bound up in the Duke, bravely dramatizing the danger and the impossibility of clinging to the past.

At the outset the Duke, like Carlyle in *Past and Present*, seeks to use the past as model for the present. Here I must touch again on ground already covered in John Hagan's indispensable article on *The Duke's Children* as Trollope's "psychological masterpiece."[3] Trollope reminds us constantly that the Duke sees his own marriage – an arranged match between a thoroughly respectable heir to a title and an heiress who had unfortunately been infatuated first with a quite unsuitable spendthrift – as a paradigm for marriages of people of his class. His boys are to be Plantagenet Pallisers, his girls Lady Glencoras, and they are to enact again the suitable marriage that follows on an unsuitable attachment: thus his past is to be justified.

This pattern is of course most evident in his opposition to Mary's engagement to Tregear. Glencora there had been guilty of her own machinations – she had promoted the match, seeing Tregear as a reincarnation of her beautiful Burgo, as a late compensation for her loss of her first love. The Duke divines this, but won't allow himself to believe it: hence his injustice to Mrs. Finn, whom he wants to blame instead of his wife. But he nonetheless makes it a crusade to end the unsuitable engagement, consciously following the same precedent. Glencora had wanted to undo the past, but the Duke insists on doing it again. He draws on "his own personal history" to convince himself that Mary must be separated from Tregear, and married to some young version of himself.

> Surely that method of bargaining to which he had owed his own wife would be better. . . . Let it be said, – only he himself most certainly could not be the person to say it, – let it be said to some men of rank and means and fairly good character: 'Here is a wife for you with so many thousand pounds, with beauty, as you can see for yourself, with rank and belongings of the highest; very good in every respect; – only that as regards her heart she thinks she has given it to a young man named Tregear. No marriage there is possible; but perhaps the young lady might suit you?' It was thus he had been married. (I, 109)

Even in his reflections he is unconsciously embarrassed to think about this touting – ("he himself . . . could not be the person to say it"); but he still proceeds on the irreversible principle that since his marriage had been made that way, and since his marriage was a good marriage (a proposition he clings to), therefore that is the way good marriages are made.

In the matter of opposition to Tregear, he takes the labour on himself; but in the other part of the transaction, the enticing of a suitable young man to play his own role, he leaves the dirty work to Lady Cantrip. She goes about the task with devotion, though with some qualms: Popplecourt is to be the latter-day Palliser – and it is amusing to see how, once his counterpart has been found, the Duke despises him. "He hardly liked to look at the fish whom he wished to catch for his daughter" – the "fish" is himself in this reenactment. "Whenever this aspect of affairs presented itself to him, he would endeavour to console himself by remembering the past success of a similar transaction" (II, 62). The endeavour at consolation can hardly be very successful while he sees himself in this respectable but despicable young man, "who was not fast only because he did not like to risk his money" (I, 297). Although his enterprise to reconstruct the past proceeds partly from his pride, the Duke's reaction to his reintroduced self is a touching reminder of his innate modesty. It confirms what we hear elsewhere, "he had by no means regarded his own mode of life with favour" (II, 206). He is not prone to self-love, although he wants to impose his own history on his children.

Lady Mary, however, though she resembles her mother in appearance, is quite different in temperament. She has neither Glencora's sparkle, nor her pliability. Glencora as we came to know her seemed strong and forceful enough, but her strength was not in steadfastness: it was part of her charm to be wily and adaptable. She was persuaded by family pressure to give up Burgo, but she managed to make a success – almost – of her subsequent marriage; she was the sworn enemy of Marie Goesler, but later made her her bosom companion. Politics bored her stiff, but she became the most ambitious and astute of political wives. Mary is different. Heaven and earth won't make her give up Tregear – the united forces of her father, her brother and Lady Cantrip certainly cannot compass it. The Duke, who has always eventually extracted obedience from Glencora, cannot move her. We hear at the outset, "Of one thing she was very sure, that under no pressure whatsoever would she abandon her engagement with Mr. Tregear" (I, 43). She refuses outright to be proposed to by Lord Popplecourt. And when Lady Cantrip tries a little persuasive pressure, expressing "a hope that her dear Mary would think over these things and try to please her father," Mary's resounding response is, "Why does he not try to please me?" (II, 81). Lady Cantrip, burdened with her recalcitrant charge, finds that "she had to deal with a very self-willed young lady indeed. . . . 'One doesn't know which she is most like, her father or her mother. . . . She has his cool determination, and her hot-headed obstinacy'" (I, 225–6). But when she takes Mary's side with the Duke, arguing "If she is firm, Duke, you must yield," he replies "Never!" (I, 228). Between them, father and daughter seem to be the proverbial irresistible force and immovable object.

Mary as the immovable object does not have much dramatic interest; the drama lies in the successive defeats of her antagonist, the Duke, as he batters himself against his daughter's unyielding determination, and is forced finally to negotiate and then withdraw. The great scene of his capitulation – the "attack", as Trollope calls it in his chapter heading, that determines his defeat – is the one with Mrs. Finn. It is a fine example of how Trollope can dramatize his theme, and maintain his thread of ideas even as he composes a dialogue that involves his reader in the urgency of the experience. The scene at chapter 66 deserves some close analysis and ample quotation.

To begin with, we need to remember that Mrs. Finn speaks from a position of unique strength. With a sensitivity of scruple to match the Duke's own, she has maintained her position of absolute irreproachability in her relation to the Duke's family. She refused the old Duke's offer of marriage when she might have cut out Palliser, Glencora, and the young hopeful, Silverbridge. She selflessly devoted herself to the old man, tending to all his needs and sacrificing all her own. She refused to accept the legacy of diamonds, which might have cast the slur of self-interest on her previous dealings, and she was indispensable but forbearing and discreet in all the years of Glencora's reliance on her. All this was past history at the beginning of the present novel; but the Duke, who has so specialized in being scrupulous himself, has not fully appreciated the quality in another, and – partially from jealousy, it is easy to surmise – he still distrusts her as "an adventuress" (I, 67), and wants to blame her instead of his wife for Mary's engagement to Tregear.[4] But

she is the one character in the novels who can match him for scruple and
sensitivity, who can not only know she is right, like Louis Trevelyan, but
be right. "She could tell herself with pride that her conduct towards him
had been always such as would become a lady of high spirit and fine
feeling. She knew she had deserved well of him" (I, 124). But for all this
he, Aristides the Just, has been unjust to her. Prompted by his need to
justify his wife and preserve his past, he blames her for an offence she
never committed: and her crusade to extract an apology from him is
pursued with great fervour on her part and related with some delicacy
on Trollope's. When she receives his apology, coldly worded though it
is, her eyes fill with tears. Aristides has become just again, and she
herself is justified.

So Mrs. Finn, as one of the few people who have managed to impress
the Duke as being fully in the right, has a special persuasive power with
him. But when she takes Mary's cause in hand, she treads carefully:

> 'I feel that I am bound to tell you my opinion.'
> 'Oh yes.'
> 'You think that in the end Lady Mary will allow herself to be
> separated from Tregear. I think that in the end they will become man
> and wife.'
> This seemed to the Duke to be not quite so bad as it might have
> been. Any speculation as to results were very different from an
> expressed opinion as to propriety. (II, 245)

One realizes from that shrewd discrimination in the narrative comment
just how clever Mrs. Finn has been in her approach to the subject. She
has not girded her loins to do battle with the Duke on the principle. On
the principle, as she knows very well, he will not bend, though he has
already faced possibilities as to an inevitable outcome:

> Were he to tell the truth as to his own mind, he might perhaps have
> said the same thing. But one is not to relax in one's endeavours to
> prevent that which is wrong, because one fears that the wrong may be
> ultimately perpetrated. 'Let that be as it may,' he said, 'it cannot alter
> my duty.'
> 'Nor mine, Duke, if I may presume to think that I have a duty in
> this matter.'

Her language is deferential, but the sentiment is strong. She holds on to
her right to have a duty too, and one that is as unalterable as his. He
quickly backs down.

> 'That you should encounter the burden of the duty binds me to you
> for ever.'
> 'If it be that they will certainly be married one day–'

– here he detects her in an assumption he will not explicitly sanction, and it is she who has to back down, while changing to a logic that is personal rather than universal.

'Who has said that? Who has admitted that?'
'If it be so; if it seems to me that it must be so, – then how can I be anxious to prolong her sufferings? She does suffer terribly.' Upon this the Duke frowned, but there was more of tenderness in his frown than in the hard smile which he had hitherto worn.

By becoming personal herself, by leaving the philosophical speculation about probable outcome, skirting the ethical question of propriety and arriving at her feelings in witnessing Mary's feelings, she induces the Duke to be personal too. It is here that he is accessible to pursuasion.

'I do not know whether you see it all.' He well remembered all that he had seen when he and Mary were travelling together.

Though he remembers, he does not say so. He feels, but he is as usual reticent in expressing his feelings. It is Mrs. Finn who keeps talking, the Duke who silently reacts and reflects.

'I see it; and I do not pass half an hour with her without sorrowing for her.' On hearing this he sighed and turned his face away. 'Girls are so different! There are many who though they be genuinely in love, though their natures are sweet and affectionate, are not strong enough to support their own feelings in resistance to the will of those who have authority over them.' Had it been so with his wife? At this moment all the former history passed through his mind. 'They yield to that which seems to be inevitable, and allow themselves to be fashioned by the purposes of others. It is well for them often that they are so plastic. Whether it would be better for her that she should be so I will not say.'
'It would be better,' said the Duke doggedly.
'But such is not her nature. She is as determined as ever.'
'I may be determined too.'
'But if at last it will be of no use, – if it be her fate either to be married to this man or die of a broken heart –'
'What justifies you in saying that? How can you torture me by such a threat?'
'If I think so, Duke, I am justified. Of late I have been with her daily, – almost hourly. I do not say that this will kill her now, – in her youth. It is not often, I fancy, that women die after that fashion. But a broken heart may bring the sufferer to the grave after a lapse of many years. How will it be with you if she should live like a ghost beside you

for the next twenty years, and you should then see her die, faded and withered before her time, – all her life gone without a joy, – because she had loved a man whose position in life was displeasing to you? Would the ground on which the sacrifice had been made then justify itself to you? In thus performing your duty to your order would you feel satisfied that you had performed that to your child?' (II, 246–7)

Bravo, Mrs. Finn! But bravo Trollope, too. How brilliant she has been – and he in showing it – at touching on that one dominantly vibrating chord of the Duke's consciousness, his need to justify his past. What she says is simple enough: "Girls are so different!" All along the Duke has defended his psychological need to reenact the history of his marriage by making a principle out of the individual case and so calling the reenactment "duty." "If it were right, he must still do it," he tells himself (II, 95). To tell him his general rule is merely an individual variation is to pull the carpet out from under his feet. Lady Cantrip had tried to tell him the same thing, but failed: "Why should she not be like others?" he kept insisting (I, 228). It takes Mrs. Finn to bring the proposition before him in such a way that he can accept it, and it takes her skill and tact in making the application. With infinite delicacy, and without even mentioning the name, she reminds the Duke, Glencora was Glencora, and we loved her as she was: – evoking the memory so vividly that "at this moment all the former history passed through his mind," as though he were taking that last farewell of life that is supposed to be permitted to a drowning man. But, she proceeds, Mary, for better or worse, is not Glencora. Mary is Mary, not conveniently plastic, but determined. Girls are so different.

"I may be determined too," insists the Duke. I may make her be plastic, be Glencora, for her own good. "It would be better" for her to be Glencora, to give up Burgo, to marry Palliser, to justify the past. Then Mrs. Finn makes him look at a horribly vivid picture of the future, and of what it is he is proposing to do to his daughter. It is a vision touched with the horror or Donne's "Apparition", of a tomorrow that is to be haunted by the ghost of today's wronged soul. And now she is bold enough to come onto his own ground of principle and duty, and to assert that not only are girls different, but so also are duties, and sometimes they conflict. "In thus performing your duty to your order would you feel satisfied that you had performed that to your child?" And through the scene runs the constant concern to be justified, to be made right – the urgent and compelling desire that they share. "What justifies you in saying that?" "I am justified." "Would the ground on which the sacrifice had been made then justify itself to you?"

Mrs. Finn has achieved a great deal. She has invoked his past for him, not to make him confirm it and again determine to reenact it, but to

make him ready to relinquish it; and, like Dickens's Ghost of Christmas
Yet to Come, she has also invoked a future, one that is so forbidding
that it makes possible the relinquishing of the past and the changing of
the present. In the long moment during which the Duke looks into the
fire, though we have no analysis of his feelings, we are to suppose that
something of Scrooge's experience is settling itself in his mind. "I am
not the man I was," Scrooge tells the Ghost. ". . . I will live in the Past,
the Present, and the Future. . . . I will not shut out the lessons that they
teach. Oh, tell me that I may sponge away the writing on this stone!" (*A
Christmas Carol*, IV). Trollope is not Dickens, and he does not write that
scene. But he writes his own low mimetic version of it; and though the
Duke undergoes no such total conversion as Scrooge, still the same
theme informs the two scenes. Mrs. Finn, like Scrooge's ghosts, has invoked the Duke's past and laid it to rest; reminded him of the present
sufferings of his daughter that he could assuage; and summoned up a
vision of the bleak future that will be the result if he continues in his
course.

In his formal leave-taking, which is so moving to her, the Duke tells
her, "all that you have troubled yourself to think and to feel in this
matter, and all that true friendship has compelled you to say to me, shall
be written down in the tablets of my memory" (II, 248). The archaic,
almost biblical, phrase has its appropriateness, for he has indeed made a
set of commandments out of the tablets of his memory. It is heartening
to think that there is room for additions, and that Mrs. Finn, with her
doctrine of tolerance and her plea for the individual case, has found a
place there.

Some time later he is able to tell his son about his changed views on
Mary's engagement to Tregear: "When I became convinced that this was
no temporary passion, no romantic love which time might banish, [like
Glencora's for Burgo, is his unexpressed thought,] that she was of such a
temperament that she could not change [unlike Glencora, after all], –
then I had to give way" (II, 321). All is put in rational perspective, and
he plausibly accounts for his humane decision to change himself when
he found his daughter incapable of doing so. It is a piece of recollection
in tranquillity, and is not quite accurate. Before the scene with Mrs. Finn
he had obsessively determined, "If he were to find that by persevering in
this course he would doom [his daughter] to death, or perchance to
madness, – what then? If it were right, he must still do it" (II, 95). Mrs.
Finn had exorcised a ghost, and only then was he able to act rationally
and humanely.

But the Duke, though he gives way, has by no means become a glib
and rootless modern: Trollope reminds us how he still honours the
past, still recognizes the binding power of sanctioned ritual and due
ceremony, even though he has rid himself of his pathological need to
repeat history. This is his formal recognition of the man he has so long

opposed as his son-in-law elect:

> 'Tregear,' he said, – and even that was an effort, for he had never hitherto mentioned the man's name without the formal Mister, – 'Tregear, as this is the first time you have sat at my table, let me be old-fashioned, and ask you to drink a glass of wine with me.'
>
> The glass of wine was drunk and the ceremony afforded infinite satisfaction . . . (II, 327)

He is to progress even further than this, and Trollope marks the stages of his concessions with minute precision. That wincing at the intimacy of the informal "Tregear" has to be conquered – and presently the Duke, more modern than his children, proposes to update the common usages: "I will call you Frank, if you will allow me. The use of Christian names is, I think, pleasant and hardly common enough among us" (II, 373). The familiarity is a preparation for the final news that when Mary and Tregear are married, "Perhaps the matter most remarkable in the wedding was the hilarity of the Duke" (II, 378) – he has been able to change and progress from the middle-aged widower obsessed with the need to repeat his past to the tolerant father-in-law who will make a benign and even jocular grandfather.

As the Duke opposes Mary's marriage to Tregear because that equals Glencora marrying Burgo, so he favours Silverbridge's match with Lady Mabel Grex, because that equals Plantagenet Palliser's match with Lady Glencora McCluskie. In this case the Duke does not consciously make the application, but Trollope certainly intends the reader to make it. The old triangle pattern is still in operation – we are still observing a girl who is supposed to abandon the man she loves in order to make a more socially acceptable marriage. The pattern has a certain neatness in that Tregear plays Burgo, the handsome first love, to both Lady Mabel and Lady Mary,[5] and Silverbridge is cast in his father's role as eligible second suitor.

"Ah, – if I could be like you!" Silverbridge once says spontaneously to his father – who is so touched that he at once gives permission for the purchase of a four-in-hand (I, 165). Silverbridge, without being at all like his father, at least loves him enough to want to resemble him; and he too does what he can, though unconsciously, to repeat the old pattern and marry his latter-day Glencora. But this will not do. Though he tries to press his ring on Lady Mabel, preparatory to marrying her, (it is a ring that has belonged to his forefathers, who had also united themselves with Lady Glencoras and Lady Mabels) the ring will not fit; and when it is reset for a lady's hand, still she will not accept it. Time and change assert themselves. And indeed were Silverbridge to marry Lady Mabel, the marriage would be too like his parents' for comfort.

He was aware, however, of a certain drawback. Lady Mabel as his wife would be his superior, and in some degree his master. Though not older she was wiser than he, – and not only wiser but more powerful also. And he was not quite sure but that she regarded him as a boy. . . . He was already jealous of his own dignity, and fearful lest he should miss the glory of being loved by this lovely one for his own sake, – for his own manhood, and his own gifts and his own character. (I, 180)

Glencora was certainly not wiser than her husband, but she was in some spheres more powerful; often made him jealous of his own dignity; and was far from loving him, at the outset at least, for his own sake. Her patronage of him as "a stick" would parallel Lady Mabel's patronage of Silverbridge as "poor boy" – neither the best foundation for a happy relationship, especially for someone like Silverbridge, who does not have his father's devotion to public life to compensate for a loveless home.

So the reader understands that Silverbridge's change to Isabel is a happy one, another fortunate rejection of the old paradigm. The Duke clings to his hopes for the marriage to Mabel, which is so *comme il faut*, and opposes the choice of Isabel. When Silverbridge argues, "I suppose a man ought to marry the woman he loves, – if he can get her," his father eagerly disagrees: "No; no; not so; not always so. Do you think that love is a passion that cannot be withstood?" (II, 201). He still argues from his old model. Nevertheless, he is much more easily reconciled to Isabel than to Tregear. For one thing the myth of the low-born maiden who marries a prince is more acceptable than that of the fortune-hunting admirer who carries off the princess: for, as Silverbridge (like Richardson's Mr. B) points out, the man raises his wife to his own station, but the wife cannot do as much for her low-born husband. But for another, of course the Duke is susceptible, and confesses, "I know that I can love Isabel" (II, 322). However, there is still a struggle, and the scene of his capitulation, though not as impressive as that on Mary's engagement, is tellingly narrated:

'My opinion is to go for nothing, – in anything!' The Duke as he said this knew that he was expressing aloud a feeling which should have been restrained within his own bosom. It was natural that there should have been such plaints. The same suffering must be encountered in regard to Tregear and his daughter. In every way he had been thwarted. . . . Silverbridge was now standing before him abashed by that plaint, inwardly sustained no doubt by the conviction of his great success, but subdued by his father's wailing. 'However, – perhaps we had better let that pass,' said the Duke, with a long sigh. (II, 294–5)

It is another fine moment: in its place in the conversation, those last words sound automatic enough – "perhaps we had better let that pass"; but in the larger context of all we know of the Duke and his enterprise to make his son reenact his own history, the phrase has its special weight. Let that pass – let the past *be* past. Marry your Isabel rather than my Glencora. And presently we find him producing, as from the wide variety of his own experience, the piece of wisdom, "Some girls are fools –", but not Isabel. Girls are so different.

And in his yielding, again he is to be rewarded. As George Butte points out,[6] in the scene in which he presents Isabel with Glencora's ring, we are to suppose he has found some compensation for his loss, a replacement for Glencora at last (II, 305).

In politics too the Duke has to abandon his declared resolution and take office. This is a little piece of business left hanging over from *The Prime Minister*, but we know he has been under pressure through the later novel too, although his domestic worries have largely displaced his political ones. Early in the novel he receives two letters which he finds himself unable to answer, and they both tell this scrupulously just man that he is wrong. One is from Mrs. Finn asking for his apology, and the other is from the Duke of St. Bungay asking him to revise his decision to withdraw from the government. We hear the full history of the writing and response to the first, but the letter from the old duke recedes into the background, and is eventually answered in action rather than words: in one of the last chapters, "The Duke Returns to Office", he joins Mr. Monk's cabinet. Trollope reminds us again how in this too the Duke has to give way and reverse his declaration, but again the yielding and change are fortunate: "He had had many contests with himself before he could bring himself to this submission. . . . He had in his soreness declared to himself that he would never more take office. He had much to do to overcome this promise to himself; – but when he had brought himself to submit he was certainly a happier man" (II, 365–6).

In the Duke Trollope has painstakingly represented a man of principle, a man who has been strong in leading his life according to certain unchanging ethical precepts, who has always, against whatever pressure, insisted on doing his duty as he sees it – his duty to his country, to his class, to his family. We have learned to admire him for his steadfastness, his steady refusal to give way to any motive of self-interest. In this novel too we see how his principles remain a force for good: Silverbridge weeps and gives up racing and Gerald forswears gambling because they are so won over by their father's eloquent moral lectures. When we have so come to admire the man for his unswerving integrity, it was a brave undertaking on Trollope's part to show how the same man must be made to surrender his principles, some of which have become a mask for his own psychological needs, and become flexible. The changes in the younger generation are as nothing in comparison – they are supple as a matter of course. But in this bildungsroman the hero who receives the education is a middle-aged man; and what he has to learn is not how to live steadily according to principle, but how to surrender a principle and adapt. George Eliot undertook a similar task into showing how Adam Bede, a strong and righteous man, had to accommodate himself to the weak and the erring – and was in this part of her story I think less successful than Trollope. In lighter vein, Lewis Carroll had exploited the potential absurdity of the flexible old man in his immortal parody, "You are old, Father William," in which the prim young son asks his white-haired old father how he manages to stand on his head and turn back flips.

"In my youth," Father William replied to his son,
  'I feared it might injure the brain;
But, now that I'm perfectly sure I have none,
  Why, I do it again and again."

One can imagine the Duke reciting those verses to his grandchildren with a certain zest. He has certainly proved himself more flexible than the young people on the other side of the generation gap.

Lady Mabel Grex is another character who is committed to the past, though not, like the Duke, by principle and temperament. In fact in all her level-headed calculations she is determined to be an adaptable modern, to shake off her past unsuitable attachment, and espouse a prosperous future as the wife of Lord Silverbridge and the destined Duchess of Omnium. She has mapped out for herself a life like Glencora's, a programme according to which she is sensibly to abandon her first love and prudently marry a Palliser who, though she does not love him, will make her a stirling husband and raise her social status. But in practice she finds herself incapable of living up to her programme of change. She is faithful in spite of herself, and we see her at last, not clinging to the past like the Duke, but chained to it, crucified on it.[7]

In launching into the section of the novel that is the story of Lady Mabel, Trollope has played a little technical trick of a kind more subtle than he usually attempts. In general, as his critics have noted, there is a comfortable uniformity about his way of going about the business of telling a story, and of unfolding different areas of it. "The old way, 'Once upon a time,' with slight modifications, is the best way of telling a story," he told Kate Field, warning her against the dangerous device of a first-person narrator (*Letters*, 217). And the old way is usually his way – to begin at the beginning and, with only occasional and clearly-marked interruptions in the chronology, to proceed steadily to the end. He equally avoids Thackeray's complex redoublings and superimpositions of past on present, and Dickens's more flamboyant eccentricities of style and presentation. But in the early chapter, "In Medias Res" he permits himself a discourse on narrative technique and simultaneously exemplifies the benefits and dangers of the dramatic mode he is discussing.

"Perhaps the method of rushing at once 'in medias res' is, of all the ways of beginning a story, or a separate branch of a story, the least objectionable," he begins. Then he shows the problems inherent in skipping the preliminary matter about characters and relationships, and concludes, "I have always found that the details would insist on being told at last, and that by rushing 'in medias res' I was simply presenting the cart before the horse. But as readers like the cart the best, I will do it once again, – trying it only for a branch of my story, – and will endeavour to let as little as possible of the horse be seen afterwards" (I, 83–4). And then he plunges straight into the middle of a dialogue between Lady Mabel Grex, now first introduced (but that she gets no introduction) and Lord Silverbridge. He maintains his figure of the cart and the horse, and from time to time acknowledges in asides that his narrative, which occasionally refers to surrounding circumstances or events antecedent, is lapsing from the dramatic mode: "A little bit of the horse is appearing . . . This is another bit of the horse."

In all this horsing around, so to speak, it is easy to miss what Trollope is conveying obliquely: that Lady Mabel Grex is a girl with a past, and that we have not yet been told about it. Lord Silverbridge's approach to Lady Mabel is very much "in the middle of the matter" so far as her history goes. And although her first words to him are about Frank Tregear, the reader has yet to learn (unless this is not his first reading; in which case he can savour his knowledge and the dramatic irony) that Lady Mabel, who talks so vivaciously about her cousin and his aspirations to the hand of Lady Mary Palliser, is irreversibly in love with him herself. "Poor fellow! I wish he had a little money; he is so nice," she says lightly (I, 86). For that want of money she had broken their engagement, ruined her own life and scarred his.

We are eventually shown the horse that came before the cart. We know that she and Tregear had been happily and completely in love; and that, like Laura, she had then refused to marry him because it would never do for the two of them to share their nothing. When we meet her she is proceeding in her plan to catch a more eligible husband, and Lord Silverbridge is quite willing to be caught. She claims to be heart-whole, with emotions sensibly subordinate to prudence: "It would not suit me to marry a poor man, and so I don't mean to fall in love with a poor man" (I, 184). "She thought that she could arrange her future life in accordance with certain wise rules over which her heart should have no influence" (I, 374), explains the narrator. But of course she cannot, and in all her big scenes we see how she breaks her own rules and resolutions, and keeps only enough of them to destroy her happiness.

It takes her some time to learn about herself, and she never fully learns, for all her vaunted openness. When Silverbridge obligingly springs into her net, a willing fish, she throws him back in. She is evidently rather surprised at her own action, but explains it, "I spared him; – out of sheer downright Christian charity! . . . Though I had him in my net, I let him go. Shall I go to heaven for doing that?" (I, 194). But Christian charity had nothing to do with it, and Lady Mabel is not destined to win heaven for that act, at least. Recognizing her imprudence, she promises herself and her lady companion, Miss Cassewary, "I shall not spare him again" (I, 196). But she does; she keeps doing it. She balks Silverbridge's approaches to a proposal at every turn. She refuses to walk with him at the garden party when he has his proposal on his lips, and, when he insists, she brings her chaperone with her; she refuses to play tennis with him, refuses to dance. True to her resolution, she asks for his ring, which he at once hands to her; but then she rejects it because she says it won't fit, and returns it when he has it reset to fit her. She is simply incapable of accepting him. In fact she does more than a little to thrust him into the arms of her rival. She spreads rumours about their love before she has any warrant, and the narrator acknowledges, "This was very imprudent on the part of Lady Mabel, who, had she been capable of clinging fast to her policy, would not now in a moment of strong feeling have done so much to raise obstacles in her own way" (I, 377). But she never fully knows herself in her inability to accept Silverbridge. Even in her last scenes with Silverbridge and Tregear, when she thinks she is laying bare the whole truth, she talks only of the single occasion on which she "spared him" as though it were the decisive incident. "There is a tide in the affairs of men –!" she quotes (II, 317), but not really appropriately. That tide was at the flood several times for her, but she never really wanted it to lead on to fortune. It was the other tide that she had missed, in not marrying Tregear, and that was an act of will. In her inability to square her conduct with her policy she is again like the Duke, whose liberal principles are so at odds with his conservative practice.

Once Silverbridge has made his change to Isabel, her resolution is again strong, and she makes two great bids, one by the falls at Killancodlem and the next by the icy stream at Matching, to net him for herself. But these, though fine scenes, are not real attempts. She is going through it for the form's sake, but she can summon up the energy to try for him only when he is already out of her reach.

Lady Mabel is attached to place – it is part of Trollope's use of significant detail to create her settings, and make them consonant with her character and mood. She herself has a feeling for appropriate surroundings, and generally takes her men to this place or that to accomplish certain ends. She brings Lord Silverbridge to the stream at Killancodlem and looks at the running water at a time when she is working up her energy and her passion for assault and change (II, 29–32). And again she takes him "to the seat over the river" at Matching in the winter to call him, "Oh, Silverbridge; – oh, my loved one!" It is a premeditated falsehood, and also guileful is her calculated use of the pathetic fallacy: "Cold; – of course I am cold; – cold through to the heart. . . . You have left me – utterly in the cold – more desolate than I am here even though I should spend the night among the trees" (II, 183–8). We hear later, "She had not been cold. She could still feel the tingling heat of her blood as she had implored him to love her" (II, 194).

These two attempts to change the course of her life are undertaken near running water; but Mabel is really at home in Grex, "the home of her ancestors," the ruinous old estate that expresses her family and herself. The Duke acknowledges that Grex has a more venerable antiquity even than Matching, and, in sympathy with his love for the past, she tells him, "Grex is very old, and very wild, – and very uncomfortable. But I love it dearly" (II, 175). It is here that she can indulge the sombre side of her temperament: "With all her lightness of spirit she was prone to memories, prone to melancholy, prone at times almost to seek the gratification of sorrow" (I, 352).

In the scene at Grex she finds her place on a rock near the lake of still if not stagnant water: it best expresses the stasis at which she has arrived. Here she tells Tregear of her unalterable love for him, the love that she had sought to put behind her and make past, but which is still so insistently and unquenchably present. After her avowal, her scene of anger and confession, she comes back to tell Miss Cassewary, "We have been to the lake . . . and have been talking of old days" (I, 358). Afterwards she returns to sit on the same rock, "thinking of her past life and trying to think of that before her. It is so much easier to think of the past than of the future" (I, 360). Lady Mabel is anchored, unable like Tregear and Silverbridge to look and move forward into a future that is pregnant with promise. "To the end of time I shall love Frank Tregear," she says, with a dreary certainty of her ineluctable destiny (II, 316); and love, which is so joyful for the other young people at the end of the novel, is to her a virulent malady (II, 355).

But she is not young; though Silverbridge knows he is actually slightly her senior in years, "there had always been present to him a feeling that she was old" (II, 271). Her dilapidated estate and her degenerate father and brother are among her appurtenances that remind us she and her like are in a state of decay, a generation and a way of life that are outmoded and doomed. Her father Lord Grex dies, her brother, Percival, a "nasty fellow" and "heir to a ruined estate and a beggared peerage," is unlikely to marry; and she herself will be childless. When her father dies at the end of the novel, she seems to have aged ten years (II, 349). When Silverbridge tries to persuade her that time will cure her sorrow, she rejects the proposition scornfully: "Yes; time, – that brings wrinkles and rouge-pots and rheumatism" (II, 317). Time for her is not the healer, but the destroyer. And at the last we see her, in her sitting-room in London – the other location which is haunted by ghosts of past experience – weighed down with her burden of painful memories. She is not even to keep Grex, the family estate (II, 351). Here she is unlike Lady Laura, who in many respects she resembles: Lady Laura rejected Phineas whom she loved in order to marry Mr. Kennedy, whom she soon grew to hate. And when Kennedy dies she becomes a rich widow, burdened with Loughlinter, the property for which she had sold herself, and longing to share it with Phineas. But Lady Mabel is to end up with nothing and share it with nobody.

John Hagan takes Trollope to task for his harsh dealing with Lady Mabel. He suggests that Trollope is heavy-handed in meting out Victorian poetic justic on this sinner: "Conventional Victorian morality demands that whoever attempts to marry for money rather than love must be frustrated and punished, and Trollope follows out this code to the letter."[8] He feels Trollope should have allowed the rehabilitation and eventual happy marriage of Lady Mabel. But I think this is a case where the modern critic is being more sentimental than the Victorian novelist. Trollope is not so much meting out poetic justice, Victorian or otherwise, as suggesting that if you repress a strong and lasting love you are likely to end up frustrated. There is, after all, a tough and undeniable logic to that proposition that would make it apply to any age: or at least to any age that can accept the possibility of enduring love.

Lady Mary Palliser does not change either, and is as constant to Tregear as Lady Mabel: (Burgo Fitzgerald might well have envied his counterpart the constancy of his women.) All the people who surround her expect her to be pliable like her mother, and in fact she is rigid like her father – so rigid that even he has to give way to her. At the outset she tells him,

> 'I shall always intend to marry Mr. Tregear.'
> 'No!' he exclaimed.
> 'Yes; – always. I want you to understand exactly how it is. Nothing you can do can separate me from him.'
> 'Mary, that is very wicked.' (I, 110)

But she is steadfast and wins through, though at the cost of some suffering. Her first love is attained, by strong struggle, and we are told it will be sweet and lasting. "With her it had been all new and all sacred. Love with her had that religion which nothing but freshness can give it. That freshness, that bloom, may last through a long life. But every change impairs it, and after many changes it has perished forever" (I, 43). Trollope recalls this passage much later in order to contrast Lady

Mabel with Lady Mary – "That bloom of her maiden shame, of which she quite understood the sweetness, the charm, the value – was gone when . . . loving one man, she should be willing to marry another" (II, 181). After her period of trial, Mary's life is to be a happy one. Unlike Mabel, who tries to change and cannot, and unlike Silverbridge and Tregear, who do change, she is to live forwards into her life with no regrets, no embarrassing lapses to remember, no qualms about what might have been. Past, present and future are to be all of a piece for her. As the exemplum of the person who does not change she is thematically necessary in Trollope's scheme; but her constancy makes her an undramatic and not very sympathetic character.

It is the men who change. And in Silverbridge and Tregear Trollope presents studies in how the bloom and freshness are impaired by change, and the ways in which change can be vital and beneficial.

Silverbridge at the start of the novel is a mere adolescent, recently sent down from Oxford for the schoolboy prank of painting the dean's house red. If he were of Johnny Eames's or Trollope's own class, he would be a hobbledehoy. Much of the development that we see in him is simply a matter of his growing up, and Trollope has invested a good deal of time and attention in examining the ways in which he matures, as man, social being, politician and lover. We are given the whole chronicle of how he learns to abandon his silly bachelor ways of racing and gambling (hunting is different), and is drawn from the purely masculine worlds of Major Tifto, the Beargarden and Crummie-Toddie into the female sphere of Lady Mabel, Killancodlem and Isabel Boncassen – a development that Trollope sees as all to the good. His growth from the social ineptitude displayed before Lady Mabel to the witty conversational play he can achieve with Isabel is nicely managed, and we are convincingly shown how his experiences "were giving him by degrees age and flavour" (II, 28).

To begin with he is not only boyish and inchoate, but irresponsibly changeable. Trollope introduces discussions on constancy and fickleness to keep his theme to the fore. Such is this exchange between Lady Mabel and Silverbridge:

> 'I wish I knew your sister. Is she – firm?'
> 'Indeed she is.'
> 'I am not so sure that you are.'
> 'No,' said he, after considering awhile; 'nor am I. But she is not like Gerald or me. She is more obstinate.'
> 'Less fickle perhaps.'
> 'Yes, if you choose to call it fickle. I don't know that I am fickle. If I were in love with a girl I should be true to her.'
> 'Are you sure of that?'

'Quite sure. If I were really in love with her I certainly should not change.' (I, 182)

And so they go through the declension of firm, obstinate, pig-headed; adaptable, fickle, flighty; and rehearse in advance the debate on Silverbridge's moral justification in changing from Mabel to Isabel. For all Trollope's leisurely pace, his novel is tightly organized, and his characters work for him, doing the work of the novelist in expatiating on his moral themes.

Silverbridge is quite humble about his weakness: "I'm soft. I can't refuse" (I, 342), he acknowledges. And he does change. On that memorable day when he goes over to Killancodlem with the intention of proposing to Mabel, he ends up, on the same evening, by proposing to Isabel. Now that does look like being fickle. Nevertheless, he tries to live up to his rather loosely worded claim, "If I were really in love with [a girl] I certainly should not change." He has some justification: we have seen how Mabel never gave him a chance, was ungracious to him, and pushed him into Isabel's arms. But he is made justifiably uncomfortable when, having given his father to suppose he was courting Mabel, he asks for his sanction for a marriage to Isabel. "I have rather changed my mind, sir," he confesses inadequately (II, 198).

> 'I cannot give you my consent.'
> 'Then I am very unhappy.'
> 'How can I believe as to your unhappiness when you would have said the same about Lady Mabel Grex a few weeks ago?'
> 'Nearly eight months,' said Silverbridge.
> 'What is the difference? It is not the time, but the disposition of the man! I cannot give you my consent.' (II, 202)

Frailty, thy name is Silverbridge, the Duke bitterly reflects. And yet in a good deal less than eight months he will reverse his own decision to withhold his consent. And in this scene of announcing his change Silverbridge shows a certain firmness that approaches his sister's: "my mind is made up about this, and I thought you had better know how it is" (II, 203). He has changed once, but he is not going to keep on changing. And he has an access of strength in defending himself: " 'You are as weak as water,' said the unhappy father. . . . 'I am not weak in this' " (II, 201).

His arrival at maturity is seen in terms of his ability to stick by his decision once he has, through whatever wavering, arrived at it. When Lady Mabel puts her greatest pressure on him, pretending to love him – a situation in which Phineas Finn would have felt himself compelled almost to commit bigamy – Silverbridge is unexpectedly strong, declaring his determination to give up everything and everyone sooner than lose Isabel: "Now at any rate he was a man," Mabel perceives (II, 187). Silverbridge has in fact developed a kind of strength from his change that Trollope expects us to admire. Mary would break before she ever gave way; but Silverbridge, who has changed once but then stands firm, has a special resilience that is valuable; and his ability to adapt and accommodate certainly makes him more *commode à vivre* than his sister.

It is not only to the Duke that he has to confess to changing his mind. Mabel, the lady left in the lurch, herself extorts the admission, and is astounded at the simple honesty of his wording. In discussing the occasion with Tregear later she obsessively dwells on his declaration, quoting it five times within a few pages.

> ' "I have changed my mind." There is something great in the courage of a man who can say that to a woman in so many words. Most of them, when they escape, escape by lies and subterfuges. . . . Yes; – when I taxed him with his falsehood, – for he had been false, – he answered me with those very words! "I have changed my mind." He could not lie. . . . I think I loved him then as nearly as ever I did.' (II, 352–4)

Lady Mabel, who is herself so irrevocably chained to the love she had tried to renounce, cannot but admire his facility. But though she claims to be so honest herself in this scene, to reveal her own inmost secrets, we should beware of swallowing it all whole. Silverbridge was not false to her as she claimed: there was never an acknowledged pledge between them, and when he tried to make one she balked him. She is a sympathetic and mainly honest figure, but she is unreliable at certain key points: when she told Silverbridge she never really loved him he responds, with the same simple honesty that she has admired, "I am glad of that" (II, 315). But when she narrates the scene afterwards to Tregear she says, "Then, – I told him I had never cared for him, and that he need have nothing on his conscience. But I doubt whether he was glad to hear it. Men are so vain!" (II, 354). Silverbridge does not deserve that particular sneer. But she cannot help resenting him – Trollope shows this, I think, though he doesn't tell it explicitly – not because he failed to propose to her, but because he could change his mind, and she never can.

Like his father, Silverbridge has also to reverse a political decision. Although in this novel Trollope often makes it clear that not only he but also his characters subordinate political concerns to domestic ones, there is still enough left of the "parliamentary" aspect of the series to make politics a continuing thread of interest. The borough of Silverbridge, which has so often been an issue, is now represented by Lord Silverbridge, the Duke's son, and at the outset Silverbridge makes a great ado about his political "convictions," and decides he must reverse the habit of generations of Pallisers and be a Conservative. "I haven't stuck to the Palliser politics. Just at present I think that order and all that sort of thing should be maintained" (I, 136) – such is the trenchant statement of his "conservative convictions." But one can hardly be a very thorough conservative on a "just at present" basis, and Silverbridge's change from the allegiance of his ancestors is seen in this instance as flighty and irresponsible. In the course of the novel he does gain some political maturity: he learns that the Conservatives rejoice at his defection from his family politics not so much because they gain him as because it spites his father, their political enemy (II, 259–60). (This aspect of his development was to have had more prominence in the uncut version of the novel.[9]) At the end, when the Conservatives go out and the Liberals come in, and when his father too has reversed his political decision, there is this emblematic little exchange between them:

> 'I am the only man who does not mean to make any change' [says Silverbridge].
> 'How so?'
> 'I shall stay where I am, – on the Government side of the House.'
> 'Are you clear about that, my boy?'
> 'Quite clear.'
> 'Such changes should not be made without very much consideration.'
> 'I have already written to them at Silverbridge. . . . I have had my little vagary, and I don't think that I shall change again.' (II, 367)

Silverbridge, for all his vagaries and vacillation, has paradoxically become a centre of stability, while the political world around him plays its game of musical chairs. His change from Conservative to Liberal is in fact not so much a change as a restoration. In making it, Silverbridge has discovered his equilibrium, and is not to change again. The same – though more suffering and damage are caused in the interval – might be said of his change from Mabel to Isabel. He did waver, but we are to believe in the achieved stability of his second choice.

Tregear, the other man who had Lady Mabel for a first love and then changed to a second, is less fortunate and happy in his change than Silverbridge, and the excision from his consciousness that has to be effected in the banishing of his first love is more severe.[10] When Lady Mabel told him in effect, "Shake hands forever, cancel all our vows," he took her at her word and did so. But after his final interview with her, when he realizes that in doing her "the terrible evil of ceasing to love [her]" he has caused the "great shipwreck" which is her life (II, 356, 360), he feels the need to justify himself. He knew that by any rationally applied moral standard "He certainly had not derogated in transferring his affections," and yet he feels compromised, embarrassed at his own facility in change:

> Perhaps the bitterest felling of all was that her love should have been so much stronger, so much more enduring than his own. . . . Which nature must he now regard as the higher? She had done her best to rid herself of the load of her passion and had failed. But he had freed himself with convenient haste. All that he had said as to the manliness of conquering grief had been wise enough. But still he could not quit himself of some feeling of disgrace in that he had changed and she had not. (II, 361–2)

His internal debate on which is the higher nature – the one who is constant or the one who cures himself of the past and proceeds with the present – is carried on at large in the whole novel. And Tregear brings to a conscious level the issue of the place the past is to have in the present consciousness. The Duke tries to make the present conform to his past; Lady Mabel tries to rid herself of her past and cannot; Silverbridge lives forward into his future, and is able to shake off inconvenient memories without much difficulty: his past courtship of Lady Mabel, he resolves, (at the time he is walking with Tregear who is deeply shaken by his interview with Mabel) "was a matter which must henceforward be buried in silence" (II, 362). But Tregear manages to be something of a temporal amphibian. Like Silverbridge, he has successfully effected a fortunate change; but like Mabel, though he carries his memories more lightly, he is to acknowledge that his past love was a more vivid and ecstatic experience than he will achieve again, and cannot be entirely displaced by the new love. When, early in the novel, Mabel asks him if he will be glad to see her marry Silverbridge, he replies, "As you must be somebody's wife, and not mine . . . I will endeavour to be glad. Who can explain his feelings in such a matter? Though I most truly love the girl I hope to marry, yet my heart goes back to former things and opens itself to past regrets" (I, 100). At moments his old love and his new love can coexist in his mind.

It is a theme familiar in the novels of Thackeray, who reiterates "we forget nothing," and shows again and again characters for whom memory is so powerful that it displaces present experience.

When Lady Mabel witnessed Mary's brave gesture in throwing herself into Tregear's arms in the middle of a room full of people, she asked herself, "She loves him almost as I have loved him. . . . I wonder whether he can love her as he did me?" (I, 282). It is a reverberating question. Tregear is aware of some infidelity in being accessible to two loves at a time; and his new love for Mary is to be to some extent qualified and overshadowed by the old love for Mabel, which is to remain a constituent of his consciousness.

It may be doubted whether in his second love he had walked among the stars as in the first. A man can hardly mount twice among the stars. . . . He tried to comfort himself with reflecting that Mary was all his own, – that in that matter he had been victorious and happy; – but for an hour or two he thought more of Mabel than of Mary. (II, 361–2)

Mary's love is to belong totally to Tregear, because she never changed, and her past, present and future are all the same fabric. But Tregear's love is to be divided to this extent. The ring that Mabel gives him at his marriage to Mary – a ring that was to have been a gift to him as her husband – is to remain as a reminder of a past from which he cannot quite sever himself.

Isabel Boncassen is a successful creation in many ways: her vitality is real and convincing, and we are satisfied that the naive and likable Silverbride should be united with her, and her gaity, and her youth, rather than with Lady Mabel, and her "blasé used-up way of life" (II, 26).[11] Silverbridge, who so bungles matters with Lady Mabel, can rise to wit and pace in his exchanges with Isabel; and he deserves to be loved as she loves him, for himself and not as the future Duke of Omnium. And Trollope makes us approve of the match as an alliance, too. As the father had needed the liveliness of Glencora to complete and express his high position, so the Pallisers again need a little cross-breeding with this vital young American, to keep the strain from becoming inbred. The shades of Gatherum will not be polluted by the new Duchess of Omnium, any more than the shades of Pemberley were polluted by the new Mrs. Darcy in *Pride and Prejudice*.

Nevertheless, I find Trollope lapsed in his management of Isabel as a character in this novel. Bradford Booth, though he admires the characterization of Isabel, admits to "a predictive inevitability in the love story," and draws attention to the parallel between Isabel and Lucy Robarts in *Framley Parsonage*.[12] Trollope is usually able to handle old situations he has treated in previous novels with just enough variation to make them new and interesting: so, for instance, the Duke's opposition to Mary's engagement is comparable with Mr. Wharton's to Emily's, but interestingly different. But in the case of Isabel and her insistence that Silverbridge must get the approval of his father before she will consent to marry him, Trollope has got stuck in a groove at the expense of consistency to what he has shown of women and engagements in the rest of this novel. The world of *The Duke's Children* is different from the Barsetshire world inhabited by Lucy Robarts and Lady Lufton. Here we are given the strongly-imagined picture of what would happen to Lady Mary if she were to give up the man she loves: her life will be "barren," and in all likelihood she would die, "faded and withered before her time, – all her life gone without a joy." And we have the history, more vivid yet, of the shipwreck of Lady Mabel, whose life is to be bitter and joyless because, from motives of what she thinks is prudence, she crushes her love. In such a context, how can the reader slip back to admiring the principle of Isabel in refusing Silverbridge because his family would disapprove? "I will not marry you to be rejected by your people. . . . Lord Silverbridge, if [your father] will tell me that I shall be his daughter I will become your wife, – oh, with such perfect joy, with such perfect truth! If it can never be so, then let us be torn apart, – with whatever struggle, still at once" (II, 121). Trollope expects us, apparently, to find this heroic, in the old Lucy Robarts vein. Silverbridge himself certainly does, and is all the more eager to make her his own. The familiar business is needlessly prolonged. In a subsequent scene she wonders what would happen to their marriage if it were deemed a mistake by the world at large:

> 'You would be still what you are, – with a clog round your leg while at home. In Parliament, among your friends, at your clubs, you would be just what you are. You would be that Lord Silverbridge who had all good things at his disposal, – except that he had been unfortunate in his marriage! But what should I be?' Though she paused he could not answer her, – not yet. (II, 268)

Her question is meant to be a weighty and impressive one. But the reader of the present novel is apt to be impatient. What is the alternative, Isabel, which is to face you when you tear yourselves apart? You will spend a life of sick headaches and die withered and repressed, as Mary would have; or you will remain lonely and embittered, as Mabel does. We are certainly not led to suppose that Isabel's love is any less lasting than theirs: and though the motive that prompts her rejection is not financial like Mabel's, it is none the less one of prudence. Her position is an inept reversion to the Barchester kind of heroine, and it contravenes the logic of the rest of the novel.

Trollope's instinct had been truer with Lucy Morris, in *The Eustace Diamonds*, who is similarly rejected by her suitor's family. It occurs to her to refuse Frank for his own and his family's good, but, as we saw, she rejects the notion as perverse and untrue. She knows she wants to marry him, so she agrees to do so. Trollope partly recognized his mistake, I think, in making Isabel declare to her father, "But if he is man enough to be firm I shall not throw him over, – not for all the dukes in Europe. . . . I will go back home. If he follows me then I shall choose to forget all about his rank. If he loves me well enough to show that he is in earnest, I shall not disappoint him for the sake of pleasing his father" (II, 129). But this hardly mends the matter: after all, it is spoken to her father, not Silverbridge, who is kept in the dark about this fail-safe plan. And it seems hard that Silverbridge should have to prove he is in earnest by assuming *she* is not.

Nevertheless, in other respects Trollope has fairly neatly incorporated her into his thematic structure. "A progressive American," she is a child of the present and confidently bound for the future. In her ability to visualize the future, to make plans and live up to them in performance; in her youth (she is "young as Hebe" [II, 271]); and in her advent from a young country and a new and energetic family (her father is no degenerate has-been like Lord Grex, but likely to be the next President of the United States), she is the proper contrast to Lady Mabel, who is old, used-up and bitter. "The present moment is always everything to me," Isabel says at one point (I, 314). It is a playful hyperbole at the time, but the comment has its significance. Then in contrast with Mabel's tendency to stasis, Isabel is characterized as being swift and agile in her movements. When Dolly Longstaff is slow in ringing the bell she does it herself: "Dolly sank back again into his seat, remarking in his usual apathetic way that he had intended to obey her behest but had not understood that she was in so great a hurry. 'I am always in a hurry,' she said. "I like things to be done – sharp.' And she hit the table a crack" (I, 318). Isabel plays tennis with Lord Silverbridge all afternoon – and plays better than he – while Mabel characteristically sits still and watches. Isabel dances – "One dance after another" – while Mabel refuses.

In all this Trollope has steadily developed his theme and balanced his characters, defining them and opposing them according to their relation to the past and their capacity to be constant, to adapt, and to change. Back in *Can You Forgive Her?* we were told, "Mr. Palliser was one of those politicians in possessing whom England has perhaps more reason to be proud than of any other of her resources, and who, as a body, give to her that exquisite combination of conservatism and progress which is her present strength and best security for the future" (I, 302). At that stage it was only an assertion, as Palliser had yet to live out his role. But by the time we have read *The Duke's Children* the proposition has been amply dramatized, and Trollope has demonstrated at large how this combination of conservatism and progress can indeed be exquisite, a matter of present strength and security for the future. The series has its unity.

In examining the relation of past and present, Trollope, as the creator of a series of long novels, had special advantages: he had already created his characters' past histories, and they have become part of his readers' consciousness as well. His old resource, the eternal triangle, does duty again as a structural device, as the past triangle of Glencora, Burgo and Palliser is superimposed on the new triangles, Mabel, Tregear and Palliser's son, and Popplecourt, Tregear and Glencora's daughter. By this diagrammatic superimposition, the new triangles can be examined as they fit the old model, so that changes can be exactly measured. It is neatly done. The model is in both cases rejected, and the new generation creates its own pattern; but what is left of the Duke's model survives in his person, and is valuably assimilated into the new pattern.

In its acceptance and even championing of change, and also its continued sympathy and honour for the past, *The Duke's Children* is a humanely progressive and hopeful book. The two generations of the title can be reconciled and come to accord only by some accommodation, but love and understanding successfully mediate. Only Lady Mabel, left motionless and portionless on her sofa in the middle of the room where the very furnishings are changing and being taken away, remains as an uncomfortable vestige of a past best abandoned. The other major characters, both the older generation and the younger, move hopefully but faithfully forwards towards a future that is filled with promise. It is a cheerful book for an old man to have written.

8   The Men and Women

"There is nothing in the world so difficult as the task of making up one's mind," we hear in *Phineas Finn*, when Marie Goesler is debating with herself on whether to accept or reject the Duke of Omnium's proposal.

> Who is there that has not longed that the power and privilege of selection among alternatives should be taken away from him in some important crisis of his life, and that his conduct should be arranged for him, either this way or that, by some divine power if it were possible, – by some patriarchal power in the absence of divinity, – or by chance even, if nothing better than chance could be found to do it? But no one dares to cast the die, and to go honestly by the hazard. There must be the actual necessity of obeying the die, before even the die can be of any use. (II, 252)

Trollope's fascination with the mind in process of decision is one of the constant elements in his novels, and one of their characteristics which makes them endlessly readable – the characters are so constantly choosing between the two horns of their multitudinously varied dilemmas that we must keep turning the pages in quest of the outcome. It is as simple and irresistible a formula as the courtroom scene in a television series – a verdict is always pending, and we must know what it is to be.

But Trollope's exploitation of the decision situation is no mere device for maintaining suspense – suspenseful, in their quiet way, as his novels certainly are. It is essentially in their decisions that his characters act, and so these cruxes are the major meeting place of character and action. It is in making a decision that a character defines himself; and as in taking the decision he is subject to the multiplicity of external pressures, his decision also reflects the world he inhabits. The decision in a Trollope novel is then the intersection of character and plot, and the signficant meeting point of individual psychology with the surrounding envelope of circumstances. No wonder he concocts one difficult choice after another, and is always inventing alternatives for his people to hesitate between – the two women for the man, the two men for the woman, the invitation list for the hostess, the division at the end of the debate for the politician. The very act of mailing a letter – the moment at which the fingers release it into that convenient slot in the pillar box, whereby the carriage and receipt of the document sealed and signed become irrevocable, is fraught with implication enough to raise trepidation in his characters and readers alike. George Vavasor, like those of us who want to trust the decision to the cast of the die, derogates his decision to a coin:

> 'Jem,' he said to the boy, 'there's half a crown lying there on the looking-glass. . . . Is it a head or a tail, Jem?' asked the boy's master. Jem scrutinized the coin, and declared the uppermost surface showed a tail. 'Then take that letter and post it,' said George Vavasor. (*CYFH*, I, 390)

The letter contains his proposal to Alice. But even George Vavasor had to make the decision to leave the decision to the coin, and thereby again he defines himself: that is the sort of character he is.

We usually think of George Eliot as the author who most subtly depicts this minute interaction of character, chance and circumstance by which the course of lives is changed and determined. Maggie Tulliver does not decide to leave her dicision to the accidental fall of a coin, but she submits herself to the current of the river. Gwendolen Harleth, "conscious of being at the turning of the ways" in debating like Madame Max on whether to accept her aristocratic suitor, allows the mere wording of his proposal to determine her answer, which is contrary to her prior resolution. But we know it was in her to do it: "drifting depends on something besides the currents, when the sails have been set beforehand" (*Daniel Deronda*, chapter 27).

But Trollope too shows how large is the role of chance in most decisions, even where the sails have been set beforehand. His men, particularly, debate issues within themselves, and postpone decision, until at last some hair's-breath accident of timing or expression tilts the balance, and the momentous thing is done. Often, indeed, the men have taken prior resolutions on what they think are strong rational bases, and yet when the moment comes, their reasons are utterly dispersed, and they take exactly the course they had resolved against – like Johnny Eames with Amelia Roper. It is like Jove's scales in *The Rape of the Lock*, where the men's wits are weighed against Belinda's lock: the doubtful beam long nods from side to side; At length the wits mount up, the hairs subside. So much for rational calculation, Trollope often reminds us.

George Eliot dwells on the complicating factors in Lydgate's choice

between the two candidates for the hospital chaplaincy in Middlemarch.
He knows that Farebrother is the most decent man, but Farebrother,
like everyone else, has faults. Tyke also has faults, but Tyke is with
Bulstrode, and Lydgate's interest is with Bulstrode. So the matter stands
when Lydgate is called upon to make the casting vote:

'The thing is settled now,' said Mr. Wrench, rising. 'We all know
how Mr. Lydgate will vote.'
'You seem to speak with some peculiar meaning, sir,' said Lydgate,
rather defiantly, and keeping his pencil suspended.
'I merely mean that you are expected to vote with Mr. Bulstrode.
Do you regard that meaning as offensive?'
'It may be offensive to others. But I shall not desist from voting
with him on that account.'
Lydgate immediately wrote down 'Tyke.' (*Middlemarch*, ch. 18)

Lydgate is not really so unscrupulous as to vote predictably merely
where his interest lies. But he does vote as the cynics predict, because
they predict it, and because he is too arrogant to seem to be deterred by
their prediction. It is a finely complex point, and of course a scene often
and deservedly resorted to by those who teach or write on *Middlemarch*.
A couple of years earlier Trollope had enlarged on just such a process
of the small reason taking precedence of the greater, in Phineas's decision on whether to vote with Mr. Monk and against his party on the
issue of Irish tenant right, or whether to stick with his party and so retain his post in the Government. It is the little men with their needling
who carry the day, not Phineas's own native principle or the reasoned
arguments of his respected advisers. Bonteen and Ratler, his despised
colleagues, go to work on him in the club. Trollope makes sure we understand their littleness by his maintained image of them as insect pests.

They instantly attacked him, first on one side and then on the other.
'So I am told you are going to leave us,' said Bonteen. . . .
'The whispers are very loud, I can tell you,' said Ratler. 'I think I
know already pretty nearly how every man in the House will vote, and
I have not got your name down on the right side.' . . . [Their nagging
continues, until Bonteen delivers the final sting.]
'. . . I'll bet you a sovereign Finn votes with us yet. There's nothing
like being a little coy to set off the girl's charms. I'll bet you a
sovereign, Ratler, that Finn goes into the lobby with you and me
against Monk's bill.'
Phineas not being able to stand any more of this most unpleasant
raillery, got up and went away. . . . The last words which Bonteen had
spoken made it impossible to him now not to support his old friend

Mr. Monk [and so vote against his party]. It was not only what Bonteen had said, but that the words of Mr. Bonteen so plainly indicated what would be the words of all the other Bonteens. He knew that he was weak in this. He knew that had he been strong, he would have allowed himself to be guided, – if not by the firm decision of his own spirit, – by the counsels of such men as Mr. Gresham and Lord Cantrip, and not by the sarcasms of the Bonteens and Ratlers of official life. But men who sojourn amidst savagery fear the mosquito more than they do the lion. He could not bear to think that he should yield his blood to such a one as Bonteen. (*PF*, II, 364–7)

The scene of Lydgate's vote for the hospital chaplain is a brilliant dramatization of a similar process. But for once Trollope has been more fully analytic than George Eliot, if – in this case – less dramatic. He loves to dwell on the mind in process of decision, and trace each nuance of an influence. And even the insects who carry the day have their little measure of complexity: although Bonteen and Ratler are Liberals too, and are ostensibly motivated by party loyalty, their real intention is to make Phineas vote on the other side, because they are personally envious of him.

It is of course in the realm of courtship that Trollope gives himself most scope for the study of the mind in process of decision. A proposal is just the kind of situation he delights in, not simply for its romantic interest – though he never scorned that either[1] – but because it is for both principals so major and so visible a turning point in their lives, a commitment that is at least expected to be final and irreversible. In *He Knew He was Right*, for instance, where he most especially indulged his propensity, there must be a dozen proposals at least, counting the second tries by persistent suitors. And Johnny Eames and Lily Dale virtually make careers out of proposing and refusing.

In courtship, where the principals have to make their decisions in concert, Trollope's general rule is that men are more subject to accident and the chance fluctuations of the occasion that women are. Women can know whether they are in love, and act according to that knowledge; but being in love, for the man, is not so definable a state, and certainly his actions in courtship are apt to be erratic and unconsidered. Such is the general rule, as stated by the narrator in *The Eustace Diamonds*, in the context of Lucy Morris's conscious and unswerving love for Frank Greystock. "It comes more within the scope of a woman's mind, than that of a man's, to think closely and decide sharply on such a matter. With a man it is often chance that settles the question for him. He resolves to propose to a woman, or proposes without resolving, because she is close to him" (*ED*, 30).

We see many scenes of this kind, where the man is twitched this way and that by contiguity, the influence of surroundings, the working of appeal or embarrassment – by anything but his own resolution. Crosbie proposes to Lily Dale in his bucolic phase in Allington, but in Courcy Castle is induced by the atmosphere and his own perversity to propose to Lady Alexandrina – without even the prior formality of ending the first engagement. Lord Silverbridge is almost a case study in such helpless subjection to external circumstance, giving Mabel ample grounds for her pointed strictures. When Tregear asks her what Silverbridge meant by his clumsy approach to a proposal, she returns, making her reply a general comment on his sex, "Such young men seldom mean. They drift into matrimony" (*DC*, I, 293). Though as we have seen Silverbridge does eventually do something more active than drifting, there is some justice in the comment: though he goes to Killancodlem with the fixed intention of proposing to Lady Mabel, by the end of one day of contiguity with Isabel, he has proposed to her instead. Phineas's engagement to Mary Flood Jones is again largely a matter of chance – it goes along with his also accidental commitment to support the tenant right bill. And when, like Crosbie under pressure from the De Courcy faction, he is tempted by Madame Max to marry her instead, the beauty of the woman, the temptations of a renewed chance in politics, and the heady influence of the rich appointments of her Park Lane house, all so act on him that for a moment it is touch and go whether Mary Flood Jones is to have her heart broken or not:

'You will not take money from my hand?'

'No, Madame Goesler; – I cannot do that.'

'Take the hand then first. When it and all that it holds are your own, you can help yourself as you list.' So saying, she stood before him with her right hand stretched out towards him.

What man will say that he would not have been tempted? Or what woman will declare that such temptation should have had no force? The very air of the room in which she dwelt was sweet in his nostrils, and there hovered around her a halo of grace and beauty which greeted all his senses. She invited him to join his lot to hers, in order that she might give to him all that was needed to make his life rich and glorious. . . . Whom need he fear? Who would not praise him? The story of his poor Mary would be known only in a small village, out beyond the Channel. The temptation certainly was very strong.

But he had not a moment in which to doubt. She was standing there with her face turned from him, but with her hand still stretched towards him. (*PF*, II, 394–5)

What a cliff-hanger! Trollope certainly knows how to keep his reader reading.

For this time, Phineas, unlike Crosbie, manages to be faithful to his country girl, but he is almost overcome. On the other hand, would Lily Dale, or Mary Flood Jones, or indeed most of Trollope's women, once they have engaged themselves, have a moment's doubt? Very few of them. No heady aroma of wealth and success would tempt them – in general, quite the contrary: many women, like Bell Dale, take a severe pleasure in privation, and a poor suitor to them even has an advantage over the rich one. Even Lady Mabel, who on principle means to follow rank and money, finds herself faithful in spite of herself, as we saw. And she sees her burden of fidelity as part of her woman's lot. "A woman cannot transfer her heart," says Violet Effingham, and although "Phineas was well aware that many women do transfer their hearts," in Trollope the one who does is the exception rather than the rule (*PF*, II, 308–9).[2]

But although Trollope goes on insisting that constancy comes more naturally to a woman than to a man, his attitude to this constancy changes. In Mary Thorne and Lucy Robarts it is an admirable moral quality. Lily Dale is a transitional figure, I think, since it is possible to see her both as touchingly and properly faithful, and as morbidly perverse. One can guage the change in Trollope's attitude to her by two comments. On the completion of the serial run of *The Small House*, in 1864, he wrote to a lady correspondent who begged that Lily might be married and made happy, "a girl under such circumstances should bear the effects of her own imprudence, & not rid herself of her sorrow too easily" (*Letters*, 152–3). But after showing Lily's continued rejection of Johnny through *The Last Chronicle of Barset*, and by the time he wrote the *Autobiography*, he was tired of Lily and her everlasting moping after a self-satisfied swell. "In the love with which she has been greeted I have hardly joined with much enthusiasm, feeling that she is somewhat of a female prig. She became first engaged to a snob, who jilted her; and then, though in truth she loved another man who was hardly good enough, she could not extricate herself sufficiently from the collapse of her first great misfortune" (*A*, 154). Her constancy has become a sort of disease. *Pace* James, who enlarged on Trollope's unfailing interest in the "simple maiden in her flower," and insisted that Trollope's girls had "not a touch of the morbid,"[3] Trollope's girls had plenty in them of the morbid, and they gained more as his career progressed. (James knew more of the early Trollope than of the later, and confessed to not having read some of the political novels.) Their steadfastness, adherence to principle and readiness in self-sacrifice are increasingly viewed as psychological attributes not altogether healthy, rather than as virtues. Lily's perversity leads on to Alice Vavasor's disease of principle whereby she rejects Grey for George, and then almost refuses to be made happy again; to Lady Laura's obsessive fidelity to Phineas, in the teeth of his indifference and the disapproval of all her family; to Emily Lopez's "violence of decision" (*PM*, II, 403), which binds her to a dead husband whom she despises and makes her reject a live suitor whom she loves; and to Lady Mabel's helpless arrest in a love she has decided to crush.

Trollope's art gains in psychological depth and moral complexity for this increased ability to examine the psychological roots of moral behaviour. In his introduction to *Emma* Lionel Trilling says, with a touch of naive wonder, "The extraordinary thing about Emma is that she has a moral life as a man has a moral life."[4] That sounds rather quaint nowadays, but we know what he means. So many women in novels have *not* had moral lives as the men do. They are the endless heroines who have been classified as "Pamela's Daughters," "legless angels," cardboard heroines of romance, and so on.[5] Now Trollope has never produced those, and he deserves all the praise that James and others have given him for the depiction of those sweet English girls. But all the same, though the heroines of the Barset novels have spirit and humour and pathos, and though they are splendidly individualized, still there is a sense in which being good comes naturally to them: they do not have moral lives as the men have moral lives. They have their decisions to make, and often their decisions entail considerable suffering; but we are not usually in suspense about their temptations as we are about the men's. They act according to their natures, and their natures have somehow always been there, simply waiting to be fulfilled. They act themselves out, but we do not see their characters *in process*, as we do with the men. But by the time we come to Lady Laura, vacillating between her determination to be a good wife to Kennedy and her helpless passion for Phineas, or Madame Max, hesitating delicately on the brink of a Duchessdom, or Lady Glencora, debating with herself whether her quest for power is on her own behalf or her husband's, we are with women who are on a par with men, and for whom the moral life is a constant struggle.

Most of Trollope's overt references to the Women's Rights movement are either hostile or deflationary. "The best right a woman has is the right to a husband," he wrote in *North America*, an epigram given currency in Mencken's *Book of Quotations*. When Alice reminds her dinner companion at Matching, "Women are not allowed to be politicians in this country," Jeffrey Palliser's fervid response is, "Thank God, they can't do much in that way; – not directly, I mean. Only think where we should be if we had a feminine House of Commons, with feminine debates, carried on, of course, with feminine courtesy" (*CYFH*, I, 291). Jeffrey is a likeable fellow, and his opinions, though not world-shaking, are usually such as Trollope sympathizes with. On the other hand Mr. Spalding, the American Minister in Florence in *He Knew He Was Right*, is characterized as a thundering bore, and he is boring because he argues the cause:

'Your John S. Mill is a great man,' said the minister.
'They tell me so,' said Mr. Glascock. 'I don't read what he writes myself.'

This acknowledgment seemed to the minister to be almost disgraceful, and yet he himself had never read a word of Mr. Mill's writings. 'He is a far-seeing man. . . . He has understood that women must at last be put upon an equality with men.'

'Can he manage that men shall have half the babies?' said Mr. Glascock, thinking to escape by an attempt at playfulness.

But the minister was down upon him at once, – had him by the lappet of his coat . . . (*He Knew He Was Right*, 521–2)

And when Violet Effingham, tired of the idea of matrimony, threatens, "I shall knock under to Mr. Mill, and go in for women's rights, and look forward to stand for some female borough," she is of course joking – the proposition is so grotesque it has to be a joke (*PF*, II, 145).

In his lecture of 1868 on the "Higher Education of Women," Trollope made his statement *in propria persona* on his position on the women's rights movement: he does not believe in the equality of the sexes because, he insists, the sexes are different, and God meant them to be so. He does not admit to seeing women as inferior to men: on the contrary, he frequently emphasizes that in some things women are more intelligent and capable. But, he says, he is "not advising any woman to think herself qualified to do the work of a man. Their occupations are as useful, as noble, as various; but I, at least, am convinced that they cannot in the long run be the same."[6] At the time he was speaking to an audience mainly composed of ladies. In a letter to a man he is less guarded about male supremacy: "The necessity of the supremacy of man is as certain to me as the eternity of the soul" – a passage quoted by those who emphasize Trollope's male chauvinism.[7] But he goes on to acknowledge, "There are often matters on which one lights as on subjects which are in doubt, – universal suffrage, ballot, public education, and the like – but not as I think, on these two" (*Letters*, 418). Trollope was at least accessible to argument on matters of legislation – female suffrage and education.

Trollope's Palliser novels and Mill's *The Subjection of Women* make very interesting commentaries on one another. Mill's book was not published until 1869 (though it was written much earlier) but Trollope was using Mill as the standard source of advanced views on women's rights well before that.[8] I am not in any sense arguing either as a source for the other, but it is interesting to compare the two writers and the extent to which they wrote on the same subject, though not with the same views.

Of course much of the time Trollope is exemplifying the very attitudes that Mill is attacking. Women, says Mill, have been carefully trained in "submission, and yielding to the control of others. All the moralities tell them that it is the duty of women, and all the current sentimentalities that it is their nature, to live for others; to make complete abnegation of themselves, and to have no life but in their affections" (444).[9] One could exemplify this attitude in any number of works by any number of authors, but Trollope more than most seems to have made self-sacrifice in the woman a subject. In the awkward social scene at Guestwick, the humble and impoverished Mrs. Eames implores her grand visitors to take some wine and cake. Crosbie and Bernard Dale inexorably refuse, being not inclined, but Lily and Bell, being no more inclined, nevertheless accept the unwelcome cake because "they understood that Mrs. Eames would be broken-hearted if no one partook of her delicacies. The little sacrifices of society are all made by women, as are also the great sacrifices of life. A man who is good for anything is always ready for his duty, and so is a good woman always ready for a sacrifice" (*SHA*, I, 174). But Trollope is not quite one more of those "current sentimentalities" that Mill identifies as promulgating this view of women. As usual he can see the intricacies of the situation. It is not only that in this little incident he is evidently blaming the men as unfeeling; but there is a touch of irony in his "good woman always ready for a sacrifice" – so that we are made aware that Lily and Bell are enjoying themselves, if not enjoying the cake. And in the novel at large, as we have seen, Lily Dale's readiness in self-sacrifice is far from being endorsed.

Trollope again touches on the subject in his description of Emily Wharton, who has, we hear, "a clearness of intellect joined with that feminine sweetness which has its most frequent foundation in self-denial. . . . There was innate in her an appreciation of her own position as a woman, and with it a principle of self-denial as a human being" (*PM*, I, 47). At this stage we are invited to approve of a girl so constituted, but in the whole novel Emily comes horribly to grief because that clear intellect is vitiated by the principle of self-denial. Trollope has really ceased to like such creatures in practice, however he continues to extol them in the abstract.

Can You Forgive Her? is perhaps the most explicitly anti-feminist of Trollope's novels. Alice, though she is "not so far advanced as to think that women should be lawyers and doctors, or to wish for the privilege of the franchize for herself" (I, 136), is nevertheless too far advanced for her author's views. She almost ruins her happiness by making the unfeminine resolution that she should "do something" with her life, and by her vacillation over what it is that she should do.

What should a woman do with her life? There had arisen round her a flock of learned ladies asking that question, to whom it seems that the proper answer has never yet occurred. Fall in love, marry the man, have two children [Trollope's own number, incidentally], and live happy ever afterwards. (*CYFH*, I, 134)

8. "Yes, my bonny boy, – you have made it all right for me" – Glencora fulfilled in motherhood: Taylor's illustration for *Can You Forgive Her?*, chapter 80

Alice and Glencora, in their ways, are both to learn this "proper answer" through painful experience. Alice, who had "gloried in her independence," has to learn to rejoice in submitting to the mastery of John Grey. And in the final scene of their reconciliation Trollope does not mince the matter, but insists, in dialogue and in imagery, on the necessary subordination of Alice's will to Grey's, and on his proper exercise of authority over her: "I have a right to demand your hand," he now words his proposal. "My happiness requires it, and I have a right to expect your compliance. I do demand it. If you love me, Alice, I tell you that you dare not refuse me." Alice has to acknowledge to herself that "his power over her was omnipotent." And at her final capitulation he rejoices as victor.

> 'Alice,' he said, as he pressed her close with his arm, 'the battle is over now, and I have won it.'
> 'You win everything, – always,' she said. (*CYFH*, II, 434–5)[10]

And to round matters off and conform his story to his own formula for living happily ever after, Trollope sums up of his two heroines, after their abortive rebellions are over, "One was about to become a wife and the other a mother, and that was to be their fate after each had made up her mind that no such lot was to be hers" (II, 462).

The whole novel is such a document as might well make feminists gnash their teeth. And yet Trollope, in taking up the issue at this explicit level, was already showing himself partly sympathetic to the cause he is attacking. In entering so fully into Alice's problem he is in some measure convincing himself. Alice is among the misguided, but he understands her grounds for rebellion, even though he shows her rebellion to be excessive. She is already far more sympathetically treated than Margaret, her counterpart in *The Noble Jilt*. And even then, back in 1850, Trollope was able to create views for her that still find echoes among the pronouncements of today's feminists. Margaret does not care to be a "sex object," in the current phrase:

> I do not crave the worship of a lover;
> I hate the honeyed terms and cloying prattle,
> with which men strive to sweeten the contempt
> they feel for women. Not a compliment
> or courtly phrase but argues low esteem
> and lack of confidence. Soft mincing speeches
> and pretty words spoken with bated breath
> assure me that I'm taken for a fool.[11]

Margaret rejects the man she loves, resolving to "forget my sex and be a stirring rebel" (49). Trollope was of course hardly original in all this – Tennyson's *The Princess* came out in 1847. But, his anti-feminism notwithstanding, his continuing interest in the woman's plight, and his special sensitivity to the woman who feels and rebels against her subordinate position, make his novels, like George Eliot's, Meredith's and Hardy's, sympathetic statements on the women's cause. And they grew to be more sympathetic as his career progressed, so that by the completion of the Palliser series he was no longer a reactionary, although he never became a convert.

Just as Alice, who is put in a realistic contemporary setting, and surrounded by social and political realities that were familiar to Trollope as to his readers, is more sympathetic than Margaret, her predecessor, so the whole structure of the two series, the Barset and the Palliser, show a movement of sympathy towards women and their need for an effective role in public affairs. The central recurring figure in both series is a woman, who in each novel makes her influence felt on the many human and official dramas enacted around her, and who dies abruptly towards the end of the series. Each is the wife of an eminent public man – a bishop, a distinguished member of parliament who eventually becomes Prime Minister –, and each is ambitious of power for herself, and interferes in her husband's affairs, to the considerable embarrassment of the husband. But how differently we view Mrs. Proudie and Lady Glencora! It is almost villainess to heroine. Mrs. Proudie is the frighteningly diverting figure of the woman who wears the trousers (it is Trollope's special joke that in this case the metonymic symbol of the bishop's office is actually an apron) – she is Thalestris, or Thackeray's Campaigner, or Gilbert's Katisha, both comic and horrible. The grand climax of the action, when readers are apt to stand up and cheer, is the moment at which the quiet curate of Hogglestock bids her mind her distaff. But Glencora is another matter, though she too leads her husband a dance and gives rise to rumours of petticoat government. Her machinations are good-humoured, her intrigues conducted with a skill we can often applaud, and we are sometimes inclined to believe that she is right in thinking she would have made a better Prime Minister than her husband. "I do not know that she was at all points a lady," writes her creator, "but had Fate so willed it she would have been a thorough gentleman" (*CYFH*, II, 112). It is a warm tribute, coming from Trollope, and such as he would never have paid to Mrs. Proudie, though he is ready enough to enlarge on *her* unfeminine qualities too.

The kind of women he chose for prominent roles in the individual novels changed from one series to the next, too. The celebrated Trollopian brown girl, James's famous "simple maiden in her flower" and Sadleir's "maids in love"[12] – Eleanor Harding, Mary Thorne, Lucy Robarts, Lily Dale, or Grace Crawley – belongs much more typically to the early and Barset novels than to the later and Palliser ones. (In *The Claverings*, which came between *Can You Forgive Her?* and *Phineas Finn*, one sees a transitional phase: Florence Burton is another of the Barset girls, while Julia Ongar belongs among the Palliser women.) Of course there still are simple maidens in their flower – Violet Effingham (though she is hardly "simple") and Isabel Boncassen and, to a certain extent, Lucy Morris – but they are not typical and not central. In *Northanger Abbey* Jane Austen playfully quoted Richardson's dictum "that no young lady can be justified in falling in love before the gentleman's love is declared" (chapter 3) – playfully, because she was showing already in Catherine Morland how her heroine's love certainly predates the hero's declaration. But Trollope's English maidens of the Barset series are generally able to live up to the Richardsonian ideal whereby the girl is unconscious of any special feeling for the man until at his proposal, lo! she discovers that sweet love that had been lurking all unrecognized in her heart. Mrs. Dale is able to claim of Lily's engagement to Crosbie, "She never thought of the man till he had proposed to her fully" (*SHA*, I, 261). Mary Thorne is a little bolder in having waited until she hears Frank Gresham's "first half-joking work of love" before she discovers she is not indifferent to him (*Dr. Thorne*, 352). Lucy Robarts refuses Lord Lufton's proposal, but "That her love did cling to him, she knew even then, and owned more thoroughly as soon as he was gone" (*Framley Parsonage*, 228). Even Lady Mason in *Orley Farm*, who is a widow with a grown-up son, is subject to the same rule that a woman may not love until the man has made his declaration. When Sir Peregrine proposes, she instantly discovers, "As for herself, she did love him. If she had not loved him before, she loved him now" (I, 356). The pattern remains in some later novels where Trollope returns to the consideration of the ingenue heroine whose affections wait on a declaration. Dr. Whortle, who has been taken as Trollope's self-portrait, thus expounds the matter to his daughter Mary: "There must be a beginning to such things. A man throws himself into it headlong. . . . At least all the best young men do. . . . A young woman, on the other hand, if she is such as I think you are, waits till she is asked. Then it has to begin" (247).

In the Palliser novels the simple maidens who prove to be so good at keeping their suitors at a distance are replaced by mature and passionate women, often sexually experienced, many of whom take the initiative of courtship into their own hands. (The Signora Neroni is perhaps the closest to them in the Barset series, but there she is the exception rather than the rule, and is satirically presented.) Now the women at the forefront of attention are Lady Glencora, who loves one man and marries another; Alice Vavasor, who goes through four engagements to two different men, and a variety of responses to sexual approaches, before she is married; Lady Laura, who turns down the man she loved to marry another, and then pursues her first suitor with a series of desperate pleas for his love through her married life, separation and widowhood; Madame Max and Lizzie Eustace, quite different from each other in that one is highly scrupulous and the other totally without principle, but alike in being widows who, after a first marriage of interest, are looking for love and romance, and are bold enough to offer themselves to their men; and Lady Mabel Grex, who, though she never marries, consciously bids "adieu to the sweet bloom of her maiden shame" (_DC_, II, 182) in begging a man to marry her.

"I do love Burgo Fitzgerald. I do! I do! I do! How can I help loving him?" Lady Glencora Palliser bursts out to her husband (_CYFH_, II, 230). "You will not take money from my hand? . . . Take the hand then first," Madame Max urges Phineas. "It was not my engagement or my marriage that has made the world a blank for me," Lady Laura Kennedy tells Phineas Finn, ". . . It was, and has been, and still will be my strong, unalterable, unquenchable love for you" (_PR_, I, 123–4). "O Frank, Frank, will you give me back my heart? What was it that you promised me when we sat together upon the rocks at Portray?" moans Lizzie, as she makes one of her several pitches for Frank Greystock (_ED_, 482). "Oh, Silverbridge: – oh, my loved one!" cries Lady Mabel, with the tears streaming down her face; "Have you a right to treat me like that; – when I tell you that you have all my heart?" (_DC_, II, 186). It is a passionate chorus, and a far cry from the modest maidenliness of the Barset heroines. Even Lucy Morris, who resembles them in her stoic resolution to bear her suffering without complaining, belongs among the Palliser women rather than the Barset ones, in that her passion is not meekly attendant on the man's show of love, but is a strong and independent growth: "She had given her heart, – for good and all, as she owned to herself, – to Frank Greystock. She had owned to herself that it was so, and had owned to herself that nothing could come of it. . . . Of all men he was the last who could afford to marry a governess. And then, moreover, he had never said a word to make her think that he loved her" (_ED_, 25–6). Lucy is like that other governess who shocked the world by admitting her love for her master, and so broke the Richardson stereotype. Jane Eyre, like Trollope's Barset heroines, tries to smother her love for a man who has not declared his love and is too far above her to marry her. But then she breaks out against this decree that a woman is not to know and acknowledge her own feelings, even to herself:

> 'Did I forbid myself to think of him in any other light than as a paymaster? Blasphemy against nature! Every good, true, vigorous feeling I have, gathers impulsively round him. I know I must conceal my sentiments: I must smother hope; I must remember that he cannot care much for me. . . . I must then repeat continually that we are for ever sundered: – and yet, while I breathe and think I must love him.' (_Jane Eyre_, ch. 17).

That change from Jane's resolution that she cannot be in love to the bold acknowledgement that she _is_ in love is the change from the nice

Barset girls to the passionate Palliser women, who are often not nice at all. Trollope has liberated his women in allowing them a passional life that is independent of the moral code.

This is not to say that the moral force of his writing suffers – quite the reverse. The woman's acknowledged powerful sexuality, seen as it is in relation to all society's restrictions, gives her a new status as a responsible moral agent making choices between her passion and external sanctions. Lady Laura and Lady Mabel, except that they are not the central figures in their novels, reach almost a tragic stature.

The women remain agonizingly limited in the ways in which they can manifest their love. Some of them chafe under the restriction that decrees women should be passive in courtship. Lady Mabel complains to Frank Tregear:

> 'Only think how a girl such as I am is placed; or indeed any girl. You, if you see a woman that you fancy, can pursue her, can win her and triumph, or lose her and gnaw your heart; – at any rate you can do something. . . . You can set yourself about the business you have taken in hand and can work hard at it. What can a girl do?'
>
> 'Girls work hard too sometimes.'
>
> 'Of course they do; but everybody feels that they are sinning against their sex. Of love, such as a man's is, a woman ought to know nothing. How can she love with passion when she should never give her love till it has been asked, and not then unless her friends tell her that the thing is suitable?' (*DC*, I, 98–9)

The Barset girls had for the most part conformed to those rules without even being conscious of their existence. But Lady Mabel knows the rules, and feels them as restrictions, and breaks them. When she has decided to make Silverbridge marry her, she resolves to turn the tables on him: "She knew that . . . she must prostrate herself at his feet, – as, since the world began, it has been man's province to prostrate himself at the feet of the woman he loves" (*DC*, II, 182). In the Palliser novels this custom, however, is almost more notable in the breach than in the observance. Lizzie Eustace, of course, offers herself to Frank quite regularly, but here the narrator enters some strictures: "The offer of herself by a woman to a man is, to us all, a thing so distasteful that we at once declare that the woman must be abominable." However, he continues, with a more tolerant irony, "But the man to whom the offer is made hardly sees the thing in the same light. He is disposed to believe that, in his peculiar case, there are circumstances by which the woman is, if not justified, at least excused" (*ED*, 318). But it is not only the flattered man in the case who is disposed to be charitable: Trollope by no means means his readers to condemn Madame Max's offer of herself to Phineas. That is a true and courageous gesture, though she herself is embarrassed at it when her proposal is refused. And by the time we get to *Phineas Redux*, if we are to believe Lady Glencora, the proposal by the woman is quite commonplace. There is a pungent little scene in which she discusses Lady Laura and Phineas with Madame Max, not knowing of her friend's earlier offer to Phineas.

> 'They say she is frantic about him, my dear. . . . And she is very rich. She has got all Lough Linter for her life, and her own fortune back again. I will bet you anything you like that she offers to share it with him.'
> 'It may be so,' said Madame Goesler, while the slightest blush in the world suffused her cheek.
> 'And I'll make you another bet . . . that he refuses her. It is quite a common thing nowadays for ladies to make the offer, and for gentlemen to refuse. Indeed, it was felt to be so inconvenient while it was thought that gentlemen had not the alternative, that some men became afraid of going into society. It is better understood now.'
> 'Such things have been done, I do not doubt,' said Madame Goesler. (*PR*, II, 277–8)

Making allowance for Glencora's hyperbole, one may still acknowledge that she has a case in her observation of social change, even if. only of that which occurs within the world of Trollope's novels.

Trollope is necessarily limited in his discussion of the physical manifestation of his women's love. But one recurring element in his depictions of love and courtship is his apparent requirement that the woman should worship her man as a god.[13] It is not only Lily's Crosbie who is an "Apollo" – Lord Lufton, John Grey, Phineas, Frank Greystock, Arthur Fletcher, and Silverbridge all appear as Apollos, or "handsome as a god," to the women who love them. Lady Mabel makes it almost a principle that worship on the woman's part is a necessary concomitant to love. Finding herself not really suitable to be Silverbridge's wife because "to me he is a rather foolish, but very, very sweet-tempered young man; – anything rather than a god," she enlarges on the sort of girl he *should* marry. "She should be able not only to like him and love him, but to worship him. . . . She should have a feeling that her Silverbridge is an Apollo upon earth" (*DC*, I, 195). Later, to fulfil Mabel's prophesy and to make sure his reader knows Silverbridge is now after the right girl, Trollope introduces a little scene between Isabel and Silverbridge's sister:

> 'Is he not such a man as a girl would love?' [asks Isabel.]
> 'Oh yes.'
> 'Is he not handsome as a god?' Mary stared at her with all her eyes.
> 'And sweeter than any god those pagan races knew? . . .' (*DC*, II, 77).

To a feminist all this may be rather disgusting, a nineteenth-century version of Milton's now notorious pronouncement "He for God only, she for God in him."[14] I have found it rather distasteful myself, in some readings. But it is noticeable, I think, about this quite routine talk of worship in the context of a woman's love for a man, that it is the man's physical qualities, his appearance, rather than his moral or spiritual ones that are under observation. And, usually explicitly, it is a pagan god, not the Christian one, who is being invoked. We do hear of a mortal who is to be worshipped by his woman for moral rather than physical reasons – but here it is Palliser, who is "a dry, silent, uncongenial and uncomfortable god" (*PM*, II, 185), and Glencora is certainly far from worshipping him. Most of the time we hear of the godliness in relation to the man's features, or his dress; as with Phineas, for instance, who thus appears before Lady Laura at Loughlinter:

> At the present moment he had on his head a Scotch cap with a grouse's feather in it, and he was dressed in a velvet shooting-jacket and dark knickerbockers; and was certainly, in his costume, as handsome a man as any woman would wish to see. . . . As he spoke to her she looked at him and told herself that he was as handsome as a god. (*PF*, I, 166–7)

What Trollope is saying, I think, is not really that a woman must revere her man as a being of a higher moral and spiritual order than she is herself, but merely that she should respond to him sexually. His imagery of worship is certainly mystifying, but then he is subject to the pressure of the officially accepted doctrine (often called "Victorian" but sufficiently familiar in other periods, including our own) that women, or at least *nice* women, have no sexual appetite.[15] This is his way of doing the necessary job of etherealizing sexual desire in a woman. And if Trollope has to grope for terms to express the physical aspect of love, and resort to rather obscure metaphor, he is not alone. From "my bowels were moved for him" to "I dig you, baby," we have a history of the indirect expression of sexual desire, since frank sexual terminology is always being relegated to the category of obscene language. So, according to the expressive powers of the speaker or the writer, we have on the one hand fruitful metaphor and poetic heightening, and on the other a resort to circumlocution and euphemism. Other Victorians were moved to more poetic flights that Trollope – Christina Rossetti, for instance: "My heart is like a singing bird . . ./ Because my love is come to me"; or Tennyson:

> There has fallen a splendid tear
>   From the passion-flower at the gate.
> She is coming, my dove, my dear;
>   She is coming, my life, my fate. ("Maud," II, 908–911)

Trollope's laconic "she looked at him and told herself that he was as handsome as a god" is relatively mild, but is intended to convey the same emotion. His imagery of worship, and his women's reference to Apollos, are simply his own formula to denote the exaltation of desire. With my body I thee worship. Trollope took the marriage service quite literally.

When this is understood, I think, Trollope can be seen as fairly advanced in his depictions of women in love. His women are sensual, and deeply moved by the physical attributes of their men. Unlike many novelists, particularly male ones, Trollope is very sensitive to masculine beauty, and expands in many places on the irresistible physical attractions of men like Burgo Fitzgerald, Felix Carbury, and Phineas. "You are so handsome!" exclaims the girl on the streets to Burgo. ". . . Will you give me a kiss?" (*CYFH*, II, 324). In Trollope's novels, the men too are sex objects.

In the lecture on "Higher Education for Women," Trollope puts the case for the woman who resents her exclusion from a rewarding career:

> Why should not a woman, if she be capable, earn those rich rewards of fame, of position, and of wealth which men are on all sides obtaining for themselves? When I hear, as I often do hear, a woman urgent in this matter, anxious to press forward with her whole heart into the arena of the world's work, and thus to shake off a dependence which she feels, – but I think wrongly feels, – to be more abject than that of men, I am inclined to admire her while I oppose her. (73)

Although Trollope still holds on to his opinion that she is wrong, that admiration of his comes out quite as strongly as the opposition in the novels of the sixties and seventies, which deal very sympathetically with the frustrated ambitions of the intelligent woman.

We saw how Alice was thrust back from the political arena into the domestic – firmly, albeit tenderly. In Lady Laura Standish Trollope looks again with sympathy on a woman who would enter politics if she could. Mill enlarges on the great and legitimate pleasure of the full employment of high capabilities, and argues that it is unjust to deny that pleasure to half the human race; and on the other hand, he movingly evokes "the great amount of unhappiness even now produced by the feeling of a wasted life." He asks his reader to consider "the positive evil caused to the disqualified half of the human race by their disqualification – first in the loss of the most inspiriting and elevating kind of personal enjoyment, and next in the weariness, disappointment, and profound dissatisfaction with life, which are so often a substitute for it" (547–8). Trollope might have created Lady Laura Standish as a case history for Mill.[16] "I feel that a woman's life is only half a life, as she cannot have a seat in Parliament," she says – and that when she is still young and full of energy and enthusiasm (*PF*, I, 70). Later, when she has tried to channel her energy into support of her husband's and Phineas's careers, she discovers, "I am beginning to think that it is a great curse to have been born a woman" (I, 367). It does not much matter, in this novel, whether Trollope is opposing or admiring her attitude: but what he has done, with great power, I think, is to dramatize it.

Lady Laura is a woman painfully conscious of her disabilities, both as being denied the franchise and as being legally subject to a husband who is her intellectual inferior. We are not surprised to hear that her face "lacked that softness which we all love in women" (I, 39), for like Phineas, she "looked at the world almost as a man looked at it, – as an oyster to be opened with such weapon as she could find ready to her hand" (I, 146). It is her sense of an urgent need to do something in the world, to have some effect on public life, that makes her turn to marriage with a man of property and influence as the only outlet for her energy. She is not ambitious for social status (she generously gives away her own portion to pay her brother's debts), but for political influence. And so she marries Mr. Kennedy, with his safe constituency and his huge estate, rather than Phineas, who himself needs money if he is to continue his political career. Hence her tragedy, in her fore-doomed attempt to live a rewarding life with her dreadfully narrow-minded husband.

In the Kennedy marriage Trollope presents a fine study of the plight of the wife who, in Mill's phrase, is "the actual bond-servant of her husband" (462). Alice Vavasor had been understandably reluctant to name her wedding day when she reflected, "I haven't much of my own way at present; but you see, when I'm married I shan't have it at all" (*CYFH*, I, 35). In Lady Laura we see the process by which the wife's duty to her husband, even to one so painstakingly principled as Kennedy, becomes the experience of tyranny. This is early in their married life:

> Lady Laura, who in marrying him had firmly resolved that she would do her duty to him in all ways, even though the ways might sometimes be painful, . . . was not perhaps quite so fond of accurate regularity as her husband;.and thus, by this time, certain habits of his had become rather bonds than habits to her. . . . The Sundays were very wearisome to her, and made her feel that her lord and master was – her lord and master. (*PF*, I, 253–4)

She feels acutely the loss of the free play of mind, as does Emily Lopez, who reflects in dismay on her husband's dictum, " 'You must allow me to dictate to you what you ought to think.' Could it be that marriage meant as much as that?" (*PM*, I, 346). Lady Laura tries to explain to her husband, "There are moments, Robert, when even a married woman must be herself rather than her husband's wife." But

Kennedy admits that is a proposition that he is unable to understand (*PF*, II, 25).

As the marriage deteriorates and Lady Laura determines to separate herself from him, she finds what Mill points out, "If she leaves her husband, she can take nothing with her, neither her children nor anything which is rightfully her own. If he chooses, he can compel her to return, by law, or by physical force" (464). So Kennedy threatens, "If there be any law in the land, she shall be made [to come back]," provoking her bitter response, "Is a woman like a head of cattle, that she can be fastened in her crib by force?" (II, 374). She is forced to go abroad with her father, in order to escape his legal steps to drag her back to his house. Kennedy is like another demented husband in Trollope's novels of the same period, Louis Trevelyan in *He Knew He Was Right*. Trevelyan is Trollope's illustration of Mill's point about the custody of children. He kidnaps the baby from his estranged wife, and though he is certifiably insane there is no legal means to retrieve the child for the mother. Trollope had already supplied a number of telling case histories before Mill ever published *The Subjection of Women*.

Lady Laura, of course, comes to a bad end, and if one were reading the Phineas novels for the operation of poetic justice one would have to conclude that Trollope altogether disapproves of her. Is the true heroine, in these novels in which the women are so ambitious and so outspoken, really little Mary Flood Jones, who gets the hero at the end of *Phineas Finn*? Phineas reflects, when he is engaged to marry her, that his other women have "lacked that sweet, clinging, feminine softness which made Mary Flood Jones so pre-eminently the most charming of her sex" (II, 347). But of course this is not really the happy ending with rewards according to deserts. Phineas when he tells himself so much has a bad case of sour grapes, having found that the distinguished and forceful women, for various reasons, are out of his reach. Glencora's comment rings truer in the same novel when she lays it down, "Every man likes a clever woman the best, . . . if the clever woman only knows how to use her cleverness" (II, 216).

Glencora's reservation is an immense one, however, as it includes the proposition that the clever woman is to know how to wheedle and resort to subterfuge to make her influence felt. In the Barset series, Mrs. Grantly, with her tactful manipulation of the Archdeacon in her curtain lectures, is the really clever woman, as against Mrs. Proudie, who is by this definition clever but not clever enogh. (Mrs. Proudie, incidentally, was the example before the fact of Mill's dictum that in the existing system it is apt to be the worst wives, the shrews, who are alone able to assert their wills over their husbands': "The wife's power of being disagreeable generally only establishes a counter-tyranny, and makes victims in their turn chiefly of those husbands who are least inclined to be tyrants" [470]). Glencora has never been in favour of women's rights:

when Alice Vavasor rejoices to hear of the large number of women employed as operatives in Paris, "Lady Glencora said it was a great shame, and that they ought all to have husbands" (*CYFH*, II, 350). She is, for the most part, all in favour of the covert method of operation, by which the wife can be the effective leader by being the woman behind the man. This by-way to an influence in public affairs Mill disparages, as he points out that so long as the education and moral training of women has not prepared them for public roles, their influence is not likely to be beneficial.

> The wife frequently exercises even too much power over the man; she is able to affect his conduct in things in which she may not be qualified to influence it for good. . . . She neither knows nor cares which is the right side in politics, but she knows what will bring in money or invitations, give her husband a title, her son a place, or her daughter a good marriage. (471–2)

He might have been talking of Glencora, the Prime Minister's wife, whose political principles are much less elevated than her husband's:

> 'He is so hard to manage!'[17] Of course I don't mean about politics. . . . I don't care a straw whether it run to Radicalism or Toryism. The country goes on its own way, either for better or for worse, whichever of them are in. I don't think it makes any difference as to what sort of laws are passed. But among ourselves, in our set, it makes a deal of difference who gets the garters, the counties, who are made barons and then earls, and whose name stands at the head of everything.'
> 'That is your way of looking at politics?'
> 'I own it to you; – and I must teach it to him.' (*PM*, I, 64)

Fortunately for the good of the country, one might say, her husband proves an intractable pupil in learning her lessons. But in her favour it must be said, first, that Trollope and many of the reliable characters in the novel seem to share Glencora's rather disenchanted view that the country will get on all right whoever is in; and also that her husband, in spite of his exalted principles – and in some sense even because of them – makes no great success of doing things his way. When she tells him, in a moment of exasperation, "Really you are becoming so autocratic that I shall have to go in for women's rights" (I, 366), she, like Violet, is only joking. And yet her history seems to demonstrate that had she had some legitimate outlet for all the intelligence and energy, she might have achieved something more admirable than mere backstairs intrigue, and her husband might have led a more tranquil and rewarding political career. Poor Lady Glencora! She has to justify herself by the reflection,

"All that she did, – was it not for his sake?" – a proposition which she immediately follows by the argument, "And why should she not have her amibition in life as well as he his?" (I, 359). Her husband, in his sense of failure, has at least the consolation that he has failed in a grand enterprise, the government of a great country. But Glencora can fail only in her enormous exertions "to rule England by coaxing unpleasant men" (II, 467).

Glencora's daughter also has occasion to threaten that she will take up women's rights. "What would papa say if he heard I was going to give a lecture at an Institute?" she wonders, with a touch of her mother's wickedness (*DC*, I, 276). Lady Mary Palliser has some occasion to be dissatisfied with her lot, as she compares it with her brother's. She too is expected to conform to the requirement on women "to make complete abnegation of themselves, and to have no life but in their affections" (Mill, 444). The delicate sensibility of the woman requires that when her mother dies she should be immured for months and debarred from nearly all social contact; her father and brother, on the other hand, after a week or two of seclusion, are allowed to shed all otward signs of mourning, and to resume their normal social engagements. "How I do wish I were a man!" she tells Silverbridge when he takes her for a rare excursion in his hansom. "I'd have a hansom of my own, and go where I pleased. . . . I don't think a woman ever chooses how or where she shall live herself" (I, 276). On the other hand, Mary is in disgrace because those affections of hers which are meant to be all the life she has have been too strong. She is in love with a commoner, and means to marry him. And it is much worse for her to love a commoner than for her brother: the persistent love of a woman for someone below her in rank argues that her social instincts are subordinate to her sexual ones, and this, reprehensible but understandable in a man, is unforgivable in a woman. All that Mary does wrong in the course of the novel is insist that she wants to marry Frank Tregear, and refuse to marry anyone else. In the same time her brother has nearly proposed to an aristocratic girl and then engaged himself to a commoner; caused his brother to be sent down from Cambridge; incurred racing debts to the tune of £70,000; and become involved in an ugly scandal about disabling a racehorse. And yet Silverbridge, though he has some painful interviews with his father, is always cheerfully forgiven, while Mary is in perpetual disgrace. No wonder she wishes she were a man.

In the same novel Lady Mabel Grex rages against the miseries of being born a woman. But she is rebelling not so much against the legal subjection of women as their psychological make-up, which she finds to be different from that of men, who are less limited to the life of the affections. She cannot change her love, as Tregear can. "I thought I could. . . . But I cannot," she says bitterly. "A jackal is born a jackal, and

not a lion, and cannot help himself. So is a woman born – a woman"
(*DC*. II, 316–7).

The Palliser novels are a running commentary on the disabilities of
women. The young Lady Glencora, who was an heiress on an immense
scale, not only sees her whole fortune automatically alienated to her
husband's estate, but is expected to endure lectures from his friends on
her extravagance in keeping out his horses – (fortunately, she does not
endure it [*CFYH*, II, 41]). Later in her married life, when she proposes
to spend a lot of money on lavish entertainment in the Prime Minister's
house, we actually hear of Glencora blushing. The Duke warns her
against squandering, and she reflects,

> Though they were to squander her fortune, – that money which she
> had brought, – in the next ten years at a much greater rate than she
> contemplated, they might do so without touching the Palliser proper-
> ty. Of that she was quite sure. And the squandering was to be all in his
> glory. . . . For an instant it occurred to her that she would tell him all
> this. But she checked herself, and the idea of what she had been about
> to say brought the blood into her face. Never yet had she in talking to
> him alluded to her own wealth. 'Of course we are spending money,'
> she said. 'If you give me a hint to hold my hand, I will do it.'
> He had looked at her, and read it all in her face. 'God knows,' he
> said, 'you've a right to do it if it pleases you.'
> 'For your sake!' (*PM*, I, 114)

We get the same indication of the taboos that surround the whole
business aspect of a marriage, which in this case was immense. There are
not many subjects that Glencora is too delicate to mention, but to say
"it's my money" would be an outrage too horrifying even for her. But
Trollope, like the Duke, sympathizes with the sentiment, even if he
would not sanction the statement of it. God knows, she has a right to it,
he tacitly acknowledges: though even at that she must justify herself by
the not fully reliable plea that it is all for her husband's sake.

Alice Vavasor, when she tries to transact business, finds she has to
leave the arrangement of her money affairs to her father; and George
Vavasor, when he tries to cash a bill she has signed, finds he cannot do
so, for "the City, by one of its mouths, asserted plainly that ladies' bills
never meant business" (II, 255). Those tender affections of women that
make it "understood in the world that women mourn longer than men"
(*DC*, I, 263) also make it impossible for women to attend either funerals
or the intensely important reading of the will afterwards: Kate Vavasor
and Alice, though they are major beneficiaries under their grandfather's
will, are not allowed to hear it – and George Vavasor at least takes unscrupulous advantage of his sister's ignorance by lying to her about the
contents of the will. As the emotional delicacy of women disqualifies

them from participation in one set of activities, their physical delicacy often disqualifies them for another. Isabel Boncassen has almost to apologize for beating Lord Silverbridge at tennis: "I am beginning to think it is unladylike to exert myself," she says; but fortunately she keeps on doing it (*DC*, I, 373).

Two women in the Palliser novels deserve mention for their refusal to be frustrated and confined by the limitations of their sex: Lucy Morris and Marie Goesler. Lucy has Trollope's compassion in that she has been forced out into the labour market and made to earn her own living like a man.[18] But she is not sorry for herself, and on the contrary takes great pride in the fact that she can buy Frank Greystock a ring "purchased out of her own earnings" (*ED*, 280). It is to her credit, in the system of contrasts between her and Lizzie in *The Eustace Diamonds*, that she resolutely goes to work – even to such uncongenial work as being lady companion to Lady Linlithgow – rather than using feminine wiles to catch a rich husband, like Lizzie.

Marie Goesler is a rich widow who is entirely independent, and who is fully resourceful and self-reliant not only in the management of her own financial affairs (which involve periodic business trips to Vienna) but in finding the conclusive evidence that determines Phineas's acquittal. In this quest she exerts herself like the heroine of a ballad who saves the life of the man she loves: "It was of course known to everybody that Madame Goesler had undertaken a journey to Bohemia, – and, as many supposed, a roving tour through all the wilder parts of unknown Europe ... – with the object of looking for evidence to save the life of Phineas Finn; and grandly romantic tales were told of her wit, her wealth, and her beauty" (*PR*, II, 260). As Mrs. Finn she keeps herself fully informed about politics, and can converse on them more sensibly than most men; but she never interferes in them, as Glencora does. She asks for no privileged information from her husband, being content "to know when the proper time might come for ladies to be informed" (*PM*, II, 427). She is not resentful of being subjected to men, because she feels for the most part superior to them – she often regards them as mere boys, playing at being busy. As a woman she has been able to observe the world longer than a man of her own age, because "Young men are boys at college, rowing in boats, when women have been ever so long out in the world" (*PM*, I, 124). A passage of conversation between her and Barrington Erle deserves quoting at length, because her tone and sentiments are evidently such as Trollope approves. She has just analysed the desirable qualities in a Prime Minister.

'Mrs. Finn, you understand it all better than any one else that I ever knew.'

'I have been watching it a long time, and of course very closely since I have been married.'

'But you have an eye trained to see it all. What a useful member you would have been in a government!'

'But I should never have had patience to sit all night upon that bench in the House of Commons. How men can do it! . . . I don't believe they ever listen. It isn't in human nature to listen hour after hour to such platitudes. I believe they fall into a habit of half wakeful sleeping which carries them through the hours; but even that can't be pleasant. I look upon the Treasury Bench in July as a sort of casual-ward which we know to be necessary, but is almost too horrid to be contemplated.'

'Men do get bread and skilly there certainly; but, Mrs. Finn, we can go into the library and smoking-room.'

'Oh, yes; – and a clerk in an office can read the newspapers instead of doing his duty. But there is a certain surveillance exercised, and a certain quantity of work exacted. I have met Lords of the Treasury out at dinner on Mondays and Thursdays, but we all regard them as boys who have shirked out of school. I think upon the whole, Mr. Erle, we women have the best of it.'

'I don't suppose you will go in for your "rights."'

'Not by Act of Parliament, or by platform meeting. I have a great idea of a woman's rights; but that is the way, I think, to throw them away.' (*PM*, I, 125–6)

Evidently Trollope too had a great idea of women's rights, and it is a pity that he did not allow Mrs. Finn to enlarge on hers. From her behaviour, however, it is clear that she takes a pride in her role as woman, which she regards as high and honourable. She has an innate strength and external advantages that make her able to triumph over the disabilities that are so frustrating and so crippling to others, and make them no disabilities at all.

But there are not many Mrs. Finns in Trollope's world. We have seen how many of his women suffer under the limitations of sex. We know from his explicit pronouncements that he would not have voted for female suffrage, nor would he have encouraged his daughters, if he had had any, to become doctors and lawyers. But he gave all the advice and encouragement he could to Kate Field in her literary endeavours: "I would so fain see you step out & become one of the profession in which women can work at par along side of men" (*Letters*, 217). And his deep sensitivity to the women in his novels, both as characters "at par along side of men" and as separate beings conscious of their separateness, and his constant reference to the social structure that debarred them from men's activity, make his novels, particularly the Palliser ones, prominent documents in the women's cause, if not propaganda for women's rights. In his views on the relations of men and women, as in his views on politics,[19] we can call him "an advanced, but still a conservative liberal."

9 The Places and Things

Trollope, the unwanted son in a family that was forever trying to put down roots and forever flitting, who spent so much of his childhood in agonies of transition between one place and another, who once passed his school holidays in his father's deserted chambers because he had no home to return to, and once assisted in smuggling family trinkets through a hole in the hedge when the bailiffs had moved into possession of Julians Hill, had an acutely developed sense of belonging.[1] Perhaps it was because his family never achieved the status of country gentry which they evidently longed for that he writes so often and so warmly about the country estate, and writes with the sense that the blood of a family flows not only in their own veins, but through the bricks and mortar, the lanes and timber, of the places where they live. The first identification between the content of his life and the content of his fiction that he makes in the *Autobiography* (and he makes relatively few) is that between Julians Hill and Orley Farm.[2] The titles of many of his novels – *The Macdermots of Ballycloran*, *The Vicar of Bullhampton*, *Harry Heathcote of Gangoil* – attest his sense of the almost umbilical relation between the person and the place.

We can only speculate on whether Trollope's tenacity in grasping on place in his novels and his acutely developed sensitivity to the influence of location were born of his own need. But the sensitivity is there, and is one of the elements in his writing that gives it its special flavour; and the love for the estate and care for its disposal are among the emotions he has most specialized in portraying. When Mrs. Dale and her daughters are preparing to move out of the Small House at Allington into lodgings, there is a commonly felt pang in Trollope's description of the upheaval:

> Who does not know how terrible are those preparations for house-moving; – how infinite in number are the articles which must be

9. Orley Farm: Millais' frontispiece for *Orley Farm*

packed, how inexpressibly uncomfortable is the period of packing, and how poor and tawdry is the aspect of one's belongings while they are thus in a state of dislocation? (*SHA*, II, 261)

As we saw, Lady Mabel Grex best expresses the particular hell in which she finds herself as being "dislocated from [her] very self" (*DC*, II, 316) – and her dislocation is physically enacted in her loss of Grex, the family's shabby old country estate (*DC*, II, 351).

Trollope is very knowing about the special kind of covetousness that links a man to his house and his land, and often satirizes it. The whole institution of primogeniture, which guards the land against division and alienation, is often a butt for gentle satire, and is of central import in the plots of such novels as *Orley Farm*, *Ralph the Heir*, and *Mr. Scarborough's Family*. In *The Prime Minister* we get a close view of the world of the Whartons, and their joy when the unpleasant heir dies and the new and congenial heir, Everett Wharton, can be initiated into the mysteries of the estate and introduced to the tenants. The Wharton tribe is predictably hostile to Lopez, who as a foreigner and a Jew is *landless* in a special way, and who is further to be distrusted because the estate he deals in is anything but real.

It is not surprising that Trollope, with all this interest in location, should often make his places emblematic. They are not simply a necessary physical environment in which action proceeds and character is displayed; they are part and parcel of action and character, moral places, like Fielding's Paradise Hall or Jane Austen's Mansfield Park.[3] Many of his novels begin with an elaborate description of a house and its environs, which seems to have been as necessary an exercise to initiate his imagination of the action as his description of the appearance of his characters was necessary to his imagining their minds and lives. The layouts he gives us are often painstaking rather than vivid, and he sometimes lays himself open to the criticism Jane Austen gave her niece Anna, who aspired to be a novelist: "You describe a sweet place, but your descriptions are often more minute than will be liked. You give too many particulars of right hand & left";[4] but Trollope evidently needed to be precise about such matters, and it seems to have been one of his warm-up routines at the beginning of a novel to go into diagrammatic detail about his places. The whole first chapter of *The Small House at Allington* is devoted to a description of the Great House, its environs, and its inheritors the Dales; and even at that we have still to wait for the second chapter to get a description of the Small House of the title:

The gardens of the Great House of Allington and those of the Small House open on to each other. A proper boundary of thick laurel hedge, and wide ditch, and of iron spikes guarding the ditch, there is between them; but over the wide ditch there is a foot-bridge,

and at the bridge there is a gate which has no key; and for all purposes of enjoyment the gardens of each house are open to the other.
And the gardens of the Small House are very pretty. .... (*SHA*, I,
20–21)

This is by no means simply space-filling. The story is already under way,
if we have the ear to hear it. In the social-climbing world of the novel,
where a dowerless daughter of a younger son is jilted for the daughter of
an earl, the exact relation of the Great House to the Small House is of
considerable import. Squire Dale of the Great House is the head of the
family, and his sister-in-law and nieces in the Small House are his
dependents, living rent-free in a house belonging to him. He would like
to be loving to his nieces, but they are not his daughters: the exact
boundaries and barriers between him and them, social and psychological, are to be significant in both plots, Lily's and Bell's, and the
ditch and the bridge are the outward signs. The boundary indeed should
be a "proper" one.

As the action begins, Lily and Bell Dale are in the Small House gardens, awaiting Bernard Dale and his friend Adolphus Crosbie, who will
arrive by means of that little bridge, which makes it possible to cross that
wide ditch with the iron spikes. Crosbie enters Lily's life by way of the
Great House, and he dallies in the pretty gardens of the Small House,
and makes commitments to Lily which seem feasible because of that easy
transition between the Great House and the Small. Indeed, in later
scenes that little bridge is the chosen location of the engaged couple for
their goodnight kisses and ardent promises (I, 123; II, 383). But when
Lily's uncle tells Crosbie (in spite of there being no lock to the gate
between the two properties) that no dowry from the Great House will be
forthcoming, Crosbie becomes mindful of the social gulf and the moral
iron spikes, and moves on to a greater house still. It is almost as precise
a piece of significant landscaping as that at Sotherton, where Maria Ber-
tram, as she is subsequently to do in life, squeezes past the matrimonial
barred gate, risks the spikes that could tear her dress, and elopes across
the open field with Mr. Crawford.[5] Trollope is not as economical as Jane
Austen, and by no means all of his topographical and architectural
description would bear the same scrutiny for symbolic significance; but
still his precise layout of the physical bridges and barriers between the
two houses here has more than a mere scene-setting significance. The
barriers and communications between the two spheres of Great and
Small Houses are still the subject of the story, after Crosbie has taken
himself beyond the sphere of either, in the prolonged negotiations over
Bernard Dale's suit of Bell, and the degree of obligation that must exist
between the Squire and his poor relations. (Bell dallies on no bridges,
and stoutly refuses her suitor from the Great House, choosing instead a
country doctor from another small house.)

Portray Castle is Lizzie Eustace's place, and when she retreats there, and scuttles like Dracula or a lizard among the rocks, and totes her volume of Shelley from rock to moat garden, and keeps her necklace in its iron box upstairs, Portray is made to express her.

> Portray Castle was really a castle, – not simply a country mansion so called, but a stone edifice with battlements and a round tower at one corner, and a gate which looked as if it might have had a portcullis, and narrow windows in a portion of it, and a cannon mounted up on a low roof, and an excavation called the moat, – but which was now a fantastic and somewhat picturesque garden, – running round two sides of it. In very truth, though a portion of the castle was undoubtedly old, and had been built when strength was needed for defence and probably for the custody of booty, – the battlements, and the round tower, and the awe-inspiring gateway had all been added by one of the late Sir Florians. But the castle looked like a castle, and was interesting. (*ED*, 189–90)

That is Lizzie all right, mostly phoney appearance, with a dash of genuine beauty and talent behind it. First we are told Portray was "really a castle," and we get a list of all its castellate attributes. But "in very truth," we presently hear, the battlements, etc., were built at a time long after there was any need for defence of that kind, and are merely Victorian Gothic ornament. Her taste for romance and mediaevalism is in key with that of the late Sir Florians of the family. "The castle looked like a castle" – and that is good enough for Lizzie. Appearance has always been all that she cares about. Besides, as the Gothic ornament is consonant with her need to consider herself a heroine of romance without actually going through what a heroine must go through, there is also a kind of appropriateness in these supernumerary fortifications after all. Lizzie's position in society is by no means safe, and her hold on the diamonds by no means secure, so it is just as well that at least part of Portray was built "when strength was needed for defence and probably for the custody of booty": her Scottish estate, to which she may invite her brother-in-law the baronet's son and her uncle the bishop, and where she can keep a stable and appear with credit on the hunting scene, gives her social countenance; and it is similarly her stronghold for the custody of her plunder, where the Eustace diamonds can be kept out of reach of the grasp of the Camperdowns who besieged her in London.

Places in general have a stability that their inhabitants cannot usually achieve: the falls of the Linter will keep falling, and the view there will still be as beautiful, though Phineas should be courting Lady Laura or Violet Effingham, though Lady Laura should be accepting Kennedy's suit or loathing him. But places too can change to some extent, and so reflect the changes in the people they represent. Lizzie, who has only a life interest in Portray, can still make clandestine depredations on its timber; Johnny Eames can hack out his carving of Lily's initials from the rail of the bridge. Caversham in *The Way We Live Now* (its local deity is Lady Pomona), in being bartered by the Longstaffes to the swindling tycoon Melmotte, stands as a reminder of the way in which the country gentry have abrogated their responsibilities, like Jane Austen's Kellynch Hall; and Carbury Hall in the same novel, with its moat (a real one, not a fake, like that at Portray) is an emblem of stability, of the way we lived then as opposed to the way we live now; just as Roger Carbury, its owner, is unable to adapt or change by a hair's breadth.

One notable instance of a changed estate that reflects a changed owner is Loughlinter. At the beginning of *Phineas Finn* we see Kennedy at his most expansive and triumphant as he shows his estate to the girl who has just accepted him, and to the man he has just conquered in love.

> 'Is it not lovely?' said Laura. 'We have not been here an hour yet, and Mr. Kennedy insisted on bringing me here.'
> 'It is wonderfully beautiful,' said Phineas.
> 'It is this very spot where we now stand that made me build the house where it is,' said Mr. Kennedy, 'and I was only eighteen when I stood here and made up my mind. That is just twenty-five years ago.'
> 'So he is forty-three,' said Phineas to himself, thinking how glorious it was to be only twenty-five. . . . Then they went on with their walk very pleasantly, and the lord of all that they surveyed took them from one point of vantage to another, till they both swore that of all spots on the earth Loughlinter was surely the most lovely. 'I do delight in it, I own,' said the lord. (*PF*, I, 148–9)

Trollope's precision about times and ages is deliberate.[6] It allows us to measure change exactly, and when we get to *Phineas Redux* the difference and deterioration is the more impressive. He can hardly have looked forward to the second novel while he was in process of writing the first, but in *Phineas Redux* he is able to evoke marvellously the sense of pain and loss that goes with revisiting a site inhabited by old and happier memories. Phineas revisits Loughlinter at Kennedy's express request, and the chapter, "The Deserted Husband," is resonant with his sense of a bright lost past in contrast to a dark and desolate present. "A thousand memories crowded on his brain as he made the journey" – memories most vivid about Lady Laura's rejection of him by the falls. "He remembered the blow as though it had been struck but yesterday" (*PR*, I, 98–9). He arrives this time in the dark, still recalling the details of his previous visits, and is shown into the vast hall "which, when he had before known it, was ever filled with signs of life, and felt at once that it was empty and deserted" (I, 100). There are no fires, and no candles in

10. "The Laird of Lough Linter": Holl's illustration for *Phineas Redux*, chapter 10

the candlesticks. Everything is "cold and wretched." Trollope is unusually specific on the menu of Phineas's insultingly bad solitary dinner,
the "flabby white fish," the tough beefsteak, the crumpled tart and the
undrinkable claret, to convey the offence to senses which had been so
enchantingly indulged in this place in former days. And then we and
Phineas meet "the laird" in his domain again:

> Phineas knew the man's age well. He was still under fifty, but he
> looked as though he were seventy. He had always been thin, but he
> was thinner now than ever. He was very grey, and stooped. . . . 'You
> find me a much altered man,' he said. The change had been so great
> that it was impossible to deny it. (I, 102)

Kennedy, who had once avowed his delight in his beautiful estate, now
takes a luxurious satisfaction in conforming it to his own inner gloom.
"Not that Lough Linter can be comfortable now to any one. How can a
man, whose wife has deserted him, entertain his guests?" Because he has
been deserted, Loughlinter shall be desolate. And now it becomes clear
that there has been a certain inevitability in this devotion to pain and
self-castigation. Even in his exultant mood in the early days he had confessed, "When I come up here alone . . . I grow proud of my own, till I
become thoroughly ashamed of myself" (*PF*, I, 149). He was already
ashamed of his delight. Now his puritan rigour fully asserts itself, and
the darkness and discomfort with which he has surrounded himself
become the accurate reflection of his view of life. "Happy? What right
had she to expect to be happy? Are we to believe that we should be happy here? Are we not told that we are to look for happiness there, and
hope for none below? . . . I did not want her to make me happy. I do
not expect to be made happy. I wanted her to do her duty" (I, 104, 106).

The derangement of Kennedy's mind is enacted externally, in the
derangement of Loughlinter. And Phineas too is able to measure the
change in his own life, from the aspiring youth who wanted the moon,
and nearly always got something almost as good, to the disappointed
but still courageous man, always blamed where he has been most
scrupulous to be honourable. The experience has been resident in the
place, and the reunion with the place revives the experience. The falls at
Loughlinter are resonant with associations for several characters –
Phineas, Lady Laura, Kennedy, even Violet – and for each of them they
afford the remembrance, This is what I was. There is a certain pathos in
Lady Laura's need for Phineas after Kennedy's death. Because of that
abortive declaration, she longs not just to marry Phineas all these years
afterwards, but to endow him with Loughlinter and its falls: so she seeks
to recapture the past, and cancel out the ghastly mistake of her marriage
and the pain of the intervening years. At the end of *Phineas Redux* she is
still recalling, "it was there, standing by the waterfall, . . . that Phineas

Finn had told her of his love"; and now, a lonely widow burdened with
the estate of the man she hated, "she allowed her fancy to revel in the
idea of having him with her as she wandered over the braes" (*PR*, II,
322, 327).

There is a sequence of chapters in the middle of *The Duke's Children*
that focuses on one location after another: 'Tally-Ho Lodge,"
"Grex," "Crummie-Toddie," "Killancodlem." Each location is not just
a physical setting for character and action, but is a moral world, with its
own set of accepted values. Major Tifto in Tally-Ho Lodge, between the
stables and the kennels, with his pipes and gin within his reach, and his
clothes still redolent with the sweat of his day's labour among his
hunters, is there accessible to the persuasions of his own personal
Mephistophilis, Captain Green, and ultimately agrees to betray his
patron Silverbridge: "Square is all very well, as long as others are square
to you; – but when they aren't, then I say square be d———" (*DC*, I,
350). I have examined Grex and its peculiar appropriateness to Lady
Mabel's character in discussing *The Duke's Children* – like her it is old,
tarnished, impoverished, and full of still places and unchanging
perspectives. It is here that she can most appropriately declare her
lifelong passion, talk of "old days," and think of the past rather than the
future (*DC*, I, 357–360). Then comes Crummie-Toddie, the domain of
Reginald Dobbes, who takes his sport so seriously that he is unwilling to
allow any amenities in his household or beauty in his landscape, lest his
guests should lapse in their attention to the number of grouse to be
shot. Gerald and Silverbridge call it "ugly" and "beastly," but Dobbes
defends it, because it is pretty enough for the grouse. "There was a Spartan simplicity about Crummie-Toddie which pleased the Spartan mind
of Reginald Dobbes" (I, 365). From his businesslike masculine preserve,
he scorns the mansion of Mrs. Montacute Jones, Killancodlem, the
name of which signifies that few grouse get killed and many men get
coddled. There billiards, tennis and dancing are the order of the day.
Dobbes calls it "a very fine house for ladies to flirt in," and so it proves,
as Silverbridge is lured away from the Spartan jurisdiction of Dobbes
and his associates by the siren talents of Mrs. Montacute Jones, Lady
Mabel and Isabel, and is soon coddled into a declaration. The two es-
tates, representing two opposed ways of life, are at moral war, and there
is some deliberate mock-heroic play:

'I do not hesitate to tell you, Lord Silverbridge [says his hostess], that
I call for your surrender, in order that I may show my power over
Reginald Dobbes. Are you a Dobbite?'
    'Not thorough-going,' said Silverbridge.
    'Then be a Montacute Jones-ite; or a Boncassenite, if, as is possible,
you prefer a young woman to an old.' At this moment Isabel Boncassen was standing close to them.

11. Alice by the Rhine with George Vavasor: Browne's frontispiece for *Can You Forgive Her?*

'Killancodlem against Crummie-Toddie for ever!' said Miss Boncassen, waving her handkerchief. As a matter of course a messenger was sent back to Crummie-Toddie for the young lord's waring apparel. (*DC*, I, 371)

Although Silverbridge is not present at all these locations as the scene shifts, chapter by chapter, Trollope is nevertheless presenting a kind of moral journey for him. Major Tifto and Tally-Ho Lodge, with their shabby accompaniments of gin and shady deals, are part of his irresponsible youth that he must shake off. Grex is Lady Mabel, the possible wife for him, and we if not he find out here that she would be the wrong wife, because she is irreversibly in love with someone else. Crummie-Toddie is another version of Tally-Ho Lodge, but more respectable, as shooting is more respectable than the turf; but for a full commitment he moves on from its monastic seclusion to the complex choices involved in social and sexual life. The allegorical potential of Silverbridge's progress is made explicit in Lady Mabel's playful analysis: "Major [Tifto] is the Mr. Worldly-Wise-man who won't let Christian go to the Strait Gate. I am afraid he hasn't read his Pilgrim's Progress" (I, 278). Trollope's places are symbolic and allegorical, and as his people travel to them they move among the Hill of Difficulty, the Pleasant Meadows, the Valley of Humiliation, the Bower of Bliss.

In *Can You Forgive Her?* Alice Vavasor likewise goes on a kind of pilgrim's progress. In making her mistake and correcting it, she must trace her steps and retrace them, physically as morally. It is on the balcony at Basle overlooking the Rhine that she first listens to the song of the river, "a song full of mystery, as are all river songs when one tries to understand their words," and partly allows George to intepret the song as saying she is not fit to be the wife of John Grey (*CYFH*, I, 60ff). As a result of that ill-advised trip to Switzerland, with George and Kate as her counsellors, she breaks with Grey. Before she can repair that error, she must go to Switzerland again, this time with a couple more in favour of her worthy man than her wild man. After she has repented of breaking her engagement with Grey, she shudders at the mention of Basle (II, 269). And at the last, when she is again engaged, she brings him there as though to exorcise a ghost: "It was here, . . . here, on this very balcony, that I first rebelled against you, and now you have brought me here that I should confess and submit on the same spot. I do confess" (II, 441). In the same way Kate Vavasor, who by the stone on Swindale Fell used all her eloquence to persuade Alice to accept George (I, 403ff), must retrace her steps with George, and see the violence and despicable self-interest of the brother she has adored. "They were still on the same path, – that path which Kate and Alice had taken in the winter, – and now poor Kate could not but think of all that she had said that day on George's behalf; – how had she mingled truth and

12. Alice by the Rhine with John Grey: Taylor's illustration for *Can You Forgive Her?*, chapter 75

falsehood in her efforts to raise her brother's character in her cousin's eyes!" (II, 196). And just where she had fallen on her knees to beg Alice to accept him, George flings her on the stony ground and breaks her arm.

There is a kind of ritual which the characters themselves are sometimes aware of in this retracing of steps. They go back in time as well as in space, they face their past selves, they exorcise a ghost, they sometimes succeed in making a new start. Young Phineas, a year after his declaration to Lady Laura, needs to return to the Linter to make a new decision: "Once before when he was sitting beside the Linter he had made up his mind to declare his passion to Lady Laura; – and he had done so on the very spot. Now, within a twelvemonth of that time, he made up his mind on the same spot to declare his passion to Miss Effingham" (*PF*, I, 365). He has the same sense of the importance of location when, weary and shaken after his trial, he goes for the first time to the site of the murder, as though under some psychological urging to envisage the act of which he was supposed guilty. "Here it was," he reflects, and almost feels guilty in thus acting out the legendary compulsion of the murderer to revisit the scene of the crime (*PR*, II, 295). "On the same spot," "on this very spot" – these are frequent expressions in Trollope, testifying always to his powerful sense of the consonance of the experience with the location.

Another powerful passage in which location has almost the force of character – is in fact an extension of it – is the scene of Madame Goesler's proposal to Phineas. He is strongly tempted by the woman, but the woman and her room and her house are co-extensive. After he has felt the temptation ("The very air of the room in which she dwelt was sweet in his nostrils") and rejected her offer, he feels that he has offended not only her but her surroundings:

> He remained there, he knew not how long, standing on the very spot on which she had left him; and at last there grew on him almost a fear of moving, a dread lest he should be heard, an inordinate desire to escape without the sound of a footfall, without the clicking of a lock. Everything in that house had been offered to him. He had refused it all, and then felt that of all human beings under the sun none had so little right to be standing there as he. (*PF*, II, 394–6)

It is a shorter step than might be supposed from this to the animism of Dickens' universe, where the stairboards creak "Stop, thief!" at the guilty Pip, and a hare hanging in the larder winks its eye. Trollope does not pursue his sense of the animation in a location to the realm of fantasy, but he is similarly sensitive to the life of the mind that can flow out from itself to quicken surrounding objects.

Trollope uses his acute sense of location to convey Lady Mabel's lasting pain. Her drawing room in London, where she spends most of her time, was the site of Frank Tregear's courtship. When he returns to take his last leave of her, after being off with the old love and safely on with the new, even he is moved by the memories resident in the rooms: "He had known this house since he was a boy, and could well remember how, when he first entered it . . . he had become very much taken by the grace and good-nature of the girl who owned him as a cousin. . . . He could remember the words as though they had been spoken only yesterday" (*DC*, II, 346). He notes now that, since the death of her father, "Things were already gone which used to be familiar in his eyes" (II, 349) – Mabel's surroundings are being dislocated, as she is herself. Her residence in the room in the interim has been only a constant association with lost joys and painful memories. It was here that Lady Mary made her great gesture of flinging herself into Tregear's arms and kissing him before the assembled company, which includes his last love. That remembrance dwells with Lady Mabel, as she inhabits the room where the very furniture seems to have abandoned her: "Do you remember," she asks Frank bitterly, "when she flew into your arms in this room?" (II, 359). She is exact about such matters, the chronicle of her life being fixed in her mind by physical points of reference. So she reminds Silverbridge when he admits he has changed his mind: "there, – sitting in that very spot, – you spoke to me of your love" (II, 312).

Trollope, whose novels are so often concerned with power plays, whether at the national level between parties, or among the trivia of the individual's daily life, is particularly aware of place as territory. In the endless manoeuvres between characters trying to get the upper hand of one another, the importance of the home ground is always recognizable as a major factor in the outcome.

> The turkey-cock in his own farmyard is master of the occasion, and the thought of him creates fear. A bishop in his lawn, a judge on the bench, a chairman in the big room at the end of a long table, or a policeman with his bull's-eye lamp upon his beat, can all make themselves terrible by means of those appanages of majesty which have been vouchsafed to them. (*SHA*, II, 76)

Trollope of course can marvellously exploit these appanages of majesty for comic purposes, and in his earliest novels particularly he returns often to such scenes as Dockwrath's appropriation of the "Commercial room" in *Orley Farm*, where the real commercial gents are forced to vacate the room that is supposed to be especially set aside for their use because the determined attorney has been too many for them. The definitive little incident has its bearing on the novel as a whole. Dockwrath is Lady Mason's bitterest enemy, and the most outraged at her sin of forging the codicil in order to secure Orley Farm to her son; but here he likewise makes false claim to territory that is not his, and the sixteen little Dockwraths figure in his calculations as her son figures in Lady Mason's; but whereas Lady Mason resigns Orley Farm at last, Dockwrath is left to the enjoyment of his territorial gain.

There is much manoeuvring for territorial advantage in *The Small House at Allington*. In official life, Mr. Butterwell makes the mistake of going to Crosbie when he wants to reprimand him, instead of summoning him to his own ground:

> 'Do you know ———' said Butterwell, beginning.
> 'Sit down, won't you?' said Crosbie, seating himself as he spoke. If there was to be a contest, he would make the best fight he could. . . . Butterwell did sit down, and felt as he did so, that the very motion of sitting took away some of his power. He ought to have sent for Crosbie into his own room. A man when he wishes to reprimand another, should always have the benefit of his own atmosphere. (*SHA*, II, 253)

But it is not only in official life that the territorial imperative works: Lily in the Small House understands all about it, too, when she has to encounter the tyrannical gardener, Hopkins.

> Just at that moment Hopkins appeared at the parlour window, and signified his desire for a conference.
> 'You must come round,' said Lily. 'It's too cold for the window to be opened. I always like to get him into the house, because he feels himself a little abashed by the chairs and tables; or, perhaps, it is the carpet that is too much for him. Out on the gravel-walks he is such a terrible tyrant, and in the greenhouse he almost tramples upon one!' (II, 319)

Lily, who can articulate such a principle, is able to apply it in more serious situations, in her emotional life. When Johnny leads up to a declaration, she hastily suggests, "Shall we go into the drawing-room?" being aware that "she would be in some degree safer there than out among the shrubs and paths of the garden" (I, 283). But for this time Johnny outmanoeuvres her, stays in the garden, and gets his declaration made.

In the later novels Trollope is not so often explicit about these territorial manoeuvres, but they are going on still, and are still part of his concern with the importance of location. One of the cruellest things the Duke as Prime Minister has to bear is his visit to his own estate at Gatherum, which Glencora has had so adapted for her lavish entertainments that he finds himself a stranger in his own domain, and is snubbed by a workman (*PM*, I, 210). Phineas is similarly beleaguered by Clarkson, the bill-collector, who knows very well how to make himself obnoxious by inhabiting Phineas's lodgings, eating his bread and butter, and poking his fire (*PF*, I, 235, 313). But he finds himself unexpectedly increased in power when he faces Slide in the comforting proximity of the House, surrounded by the privileges it affords its members.

> 'I'll crush you,' said Quintus Slide, in a stage whisper; 'I will, as sure as my name is Slide.'
> Phineas looked at him and retired into the House, whither Quintus Slide could not follow him, and the editor of The People's Banner was left alone in his anger.
> 'How a cock can crow on his own dunghill!' That was Mr. Slide's first feeling, as with a painful sense of diminished consequence he retraced his steps. (*PR*, I, 290–1)

Whether the cock's own dunghill is the House of Commons or a room in a pub, Gatherum Castle or Mr. Cheeseacre's Oileymead (which is well stocked with literal dunghills), Trollope is aware of its importance, psychologically as socially.

If Trollope's novels received the intensive critical exegesis that is commonplace in studies of James, for instance, his predilection for water in his scenery would surely have attracted symbolic interpretation. Consider how much has been said on the significance of Miss Jessel's appearance by the lake in *The Turn of the Screw*.[7] Trollope's use of water imagery is similarly suggestive. He is relatively uninterested in the sea – the immense symbolic force of the sea in *Moby Dick* or *Dombey and Son*, for instance, finds no echo in Trollope. His imagery is more in tune with that in *The Mill on the Floss*. Salt water is on the whole an inconvenience, to be crossed with as little fuss as may be. The boat excursion from Yarmouth organized by Mrs. Greenow and Cheeseacre is an absurd little outing, and those who expect romance from it are resoundingly disappointed. There is a poetic attempt made to dance on the sand of the beach, but it is an acknowledged failure: "When ladies have made up their minds to dance they will dance let the circumstances of the moment be ever so antagonistic to the exercise. A ploughed field in February would not be too wet, nor the side of a house too uneven. In honest truth the sands of the seashore are not adapted for the exercise" (*CYFH*, I, 113). The sands of the seashore are in this respect no different from the lawn at Allington, which is similarly tried for dancing and found not to answer (*SHA*, I, 120). The sea and its margins have no special romance for Trollope, and among his characters it is typically Lizzie who waxes enthusiastic about waves and rocks. But inland water is another matter – streams, rivers and lakes play a significant part in his novels. When he discusses the desirable characteristics of a site for a picnic he rejects Mrs. Greenow's sea-shore situation, and describes an inland scene. "There should, if possible, be rocks, old timber, moss, and brambles. There should certainly be hills and dales, – . . . and, above all, there should be running water" (*CYFH*, I, 92–3).

That is a priority that Trollope usually observes himself in his scenery; and there seems often a connection between the running water and the state of mind of a person encountering it. Alice in making her decision on the balcony at Basle to break her engagement is responding to the Rhine as much as to the persuasions of George: "The Rhine was running at her feet, so near, that in the soft half light it seemed as though she might step into its ripple. The Rhine was running by with that delicious sound of rapidly moving waters, that fresh refreshing gurgle of the river, which is so delicious to the ear at all times" (*CYFH*, I, 59). Here, with his visible figures of assonance, alliteration, and calculated repetion, Trollope has evidently exerted himself to produce a purple passage. The following chapter is called "The Bridge over the Rhine," and Alice, agonized in the process of decision, watches the swimmers and imagines giving herself up to the current and perishing (I, 70). She is deciding on her self-destructive step to desert Grey.

Where water flows swiftly passions run high, and great changes are contemplated: the Falls of the Linter, as we have seen, seem to prompt one declaration after another; and Lady Mabel needs to lead Silverbridge to two different gushing streams to make her bids to catch him. In a memorable scene in *He Knew He was Right* Hugh Stanbury and Nora Rowley are in powerful communion, in spite of their sense of separateness, as he negotiates the rocks in the river in Devon:

> He went down, and scrambled out on the rocks into the bed of the river, while the girls above looked down upon him, watching the leaps that he made. Priscilla and Mrs. Trevelyan called to him, bidding him beware; but Nora called not at all. He was whistling as he made his jumps, but still he heard their voices, and knew that he did not hear Nora's voice. He poised himself on the edge of a rock in the middle of the stream, and looked up the river and down the river, turning himself carefully on his narrow foothold; but he was thinking only of Nora. (230–1)

Stanbury looks up the river and down the river, aware of alternatives, but coming to no decision. But bridges, which are naturally frequently present in such physical and psychological scenery, are – often though not consistently – places of decision. Lily Dale's bridge, where she kisses her lover from the sphere of the Great House and the great world, is a meeting place. Johnny Eames has his bridge too, a different bridge.

13. Johnny Eames on the bridge: Millais' illustration for *The Small House at Allington*, chapter 54

Here, in the hope of his boyhood, when Lily was scarcely more than a child, he carved his letters, LILY. In a chapter called "The First Visit to the Bridge," just before his proposal, he returns there to clean out the letters with his pocket-knife. Presently, in "The Second Visit to the Bridge," when he has been rejected, he goes back there again and, "With deep, rough gashes in the wood, cut out Lily's name from the rail," and watches the chips as they are carried away by the stream (*SHA*, II, 307, 340). The image is a familiar one: in the same way Arthur Clennam in *Little Dorrit* watched the roses and his own romantic hopes float away simultaneously down the Thames. The carving of names on wood is a custom hackneyed enough to be satirized in *As You Like It*, but Johnny is, after all, a very ordinary young man, and it is part of his appeal that he has the common touch. Trollope's imagery here is not grandly original, but it is exact and convincing in being adapted to the self-dramatizing impulse of the character at the moment. Johnny's depradations on the bridge rail are an accurate and even beautiful record of the fluctuations of his mind, and bear pondering. His excised "LILY" is like the deleted "bravo" at the foot of Yorick's sermon in *Tristram Shandy*, a touching record of a man's estimation of himself.

Trollope, as a chronicler of bureaucracy and official relations – and relations within the domestic circle can be official too – has specialized in what he calls "appanages of majesty" – the policeman's bull's-eye lamp, the clergyman's gaiters, the gardener's dunghill, the barrister's wig. In a memorable mock-heroic passage in *The Warden*, the clothing of the archdeacon receives as much attention as the armour of Hector, and Trollope has a field-day with emblems and allegory:

> As the archdeacon stood up to make his speech, . . . he looked like an ecclesiastical statue placed there, as a fitting impersonation of the church militant here on earth; his shovel hat, large, new, and well-pronounced, a churchman's hat in every inch, declared the profession as plainly as does the Quaker's broad brim; his heavy eyebrows, large open eyes, and full mouth and chin expressed the solidity of his order; the broad chest, amply covered with fine cloth, told how well to do was its estate; one hand ensconced within his pocket, evinced the practical hold which our mother church keeps on her temporal possessions; and the other, loose for action, was ready to fight if need be in her defence; and, below these, the decorous breeches, and neat black gaiters showing so admirably that well-turned leg, betokened the decency, the outward beauty and grace of our church establishment. (60–61)

Trollope would not have written such a passage in his later novels, when he has largely discarded the mock-heroic mode. But he does not cease to be conscious of the expressive paraphernalia with which his people sur-round themselves, and of the extent to which clothes, props, and ap-purtenances are of the essence of their identity. There is all the difference in the world between the Archdeacon clad in his ecclesiastical accoutrements and the archdeacon in his nightcap, as his wife knows very well. Those appanages are not mere external trappings, donned to make an impression on others. The "inner man" himself is modified by them. It is as though his veins ran through the fabric and seams of his costume, as well as within his own flesh. Chaffanbrass out of court is simply "an ugly, dirty old man" (*PR*, II, 218). But in court, where his wig is his special weapon, thrust this way and that on his head as though it were a stag's antlers, he is transformed to the great man before whom every witness must tremble.

One of Phineas's most bitter moments is that when, under suspicion of murder, he is asked by the police "whether he had any objection to change [his shirt] in their presence, – as it might be necessary, after the examination, that it should be detained as evidence. He did so, in the presence of all the men assembled; but the humiliation of doing it almost broke his heart. Then they searched among his linen, clean and dirty . . ." (*PR*, II, 96–7). That is a fine touch, allowing us to understand Phineas's acute sensitivity through the direct image of the exposure of his skin. The shirt and the dirty linen do their duty in conveying Phineas's state of mind.

I find James Kincaid's assertion, in his otherwise penetrating essay, rather surprising. "Trollope's realism . . . is oddly immaterial. It is hardly *seen* at all. Rejecting the Romantic symbol as part of a rejection of all determinant objects, Trollope seeks for a world independent of objects. . . . Dickens gives to objects a sinister and astonishing life, but Trollope simply assumes a world where objects are so unimportant as not to be there."[8] It is true that in comparison with Dickens's, Trollope's objects are tame and domesticated things. Nor does he have Thackeray's exuberance of specificity that finds expression in catalogues – catalogues of the pictures on the walls, the buttons on a jacket, the contents of a drawer. But he does very acutely place his characters among a given set of appurtenances, places and things that express and affect them, as among a given set of circumstances.

Is it true too that his emphasis is not sensuous. We do not go to Trollope for stimulation of our taste buds and olfactory organs; perhaps not much for visual satisfaction either, though he is very good at creating the sense of how one person strikes the eyes of another – Johnny Eames' shuddering memory of Amelia Roper with her hair down, or the typical male reaction to Lopez's style of good looks. One context in which he does go in for meticulous description is in the in-troduction of his characters – more than most writers he is given to cataloguing the features of his characters, and giving details as to texture of hair and whiskers, colour of eyes, thickness of lip, prominence of teeth, and so on.[9] These passages have less significance, I think, than his descriptions of houses and topography: we cannot read character from appearance as we can, say, with Chaucer.[10] But Trollope seems to have needed to go through all this before he could himself visualize his characters and so breathe life into them: the descriptions serve *his* ends, if not the reader's.

But, though so much may be granted, Kincaid's statement does less than justice to the life of the novels as it may be felt through vividly imagined settings and objects, and the way in which the physical world is enlivened by the passions and aspirations and weaknesses of the characters who inhabit it. The things are there, and are endowed with a certain life and significance by the people who encounter them. Alice's paper-knife, given her by John Grey, becomes as though red-hot when George Vavasor handles it, and learns of its donor; his own present to her, a ruby and diamond ring, is irreparably damaged by his violence, and will never be worn as a pledge of a love that does not exist (*CYFH*, II, 71–2, 77). Silverbridge's ring will not fit Lady Mabel's finger; and so on. Trollope's jewel imagery, which I have discussed as it operates in *The Eustace Diamonds*, is almost as pervasive through these novels as George Eliot's more overt symbolism of jewellery in *Romola* or *Daniel Deronda*.

Trollope's novels are more amenable to symbolic analysis, I think, than most of his critics have found them. Like so many things about him – his style, his view of his own artistic achievement, his preference for the low mimetic mode – his imagery is unobtrusive, but it is none the less effective. The places and things in his novels have their own significance, their delicately suggested part in the pattern of the novel and of his characters' lives.

The discussion between Isabel and Madame Merle on houses and things in *The Portrait of a Lady* has perhaps been overworked, but nevertheless I will venture to use it again. Isabel, the individualist, maintains her own proud separateness, insisting that her identity is an essence apart from her clothes, her possessions, her surroundings; and she says scornfully that she cares nothing for her suitor's house.

> 'That's very crude of you [replies Madame Merle]. When you've lived as long as I you'll see that every human being has his shell and that you must take the shell into account. By the shell I mean the whole envelope of circumstances. There's no such thing as an isolated man or woman; we're each of us made up of some cluster of appurtenances. What shall we call our "self"? Where does it begin? where does it end? It overflows into everything that belongs to us – and then it flows back again. I know a large part of myself is in the clothes I choose to wear. I've a great respect for *things!* One's self – for other people – is one's expression of one's self; and one's house,

one's furniture, one's garments, the books one reads, the company one keeps – these things are all expressive.' (Chapter 19)

Trollope is a novelist who takes the shell into account. It is his phoney romantic, Lizzie, who reflects, "What a tawdry world was this, in which clothes and food and houses are necessary!" Her longing for the insubstantial world of *Queen Mab*, where the soul will be "all-beautiful in naked purity," is at once invalidated when we learn she longs for it only because there "no one would claim her necklace from her, and . . . the man at the stables would not be so disagreeably punctual in sending in his bill" (*ED*, 195). Trollope sides neither with Lizzie nor with Isabel: his exquisitely acute sense of context, and his sensitivity to the relatedness of things, make him altogether of Madame Merle's way of thinking.

10 The Author

In this chapter on the author, I shall not be talking about the historical Anthony Trollope, who has received two biographical studies in recent years,[1] but rather about the authorial presence as we perceive it in the novels. Notwithstanding the critical orthodoxy of the first half of this century, which has advocated the total withdrawal of the artist from his work, I find that our sense of an authorial presence has a great deal to do with Trollope's artistic success, and with his achievement in being, as C. P. Snow calls him, obsessively readable.[2] Trollope, like most Victorian novelists, would have reacted strongly against the Joycean image for the artist as a being remote and, to all outward appearances, detached from his own work, "invisible, refined out of existence, indifferent, paring his fingernails."[3] He, like his model Thackeray, valued a close relation with his readers, and took pains to create it and maintain it. David Aitken has pointed out, "Trollope's writing has a marked personal quality, which is difficult to describe in general terms – and difficult, indeed, quite to put one's finger on at the outset – and yet is unmistakably there and unmistakably appealing."[4] I will make my own attempt at trying to characterize that personal quality in the novels.

Occasionally, as a slightly embarrassed and self-effacing figure thrust in from the wings onto his own stage, he introduces himself among his own characters, as to a cry for "Author!" from the audience. Remember Mr. Pollock, the hunting novelist in *Can You Forgive Her?* The Pollock/Trollope name juggle is not unlike the Popplecourt/Palliser one in *The Duke's Children*. We hear of one insignificant Mr. Grindley that he is inferior to a banker and to two brewers and "even to Mr. Pollock the heavy-weight literary gentleman" (*CYFH*, I, 208). That "even" is Trollope's little joke, like Johnson's definition of a lexicographer as "a poor drudge." The hunting episode at Edgehill is delightful for the Trollopian, as there Trollope puts into the mouth of his characters all the mockery that he knew his club acquaintances aimed at him. "By

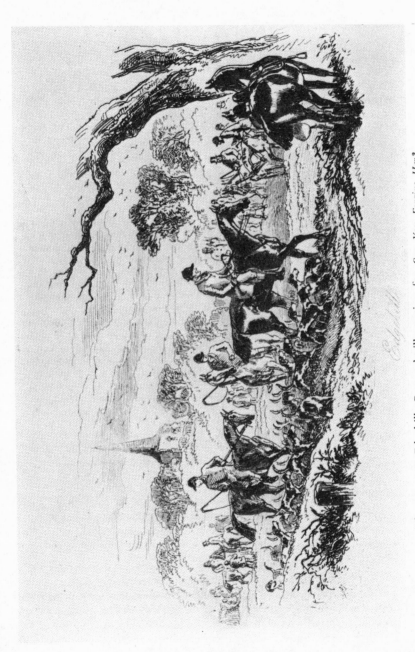

14. The meet at Edgehill: Browne's illustration for *Can You Forgive Her?*, chapter 17

George, there's Pollock!" says Maxwell. "I'll bet half a crown that he's come down from London this morning, that he was up all night last night, and that he tells us so three times before the hounds go out of the paddock" (210). True to form, Pollock burbles, "By George, . . . just down from London by the 8.30 from Euston Square, and got over here from Windsor in a trap. . . . I had to leave Onslow Cresent at a quarter before eight, and I did three hours' work before I started" (214).[5] On this occasion Pollock takes a bet that he will see more of the hunt than Maxwell, and loses it. His fifteen stone prove too much for his horse, which at last "refused a little hedge, and there was not another trot to be got out of him" (226). Trollope allows himself a little lyric outburst about his on-stage self: "few knew the sad misfortunes which poor Pollock sometimes encountered; – the muddy ditches in which he was left; the despair with which he would stand by his unfortunate horse when the poor brute could no longer move across some deep-ploughed field . . ." (221). There is the writer of the *Autobiography* plainly enough: the brash and extrovert exterior, the boasting about early morning labours, the apparent cheerful indifference to the opinion of others; and behind that, the hint of the weary effort by which it must all be maintained, and the acute sensitivity to judgment that is testified by this very image of himself as he supposes others see him.

Another novelist who appears briefly as a poor drudge, convenient to be made into mincement under Chaffanbrass's examination, is Mr. Bouncer in *Phineas Redux*. Mr. Bouncer attempts to stand on his dignity, a posture which Chaffanbrass will by no means allow. All the literary information in the examination is produced by the barrister, not the novelist, who in his extremity is "quite unable to think of the plot of a single novel" (II, 232). He makes no very brilliant showing:

> 'The plot of a novel should, I imagine, be constructed in accordance with human nature?'
> 'Certainly,' said Mr. Bouncer.
> 'You have murders in novels?'
> 'Sometimes,' said Mr. Bouncer, who had himself done many murders in his time. [A murder trial was the climax of Trollope's first novel, as well as of the present one.] (*PR*, II, 231–2)

"The unfortunate author" loses all his dignity under Chaffanbrass's questions, and is dismissed with insulting patronage.

"The poor fictionist" alike calls for our tolerant sympathy when he talks explicitly and as the present author about the pitfalls of the novelist's career. As James Kincaid has forcefully demonstrated, Trollope is very much a self-conscious author, and is not shy of talking about the process of writing while he is in the midst of it.[6] But here too his characteristic tone is self-deprecatory and apologetic:

> The poor fictionist very frequently finds himself to have been wrong in his description of things in general, and is told so roughly by the critics, and tenderly by the friends of his bosom. . . . He catches salmon in October; or shoots his partridges in March. . . . He opens the opera-houses before Easter, and makes Parliament sit on a Wednesday evening. And then those terrible meshes of the Law! How is a fictionist, in these excited days, to create the needed biting interest without legal difficulties; and how again is he to steer his little bark clear of so many rocks . . .? (*PF*, I, 325)

Of course this is to a large extent a front. Trollope, as he knows in his heart of hearts, is better able than most poor fictionists to steer his little bark through the terrible meshes of the law, as through the hunting field, the partridge-shooting, and the Cabinet meetings. In the same novel, à propos of Phineas's improvement in parliamentary speaking, he tosses off the comparison, "He knew that words would come readily enough to him, and that he had learned the task of turning his thoughts quickly into language while standing with a crowd of listeners around him, – as a practised writer does when seated in his chair" (*PF*, II, 418). The analogy comes readily to hand, because there he is, the practised writer, turning out the right rhythms at that moment. We are reminded of the passage in the *Autobiography* on the uses of familiarity, which are so to train the writer's ear "that he shall be able to weigh the rhythm of every word as it falls from his pen" (203). But the self-deprecatory pose suits Trollope, and he adopts it often. It is an appeal for sympathy.

Trollope's authorial tone is not chatty and colloquial like Thackeray's; on the contrary, his diction in the narration (dialogue is another matter) is rather formal than otherwise, and abounds in decorative inversions and slightly archaic usage. Still less is he outrageously erratic, like Sterne. And yet a close relation with his reader is as much part of his strategy as theirs. "Oh, thou, my reader, whose sympathies are in truth the great and only aim of my work," he apostrophises us, at one point (*ED*, 315). In spite of the deliberate inflation of style, I am inclined to believe that, "in truth," he meant what he said, – as much as he could mean any such large generalization. The sympathies of his reader were immensely important to him, even if they were not quite the only aim of his work. George Bartley's letter, which condemned *The Noble Jilt* on the grounds that there was no character with whom the audience could sympathize, had early been declared "critical gospel" in Trollope's creed (*A*, 74).

Can You Forgive Her?, with its personal appeal directed at the reader in the second person, is one of the few novels extant that gets the reader right into the title. That appeal is followed up in the novel itself in the discussion of Alice's misdemeanours:

> But can you forgive her, delicate reader? Or am I asking the question too early in my story? For myself, I have forgiven her. The story of her struggle has been present to my mind for many years. . . . And you also must forgive her before we close the book, or else my story will have been told amiss. (*CYFH*, I, 474)

The young James's irritable reaction to this kind of appeal – "The question is, Can we forgive Miss Vavasor? Of course we can, and forget her, too, for that matter" – is quite in character with his later strictures against Trollope for his "terrible crime" in admitting his novels are fictions.[7] Both the question and the admission are authorial intrusions of the kind that Jamesian critics deplore. But by such "intrusions" Trollope maintained his necessary contact with his reader. In his apostrophe to the reader he has included other figures of his own particular rhetoric. "Am I asking the question too early?" – he wonders, pausing, as in a lecture, for the slower students to catch up and for the faster ones to respond. "For myself, I have forgiven her" – he confesses: not that I would want to bully you into my position – I realize you have your own opinions. For himself, he is also ready to add the personal touch about the many years that Alice's struggle has occupied his mind. (He does not at this point include the painful story of the rejection of *The Noble Jilt* a dozen years before – but the acquaintance has so far advanced that the reader feels such intimate revelations are only just round the corner.) "My story will have been told amiss" – he admits humbly, envisaging the possibility of failure, in order to capture his audience's compassion. And throughout such a passage runs the earnest and almost spoken plea that we shall allow our author to convince us; that we should listen to him, hear his case, understand his point of view. That is often Trollope's tone; and not just in visible and explicit appeals like this, but invisibly, in the choice of words, the time he takes to explain, the filling in on background information, the painstaking attention he pays to the business of keeping his reader with him, even if it means repeating information. For instance, late in the same novel, and on our second meeting with a very minor character, he is cheerfully ready to furnish this timely reminder: "Then he . . . walked up the street till he reached the house of Mr. Jones, the pugilistic tailor. The reader, no doubt, has forgotten all he ever knew of Mr. Jones, the pugilistic tailor. It can soon be told again. . . ." (*CYFH*, II, 402).

His use of the summing-up final sentence of a paragraph, so that his prose moves in long rhythms like Spenserian stanzas, is another sign of the same solicitude. (It is noticeable, in his one substantially revised novel, that when he had to prune the manuscript of *The Duke's Children*

the final sentences of paragraphs are the characteristic cuts: being sum-
maries of already stated matter, they were dispensable, though he must
have regretted the sacrifice of his felicitous phrasing.)

His paragraphs are generally models of lucidity, beginning with a
sentence that introduces a proposition or a problem, proceeding with
an elaboration of its intricacies, ending with a summary or at least an
overview of ground covered. Here is an opening sentence from near the
beginning of *The Eustace Diamonds*, on Lizzie's covert use of jewels to trap
Sir Florian when she is supposed to be in mourning: "Lady Linlithgow
saw the jewels come back, one by one, ring added to ring on the little
taper fingers, the rubies for the neck, and the pendant yellow earrings."
Now the complications are unfolded: as a conscientious woman Lady
Linlithgow disapproves of Lizzie's use of lures, but she also partly enters
into Lizzie's campaign to catch a rich husband. The conflict of the guar-
dian's worldliness with her conscience is then elaborated, and in the
process we come to know a good deal of her character, and Trollope has
some fun in the crackling enumeration of her vices and virtues:

> Lady Linlithgow was worldly, stingy, ill-tempered, selfish, and mean.
> Lady Linlithgow would cheat a butcher out of a mutton-chop, or a
> cook out of a month's wages, if she could do so with some slant of
> legal wind in her favour. ... But nevertheless she recognized certain
> duties, – and performed them, though she hated them. She went to
> church, not merely that people might see her there, – as to which in
> truth she cared nothing, – but because she thought it was right.
> (*ED*, 4)

Understand this exactly, insists the narrator: it may seem like a contradiction, and certainly it is surprising that she should be both so bad
and yet by her own lights a dutiful woman; but people are not simple
organisms, and you must understand the balance of contrary motives in
this one. From your own knowledge of human nature you may conclude
that so mean and wordly an old harridan, if she goes to church, must go
there only for another wordly motive. But no, in this case that's not how
it was; strange as it may seem, in fact – "in truth" – she went there
because she thought it was right. (I exaggerate the explaining tone for
emphasis, but that tone is there, running beneath the vision and its
expression.) The final sentence neatly rounds off the paragraph,
bringing Lizzie's jewels and Lady Linlithgow's character together: "Now
a marriage with Sir Florian Eustace would be very splendid, and
therefore [Lady Linlithgow] was unable to go into the matter of the
jewels with that rigour which in other circumstances she would certainly
have displayed." But it is more than a summary (if it were that, we could
skip the body of the paragraph) – its force and irony can be grasped only
if one has carefully followed the preceding matter. The opening "now"

is characteristic too: it asserts again the stance of explainer to eager audience. The word has virtually lost its use as an adverb of time, to become a comfortable conjunction with no more force than as a mild appeal that we should pay special attention to what follows. ("Now you must know and understand, O Best Beloved . . ." – as Kipling addresses his child reader in the *Just So Stories*.)[8] Lest I should do Trollope an injustice by the insertion of such crude rewordings of what he delicately and often wittily suggests, let me add one more of his "now" sentences, which shows not only the author careful and discriminating, but also the author ironic and satirical:

> Mr. Roby had never quite seconded Sir Orlando's ardour in that matter of the four ships, and Sir Orlando in his pride of place had ventured to snub Mr. Roby. Now Mr. Roby could bear a snubbing perhaps as well as any other official subordinate, – but he was one who would study the question and assure himself that it was, or that it was not, worth his while to bear it. (*PM*, I, 438)

Trollope reminds one often of an accommodating lecturer, a personal presence responding to the needs of a present audience, humorous often, and patient and engagingly concerned with his students' full understanding of the subject in hand. Are you with me? Am I going too fast? Shall I explain that again? Don't hesitate to ask a question. Such is the tone behind the narration. And such solicitude and accommodation cannot but win the attention and the loyalty of his hearers. You have to keep listening, keep reading – the fellow obviously cares so much about you.

His tone of careful explanation is often perceptible when he is accounting to the reader for his characters' behaviour by drawing attention to their limited points of view. The reader has been given such complete information about surrounding characters and events that he has to be reminded how small a proportion of knowledge falls to the share of the participating characters. Why is Frank Greystock fool enough to be attracted by so manifest a little liar as Lizzie, the reader may wonder. The narrator explains: "It can hardly be too strongly asserted that Lizzie Greystock did not appear to Frank as she has been made to appear to the reader. In all this affair of the necklace he was beginning to believe that she was really an ill-used woman; and as to other traits in Lizzie's character . . . it must be remembered that beauty reclining in a man's arms does go far towards washing white the lovely blackamoor" (*ED*, 317). Even so disgusting a character as Quintus Slide of the People's Banner, when he is gnashing his teeth at being prevented from publishing his ugly gossip, gains this conscientious concession from his creator: "It must be acknowledged on behalf of this editor that he did in truth believe that he had been hindered from doing good" (*PR*, I, 287).

There follows a fine ironic passage, written from Slide's point of view, on the irreproachable moral standing of the editor of the People's Banner. "It must be remembered . . .," "It must be acknowledged . . ." – those are the characteristic little phrases by which Trollope keeps his reader's attention, alerts him to conflicting views and extenuating circumstances. He really is a very good lecturer.

I have drawn attention before to Trollope's characteristic phrase, "in truth." It is one more of his little holds on our attention, his signals that our author is to be trusted. A much larger proportion of the narrative commentary than one at first realizes is dramatic, in the sense that it proceeds not direct from an omniscient author but as sifted through the consciousness of the characters. Such is Slide's self-righteous reflection that I have just referred to. But Trollope is careful to flag his internal monologues as not carrying the full authority of the author. The "in truth" phrase generally marks the insight that we can rely on. So in an interview between Phineas and Lady Laura when she begins by rebuking him for the duel, and then trails off: "Neither of them knew what was taking place between them; but she was, in truth, gradually submitting herself again to this man's influence" (*PF*, II, 22).

It is not surprising that Trollope should have irritated some readers by defeating their expectation for the long-term suspense created by the whodunnit. Don't worry, he tells us; "let the gentle-hearted reader be under no apprehension whatsoever. It is not destined that Eleanor shall marry Mr. Slope or Bertie Stanhope" (*Barchester Towers*, 129). That passage, it is traditionally supposed, is the one James had in mind when he spoke of the terrible crime of the author in conceding to the reader "that he and this trusting friend are only 'making believe.' "[9] Similarly, "The reader need hardly be told that, as regards this great offence [the murder of Bonteen], Phineas Finn was as white as snow" (*PR*, II, 92). That one irritated Hugh Walpole.[10] And, in case we are fretting about the whereabouts of Lizzie's necklace, our author sets our minds at ease: "The Eustace diamonds were locked up in a small safe . . . beneath the establishment of Messrs. Harter and Benjamin. . . . The chronicler states this at once, as he scorns to keep from his reader any secret that is known to himself" (*ED*, 473). This stated policy of openness has its uses; he reminds us again that *he* is no remote and godlike artist paring his fingernails, but a very human presence, concerned for the trust and loyalty of his audience. Of course he manages to have it both ways: he enters into a compact of frankness with his readers, *and* he maintains his own kind of suspense. He tells us whom Eleanor Bold won't marry, but he keeps us interested on the question of whom she will; he tells us Phineas didn't do the murder, but not how the trial will come out; he tells us where the diamonds are, but not how they got there. He knows to a nicety just which beans he can afford to spill – just enough of them to serve his purpose.

One of his strengths is the running commentary, a kind of practical criticism on the course of an argument, the turns of thought in a passage of reflection, the composition or reception of a letter. The reader is not allowed to skim; he is made to sit down with the author and characters to respond in detail to this or that appeal or turn of phrase. The letter with commentary, for instance, is a minor genre of which Trollope must be the master. Spooner's letter of proposal for Adelaide Palliser is directly followed by a record of the argument between Spooner and his cousin on its composition. The letter ends with a postscript:

> 'As I believe that Miss Palliser is fond of books, it may be well to tell her that there is an uncommon good library at Spoon Hall. I shall have no objection to go abroad for the honeymoon for three or four months in the summer.'
>
> The postscript was the Squire's own, and was inserted in opposition to the cousin's judgment. 'She won't come for the sake of the books,' said the cousin. But the Squire thought that the attractions should be piled up. 'I wouldn't talk of the honeymoon till I'd got her to come round a little,' said the cousin. The Squire thought that the cousin was falsely delicate, and pleaded that all girls like to be taken abroad when they're married. (*PR*, I, 315)

The whole Spooner-Adelaide subplot is not one of Trollope's most successful pieces of comic writing, but it has its moments, like this debate on the art of letters of proposal. Behind such a scene is Trollope's implied faith that if you only look at something closely enough it will become interesting: something like Constable's belief that there is nothing ugly – no object or scene that the effects of light and perspective will not make beautiful and significant. It is that quality of Trollope's that James called "his great, his inestimable merit . . . a complete appreciation of the usual"[11] – (a tribute which I find more appreciative and less patronizing than some of Trollope's apologists). The commentaries on letters are often included in parenthesis in the letter itself, and again we are made aware of Trollope's painstaking concern to keep the reader with him: Lady Midlothian writes to Alice on her engagement to Grey, " 'I was heartily glad to find that your choice had done you so much credit.' (If the reader has read Alice's character as I have meant it should be read, it will thoroughly be understood that this was wormwood to her)" (*CYFH*, I, 238). In this case the commentary is explicitly directed to the reader, but often it proceeds as a running record of the correspondent's reaction, so that we have something like dialogue, but with one of the participants limited for the moment to mental notes. I allow myself one more example, from Silverbridge's letter to his father on the election campaign at Polpenno:

'It was beastly work!' The Duke made another memorandum to in-
struct his son that no gentleman above the age of a schoolboy should
allow himself to use such a word in such a sense. 'We had to go about
in the rain up to our knees in mud for eight or nine days, always
saying the same thing. And of course all that we said was bosh.'
Another memorandum – or rather two, one as to the slang, and
another as to the expediency of teaching something to the poor voters
on such occasions. 'Our only comfort was that the Carbottle people
were quite as badly off as us.' Another memorandum as to the gram-
mar. The absence of Christian charity did not at the moment affect
the Duke. 'I made ever so many speeches, till at last it seemed to be
quite easy.' Here there was a very grave memorandum. Speeches easy
to young speakers are generally very difficult to old listeners. 'But of
course it was all bosh.' This required no separate memorandum. (*DC*,
II, 154–5)

There is the author as critic of his own text, though managing the
proceeding through another character, and supplying his readers with
full and explicit notes on the minutiae of this communication and its
reception. I have used the letter with commentary as an example,
because it is convenient in being especially characteristic of Trollope;
but the same close attention to phrasing and timbre may be found in the
recording of dialogue or passages of reflection. Listen; read carefully;
respond – he keeps asking us, tacitly.

Trollope manages to maintain close contact with the reader on the
one hand, and with the content of his story on the other. He often
writes, both sympathetically and satirically, of people who buttonhole
one another: lovers do it – "she twisted one of her little fingers into one
of his buttonholes" (*Orley Farm*, II, 407) – and bores do it, like Sir
Timothy Beeswax (*DC*, II, 282) and the American minister in *He Knew
He Was Right*. But he is himself one of the most practised buttonholers in
the history of English fiction. It is his ability to stay *in touch* that partially
accounts for his obsessive readability.

The sense of touch is always important in the content of Trollope's
novels. He has a sensitivity almost like Sterne's to the human skin and
the human fingers as mediums of communication. In *The Warden* there
are audible echoes of Sterne, and Mr. Harding is a descendent of Uncle
Toby's family tree (happy thought!) as Slope is of Dr. Slop's. Uncle
Toby's whistling of Lillabullero, when at a loss for words, is echoed in
Harding's habitual gesture of playing on his imaginary violoncello, even
to the eighteenth-century usage: "The warden still looked mutely in his
face, making the slightest possible passes with an imaginary fiddle bow,
and stopping, as he did so, sundry imaginary strings with the fingers of
his other hand. 'Twas his constant consolation in conversational
troubles" (56). Like Uncle Toby, he can communicate more effectively

by gestures than by words, as in the touching little scene with the bishop: "The two old men were sitting near each other – so near that the bishop was able to lay his hand upon the other's knee, and did so with a gentle pressure. Mr. Harding well knew what that pressure meant" (38). There are many other such moments in Trollope's novels. Think of Plantagenet Palliser, Duke of Omnium, that agonizingly reticent, distant man, who has mastered the science of communicating a financial statement when on his legs in the house, but is so crippled when it comes to expressing love: "Then the father looked round the room furtively, and seeing that the door was shut, and that they were assuredly alone, he put out his hand and gently stroked his son's hair. It was almost a caress" (*DC*, I, 253). This physical communion is of course not always an expression of tenderness. Johnny Eames feels the irresistible impulse to plant his fist in Crosbie's eye, and is filled afterwards with a warm sense that *consummatum est*. (There are many such incidents in the novels, suggesting Trollope retained a belligerent public-school-boy's instinct in punching and thrashing). He felt the need for the laying on of hands, whether in tenderness or enmity. He manages touch well in a sexual context, too, where he enters into great detail on the approaches to physical intimacy. "When a woman really loves a man, as she loved this man," we hear of Emily Wharton, "there is a desire to touch him which quivers at her finger'-ends, . . . an inclination to be near him which affects every motion of her body" (*PM*, II, 311). There are memorable extensions of fingers and entwinings of hands and arms in the novels, like Frank Gresham's embrace of Mary on the donkey in *Doctor Thorne* (the donkey, reminiscent of Tristram's, evidently approves [361]); or Madame Max's irresistible pressure on the old Duke, exerted with one finger, that makes him break his rule about never dining out: " 'You must come.' . . . And she put out her finger and touched his arm as she spoke. Her hand was very fair, and her fingers were bright with rich gems" (*PF*, II, 214–5). Her finger carries the day; later she extracts a proposal from him by her masterly handling of choice grapes (II, 255). The Duke is fairly mesmerized by her hands.

The contact between the sexes can be informed by sexual aggression too, like Sir Griffin's unwelcome pawing of Lucinda, or Eleanor Bold's resounding slap in the face of Mr. Slope – the only answer she could make at the moment that would get through to him.

But I am concerned with Trollope's particular sensitivity to contact in a figurative as well as a literal sense. My comments here are bound to be impressionistic, but it is an impression I am talking about, an impression that Trollope keeps his own tenacious hand on your sleeve, a touch as irresistible as Madame Max's to the Duke, and makes you want to keep listening, keep hearing. He is like the Ancient Mariner. First he holds you with his skinny hand: then he fixes you with his glittering eye.[12]

15. Madame Goesler touches the Duke of Omnium: Millais' illustration for
   Phineas Finn, chapter 57

How does he do it? The answer must be enormous and multiform, but I think that one decisive constituent is his choice of proximity, both to his readers and to the action he describes. A writer like Fielding chooses characteristically to stand rather far from the events he describes (though close to his reader), and gives one a sense of nations and classes marshalling for and against the Jacobite cause as a continuing context for the less distanced depiction of the loves and adventures of Tom Jones. Others – say like Sterne in the eighteenth century or Virginia Woolf in our own – specialize in the close-up vision of men and women in the intimacies of their conduct, in the minute fluctuations of warmth and withdrawal that are the moment to moment history of human consciousness. Thackerary is one who, as it were, uses the zoom lens, so that he can display before us the whole panoply of the armies clashing on the field of Waterloo ("the columns of the Imperial Guard marched up the hill of St. Jean, at length and at once to sweep the English from the height . . ."), and then focus minutely on the significant detail of George Osborne, "lying on his face, dead, with a bullet through his heart" (*Vanity Fair*, ch. 32). Proust is I suppose the closest observer of the detail of human sensibility, and he includes the reflective and analytic faculty, so that the instantaneous perception of finger, tongue or nostril can become the impulse of pages of introspective analysis. More recent writers, like Robbe-Grillet and Becket, and indeed painters too,[13] have gone beyond the eyeball-to-eyeball distance to make the workings of the mind itself, unrelated to external circumstances, their subject-matter.

George Eliot, in tune with Lewes's physiological experiments as he probed the sensitive tissue of polyps and miscroscopic organisms, was alive to the fact that the thing seen itself varies according to how closely you look at it. "Whereas under a weak lens you may seem to see a creature exhibiting an active voracity, . . . a stronger lens reveals to you certain tiniest hairlets which make vortices for these victims while the swallower waits passively" (*Middlemarch*, ch. 6). Trollope, less analytical but perhaps more patiently observant than George Eliot, has made up his mind how closely he wants to watch, how much of the life of a given character he has room to show us. He has not opted for the microscopic examination of subject matter, or the most intimate proximity to his reader, as Sterne does. Sterne, or rather Tristram, attempts to involve his reader with the kind of intensity of feeling that belongs only to prolonged and intense intimacy, so that eventually "nothing which has touched me will be thought trifling in its nature, or tedious in its telling" (*Tristram Shandy*, I, ch. 6). That is an ambitious undertaking, and Sterne, to give him his due, succeeds brilliantly in his fits and starts. Trollope is not so ambitious nor so brilliant – at least not in the same way. But what he has achieved, I think, is a choice of proximity, not quite intimate, not too distant, that will have the maximum appeal for most people. We all know how we are apt to be more engaged in the workings and personal conflicts of a department or college than of an institute or a whole university, more absorbed in the life of a village or a local chapter than of a city or a national organization. Trollope certainly ranged well beyond the "two or three families in a country village" that Jane Austen said were the very thing for a novelist; but like her he had the instinct to place himself close to his subject. Though he may range over continents and aspire to describe alike low life and the conduct of cabinet meetings, whatever he observes he observes as though he were there at the same time, in the same room or the same lane, within earshot. He puts us close, close to his people and their lives. He explains, not from second to second but from movement to movement, just what motives move them, just what stimuli make them wince with embarrassment or throb with delight. He does not make them our brothers and sisters, fathers and uncles, as Sterne seems to do; nor does he try, like Charlotte Brontë, to make us identify ourselves with the characters. But he does keep us close enough to them to make us feel *in touch* – to maintain the interest we feel in friends and acquaintances who keep us regularly informed of their movements with just enough detail to maintain our absorbed interest.

Look at Sexty Parker signing a bill, for instance. Sexty Parker is only a minor character in a vast novel, and one who in aggregate, and in looking back on the novel, is perhaps not very vivid or memorable. But for the moment in which he is observed, the observation is total and engrossing.

> 'Oh, I ain't afraid,' said Sexty, taking his pen and writing his name across the bill. But even before the signature was finished, when his eye was taken away from the face of his companion and fixed on the disagreeable piece of paper beneath his hand, he repented of what he was doing. He almost arrested his signature half-way. He did hesitate, but had not pluck enough to stop his hand. (*PM*, I, 10)

Perhaps the reader does not care one way or the other about the ultimate fate of Sexty; but for these moments – watch him! will he stop in mid-signature? – we are spellbound. Just look at something closely enough, and it is bound to be interesting.

A more extended example is the scene between the Duke and Popplecourt, who are meeting for the first time. Popplecourt has been told that his suit of Lady Mary is favoured, and the Duke has on principle resolved that Popplecourt is a respectable young man, fit to fill the role of the suitable suitor for Mary to replace the unsuitable one – the Duke's own role in the courtship of Glencora. It is therefore a tense meeting for both. Poor Popplecourt is not to know that the Duke hates the very mention of Tregear's name; that he disapproves of shooting, and regrets his second son's expertise in it, which is not matched by expertise in any less frivolous pursuit; that he has his own marriage plans for his eldest son; and that he is ashamed of his daughter's predilection for a man below her in rank. But the reader knows all this – and if he has forgotten Trollope reminds him – and can savour each moment in which Popplecourt treads roughly on each of the Duke's corns:

> 'I've been shooting in Scotland with Silverbridge, and Gerald, and Reginald Dobbes, and Nidderdale, – and that fellow Tregear, who is so thick with Silverbridge.'
>
> 'Indeed!'
>
> 'I'm told that Lord Gerald is going to be the great shot of his day,' said Lady Cantrip.
>
> 'It is a distinction,' said the Duke bitterly.
>
> 'He did not beat me by so much,' continued Popplecourt. 'I think Tregear did the best with his rifle. One morning he potted three. . . . And Gerald is a regular brick.' The Duke bowed. 'Silverbridge used always to be going off to Killancodlem, where there were a lot of ladies. He is very sweet, you know, on this American girl whom you have here.' Again the Duke winced. 'Dobbes is awfully good as to making out the shooting, but then he is a tyrant. Nevertheless I agree with him, if you mean to do a thing you should do it.'
>
> 'Certainly,' said the Duke. 'But you should make up your mind first whether the thing is worth doing.'
>
> 'Just so,' said Popplecourt. 'And as grouse and deer together are about the best things out, most of us made up our minds that it was worth doing. But that fellow Tregear would argue it out. He said a gentleman oughtn't to play billiards as well as a marker.'
>
> 'I think he was right,' said the Duke. . . .
>
> 'I cannot say I [like Tregear]. He thinks so much of himself. Of course he is very intimate with Silverbridge, and that is all that any one knows of him.' The Duke bowed almost haughtily, though why he bowed he could hardly have explained to himself. Lady Cantrip bit her lips in disgust. 'He's just the fellow,' continued Popplecourt, 'to think that some princess has fallen in love with him.' Then the Duke left the room. (*DC*, II, 63–4)

It scarcely dawns on Popplecourt what a mess he is making of this interview with his prospective father-in-law. But if the reader has read the Duke's character as Trollope meant it should be read – as Trollope might have interjected again – it will be understood that all this was wormwood to him. We have been brought so close up against the conversation that we can register and make mental notes on Popplecourt's relentless progress from one faux pas to the next. Some of them are explained, in case we should miss them – "This was unfortunate, because it recalled Tregear to the Duke's mind," we are told at the beginning of the conversation (63). But some we have the pleasure of recognizing for ourselves, because we have received such careful coaching in advance, so that the termination of the scene, after the reference to princesses falling in love with Tregear, "Then the Duke left the room," speaks volumes – to the schooled ear of the reader if not to Popplecourt.

Trollope can retain our fascinated attention in passages of reflection too, like the long one in *The Prime Minister* in which Glencora ponders the Duke's charge of "vulgarity," rejects it, accepts it, justifies herself in the face of it. The mental journey is anchored at key points by reference to the physical occupation of letter-writing: "She escaped, to the writing of her letters she said, almost before the meal was done. 'Vulgarity!' she uttered the word aloud to herself, as she sat herself down in the little room upstairs." As her mind explores the charge and its implications, we keep hearing of that unfinished correspondence: "The letters remained long unwritten, and then there came a moment in which she resolved that they should not be written. The work was very hard, and what good would come from it? . . . But at last, before she had abandoned her desk and paper, there had come to her another thought. . . . Having in this way thought it all out, she took up her pen and completed the batch of letters before she allowed herself to go to bed" (*PM*, I, 214–7). The chronicle of the writing of the letters, which accompanies the more subtle but less concrete chronicle of Glencora's inward debate, is Trollope's way of fixing the attention of the novel-reader, who craves events as well as ideas. But the reflection also is dramatic and minutely fascinating, for we follow it through the fluctuations of Glencora's resolution: "Was her courage already gone from her? Was she so weak that a single word should knock her over, – and a word evidently repented of as soon as uttered? Vulgar! Well, let her be vulgar as long as she gained her object." Such a passage bears out Trollope's claim to have *lived* with his characters, "in the full reality of established intimacy."

It is so that I have lived with my characters, and thence has come whatever success I have attained. There is a gallery of them, and of all in that gallery I may say that I know the tone of the voice, and the colour of the hair, every flame of the eye, and the very clothes they wear. Of each man I could assert whether he would have said these or the other words; of every woman, whether she would then have smiled or so have frowned. When I shall feel that this intimacy ceases, then I shall know that the old horse should be turned out to grass. (*A*, 200)

His novels tell us enough of the tones of the voice, the tilt of the eyebrows, the tricks of phrasing and passing effects of gesture and expression, to bear out his claim. As sober critics we know that there is no Glencora, no Plantagenet Palliser, or the rest, only beguiling arrangements of words that create an illusion of men and women. But as Trollope's readers, the sympathetic readers that his own solicitous and disarming tone persuades us to be, we can hardly resist being convinced that they live and breathe, that we could be close to them as their author is close to them, listening in on their thoughts and entering into their motives. By creating and maintaining our sympathy, as well as by surrounding himself with his own illusion, he has endowed us with his own sense of his characters' life. That we can so respond to his characters, and become so minutely interested in their concerns, is a result both of his proximity to them, and of his proximity, created and maintained so quietly but so continuously, to us.

It behoves the writer on Trollope to have a sense of proportion. In the foregoing pages I have suggested locally that he organizes his novels thematically like Jane Austen, that he engages his reader's sympathy like Thackeray, that he occasionally has the symbolic reach of Dickens, that his psychological vision is sometimes a source for James. I don't mean to imply that he beats them all at their own game. Trollope's claims on his own behalf were modest, and though I want to claim more for him than he did for himself, my analogies are intended to give him only his due, but to give him at least that. He does have some of the strengths of each of these masters, though he deploys them unobtrusively; his work is an amalgam that has the special qualities of durability and flexibility belonging to amalgams. His strengths are not just those he has always been allowed: lucidity of style, quiet humour, gentle satire, and an insight into human motivation and behaviour that never ceases to amaze; but a close look at the structure of single novels shows too that he can organize his work, arranging theme, character, action and imagery into a mutually supportive pattern, and so shape that loose baggy monster which is traditionally the crowded Victorian novel into a muscular and coordinated beast which yet retains its energy and vitality.

Appendix

Original Publication of the Palliser Novels:

The Small House at Allington. Composed May 20, 1862 to February 11, 1863. Serial run in 20 issues of the *Cornhill Magazine*, September 1862 to April 1864. Published in book form by Smith, Elder and Co. in March 1864. 18 illustrations by J. E. Millais.

Can You Forgive Her? Composed August 16, 1863 to April 28, 1864. Published in 20 monthly parts, January 1864 to August 1865. Published in book form by Chapman and Hall (2 vols): Vol. I in October 1864 with 20 illustrations by Hablot K. Browne, Vol. II in June 1865 with 20 illustrations by Miss Taylor.

Phineas Finn, the Irish Member. Composed November 17, 1866 to May 15, 1867. Serial run in 20 issues of *Saint Pauls Magazine*, October 1867 to May 1869. Published in book form by Virtue and Co., March 1869 (2 vols). 20 illustrations by J. E. Millais.

The Eustace Diamonds. Composed December 4, 1869 to August 25, 1870. Serial run in 21 issues of *The Fortnightly Review*, July 1871 to February 1873. Published in book form by Chapman and Hall, December 1872 with imprint 1873 (3 vols).

Phineas Redux. Composed October 23, 1870 to March 29, 1871. Serial run in 26 issues of *The Graphic*, July 19, 1873 to January 10, 1874. Published in book form by Chapman and Hall, December 1873 with imprint 1874 (2 vols). 24 illustrations by Frank Holl.

The Prime Minister. Composed April 1, 1874 to September 15, 1874. Published in 8 monthly parts, November 1875 to June 1876. Published in book form by Chapman and Hall, May 1876 (4 vols).

The Duke's Children. Composed May 2, 1876 to October 29, 1876. Serial
run in 22 issues of *All the Year Round*, October 4, 1879 to February 28,
1880. Published in book form by Chapman and Hall, June or July
1880 (3 vols).

Notes

Introduction

1. *Early Victorian Novelists* (London, 1934), pp. 259, 246.

Chapter 1. *The Small House at Allington:* The Moth and the Candle

1. (I, 17). A version of this study, " 'The Unfortunate Moth': Unifying Theme in *The Small House at Allington*," has been previously published. © 1971 by The Regents of the University of California. Reprinted from *Nineteenth-Century Fiction*, Vol. 26, No. 2, pp. 127–144 by Permission of the Regents.

2. Contrast his comments in the letter of May 16, 1864, to Miss Rowe (*Letters*, 152–3), where he defends Lily's rejection of Johnny, with his later comments in the *Autobiography*, p. 154, where he criticizes it. I discuss these comments later in this chapter, and in more detail below, in Chapter 8.

3. A. O. J. Cockshut sees this phrase as giving the key to Palliser's character, and makes the point that "he has an inverted conscientiousness which finds an almost irresistible attraction in whatever is against his own interest." *Anthony Trollope* (London, 1955), p. 162. But Palliser is only one among a number of characters who, in their different ways, are "trembling with expectant ruin."

4. Robert M. Polhemus has drawn a more extended parallel of a Trollope novel with Dostoyevsky's in "*Cousin Henry*: Trollope's Note from Underground," *Nineteenth-Century Fiction*, 20 (1966), 385–89.

5. Constance Garnett, trans., *White Nights and Other Stories* (London, 1966), p. 75.

6. Ibid., p. 86.

7. William Cadbury sees Crosbie as belonging to Trollope's basic theme of "the opposition of heart and head." "Shape and Theme: Determinants of Trollope's Forms," *PMLA*, 78 (1963), p. 331. But Lady Alexandrina is neither emotionally or rationally attractive to Crosbie.

8. *Anthony Trollope* (London, 1928), p. 53.

9. *The Hero in Eclipse in Victorian Fiction*, trans. Angus Davidson (London, 1956), p. 309. E. L. Skinner, with some exasperation, also describes the dangerous

way in which Trollope's heroines jeopardize their happiness in "Mr. Trollope's Young Ladies," *Nineteenth-Century Fiction*, 4 (1949), 197–207.

10. Sir Arthur Quiller-Couch said that because of a strain of cheapness in his hero, Trollope "could not bring himself to mate his 'dear Lily Dale' with that faithful, most helpful, little bounder Johnny Eames" (*Charles Dickens and Other Victorians* [Cambridge, 1925], p. 234). And L. P. and R. P. Stebbins congratulate Trollope for not having mismatched "the fragile Lily and the boobish Johnny" (*The Trollopes: The Chronicle of a Writing Family* [New York, 1946], p. 217).

11. Bradford A. Booth says that in *The Last Chronicle* at least Johnny has become too good for Lily (*Anthony Trollope: Aspects of His Life and Art* [London, 1958], pp. 52–53). And E. L. Skinner accounts for Trollope's refusal to marry Johnny and Lily: "the reason (in my belief) being that Eames was in large measure identified with himself, and he could not tolerate the idea of being married to Lily Dale" ("Mr. Trollope's Young Ladies," p. 202).

12. *Anthony Trollope*, p. 61.

13. I have enlarged on this view of James's heroine in "The Portrait of Isabel Archer," *American Literature*, 45 (1973), 50–66.

14. The erroneous reading of "French prig," which has puzzled some readers, has been corrected from Trollope's manuscript in World's Classics editions since 1953. And see R. W. Chapman, "The Text of Trollope's Autobiography," *Review of English Studies*, 17 (1941), 90–94.

15. *Anthony Trollope*, p. 31.

16. For instance, by Cockshut, p. 31, and by Ruth ap Roberts in "*Cousin Henry*: Trollope's Note from Antiquity," *Nineteenth-Century Fiction*, 24 (1969), p. 97.

Chapter 2. Can You Forgive Her? The Meaning of Words and the Nature of Things

1. The present chapter is adapted from my article, " 'The Meaning of Words and the Nature of Things': Trollope's *Can You Forgive Her?*," in *Studies in English Literature* 14 (Autumn, 1974), 603–618, and is reproduced with the editor's permission.

2. "Of *Can You Forgive Her?* I cannot speak with too great affection. . . . That which endears the book to me is the first presentation which I made in it of Plantagenet Palliser, with his wife, Lady Glencora" (*Autobiography*, 155).

3. *Anthony Trollope* (London, 1928), p. 100.

4. September 2, 1865. This and other reviews are readily available in *Anthony Trollope: The Critical Heritage*, ed. Donald Smalley, (London, 1969), and page references for them are to this volume. The present quotation is from p. 245.

5. *Nation*, September 28, 1865; *Critical Heritage*, pp. 249–250.

6. Trollope always sold his copyright outright, and so the sales made no direct financial difference to him. His contract for *Can You Forgive Her?* was £3525, as against £3200 for *Phineas Finn* and *He Knew He Was Right*, the nearest competitors. See *Autobiography*, pp. 312–3.

7. *Critical Heritage*, p. 252.

8. *Anthony Trollope*, pp. 99–100; *The Changing World of Anthony Trollope* (Berkeley and Los Angeles, 1968), p. 110.

9. (Harmondsworth, 1972), p. 18.
10. In the opening scene her father asks her,

    Come hither, Margaret. What ails you, dearest?
    Why sits that heavy cloud upon your brow? . . .
    A life too happy – days too full of ease –
    are those the fears that make your brow so gloomy? (I, i)

    See Michael Sadleir's edition of *The Noble Jilt* (London, 1923), p. 3.
11. *Anthony Trollope: His Public Services, Private Friends, And Literary Originals* (London, 1913), p. 209.
12. *Anthony Trollope* (London, 1955).
13. Polhemus points out that in this novel Trollope shows women to be members of an oppressed second sex, which is denied most of the occupations and amusements that men enjoy. *The Changing World of Anthony Trollope*, p. 105.
14. "There is not one character, serious or comic, to challenge the sympathy of the audience." Letter from George Bartley of June 18, 1851, quoted in full by Michael Sadleir in his preface to *The Noble Jilt*, pp. xiv–xv. Trollope quotes other parts of this letter in the *Autobiography*, p. 74.
15. Bradford Booth, for instance, contends that "we are taught in this semiproblem novel that self-indulgence must yield to propriety and good sense." *Anthony Trollope: Aspects of His Life and Art* (London, 1958), p. 84. But I think Alice can hardly be called self-indulgent in engaging herself to George: quite the contrary. As Grey attests, "There has been no touch of selfishness in your fickleness" (II, 433).
16. Polhemus, op. cit., p. 111.
17. George Levine, in a full and sympathetic study of the novel, interestingly compares Alice with "Jane Austen's Emma, George Eliot's Gwendolen Harleth, James's Isabel Archer, for whom genuine freedom seems to be available only – and powerfully – through frigidity, or at least through a mistaken resistance to men who love them. The resistance to sexuality is a resistance to being mastered, penetrated, taken. . . . John Grey is really dangerous to [Alice] because she feels his sexual attraction." "Can You Forgive Him? Trollope's *Can You Forgive Her?* and the Myth of Realism," *Victorian Studies* 18 (September, 1974), p. 16. In more sensational vein, in his introduction to the Panther paperback edition, Simon Raven expatiates on Alice's sexuality: "Alice fancied her cousin George because he was tough and sexy. . . . At the beginning of the book she is now affianced to John Grey, a scholarly 'squire, having chosen him because he too is tough and sexy but *also* respectable. . . . One thing becomes very apparent: Alice, though keen on sexy men, is terrified about what is going to happen on her wedding night, and keep [sic] shuttling from George to Grey and back. . . . Well before the end you will long for Alice to be hit on the head with a mallet and then raped (which is not, I need hardly add, what happens)" (1973), p. xix. Raven has had to write in some scenes to support this interpretation in his adaptation of Trollope for the BBC television serial, *The Pallisers*. His view is a long (and dangerous) leap from Polhemus's view of Alice as "sexless"; but Alice's determined subordination of the physical to the theoretical inevitably gives rise to some rather desperate speculation among critics as well as among the characters who surround her.

18. Booth, p. 84.

19. *Critical Heritage*, p. 246.

20. Cf. George Levine, op. cit. "One of the marks of Glencora's desire for spontaneity, directness, and honesty of speech is that she is almost powerless to act out her independence any way but verbally. . . . Glencora, though she persistently violates the verbal rules, has not quite broken the rules of behavior" (p. 20).

21. *Critical Heritage*, p. 253.

22. See his advice to Kate Field: "In telling a tale it is, I think, always well to sink the personal pronoun. The old way, 'Once upon a time,' with slight modifications, is the best way of telling a story." *The Letters of Anthony Trollope*, ed. Bradford A. Booth (London, 1951), p. 217.

Chapter 3. Phineas Finn: The Politics of Love

1. *Saint Pauls*, I, (October, 1867), p. 6.

2. April 9, 1864. *Critical Heritage*, p. 197.

3. *Anthony Trollope* (London, 1928), p. 106.

4. *Anthony Trollope: Aspects of His Life and Art* (London, 1958), p. 87.

5. See N. John Hall, in his introduction to his edition of *The New Zealander* (Oxford, 1972): "Phineas Finn, who believes that 'A man who is ready to vote black white, because somebody tells him, is dishonest,' agonizes over the problem of party loyalty" (p. xxvi).

6. *Spectator*, March 20, 1869. *Critical Heritage*, p. 311.

7. Walpole, p. 107.

8. See John Sutherland's perceptive study of Lady Laura in his introduction to the Penguin *Phineas Finn* (Harmondsworth, 1972), p. 25ff.

9. *Critical Heritage*, p. 310.

10. *Anthony Trollope*, pp. 107–8.

11. *Anthony Trollope* (London, 1971), p. 282.

12. I suspect that Trollope chose the confusive series of names, Loughshane, Loughlinter and Loughton (one for each of Ireland, Scotland and England, and no doubt with a different pronunciation for the first syllable to reflect the nation) for the same reason that Conrad placed Lord Jim first on the *Patna* and then in Patusan. They are superficially varied scenes for the same action – success in Phineas's case, failure in Jim's.

13. Trollope's depiction of Phineas and Lady Laura often brings to mind Thackeray's treatment of Henry Esmond and Rachel, Lady Castlewood, in Trollope's favourite novel. Like Esmond, Phineas is cruel enough to make the woman who loves him his confidante in his suit of another wife.

14. Charles Blinderman's argument that Trollope is hostile to this dark Jewess seems to me perverse: "Her beauty is fake, her wit superficial. The Jew is often in Trollope's novels a liar and impostor. [So is the Gentile, come to that.] Madame Max's conversational talents, fluency with languages and general vivacity are also tinsel." "The Servility of Dependence: the Dark Lady in Trollope," *Images of Women In Fiction: Feminist Perspectives*, ed. Susan Koppelman Cornillon (Bowling Green, Ohio, 1972), p. 64.

15. *The Changing World of Anthony Trollope* (Berkeley and Los Angeles, 1968), p. 161.

16. It is tempting to speculate on the relation between this statement of Madame Goesler's politics and Derby's famous use of the same image of the leap in the dark for the second reform bill. According to his worksheet, Trollope finished writing this novel on May 15, 1867, though this chapter was not published until January, 1869. Derby's speech came in between, on August 6, 1867. The MS shows no sign of revision here, so Madame Goesler's speech could scarcely have been influenced by the Earl of Derby's. But Trollope may well have noted the correspondence, as the first political article in *Saint Pauls*, the journal he edited and in which he ran *Phineas Finn*, was on the second reform bill, and was called "The Leap in the Dark." (October, 1867), 1–22.

Chapter 4. *Phineas Redux:* The Law's Delay, The Insolence of Office

1. Trollope's defeat at Beverley in his own attempt to enter the hallowed portals of the House of Commons no doubt had something to do with the sour view of politics in *Phineas Redux* after the relative optimism of *Phineas Finn*. But I do not like to read the novel as a prolonged and personal expression of sour grapes. Trollope's theme of change in the Palliser novels is pervasive enough to transcend the rancour of a single disillusioning experience, or even of many.

2. See the *Autobiography*, p. 128–9. Sadleir and others agree that Millais' work was particularly appropriate to Trollope's art. "Never were author and artist in greater sympathy. They worked, each in his genre, along identical lines." *Trollope: A Commentary* (London, 1927), p. 266. Holl's work, however, compared with Millais' for *Phineas Finn*, has certain advantages. His Madame Max, for instance, is certainly more graceful and attractive than Millais'.

3. The "Loughlinter" of *Phineas Finn* has become, by some printer's decision, "Lough Linter" in *Phineas Redux*, though Trollope wrote Loughlinter throughout the manuscript. I preserve Loughlinter, except within quotations.

4. See also Polhemus, *The Changing World of Anthony Trollope* (Berkeley and Los Angeles, 1968), p. 178ff.

5. It is notable that in the two encounters between rivals in love in the two novels, some ado is made about the days of the week. Phineas and Chiltern are careful neither to fight nor to travel on a Sunday, though Phineas and his second have to be back in the House to vote in the division on the Tuesday (*PF*, II, 4–7); but Kennedy, ardent sabbatarian though he is, takes the most determined and vigorous (and criminal) action of his life on a Sunday – a piece of timing "which added infinitely to the delightful horror of the catastrophe" (*PR*, II, 24).

6. See P. D. Edwards, *Anthony Trollope*, in the Profiles in Literature Series. (London, 1968), pp. 106–8.

7. See Julian Moynahan, "The Hero's Guilt: The Case of *Great Expectations*," *Essays in Criticism*, X (1960), pp. 60–79.

8. Hugh Walpole is surely crude in suggesting Trollope should have kept us guessing on Phineas's guilt or innocence. Trollope's readers are more fully acquainted with Phineas's character than the public can be, and properly

side with the hero's injured innocence. See *Anthony Trollope* (London, 1928), p. 109.

9. *Anthony Trollope: Aspects of His Life and Art* (London, 1958), p. 94.

10. Trollope was deeply impressed by this poem, which was first published in *The Cornhill* for July, 1860, and commented on it in a letter to his brother. It moved him to argue, "A man that can be a poet is so much the more a man in becoming such, and is the more fitted for a man's best work." The comment suggests again that we are to admire Phineas for his sensitivity, even though it is temporarily incapacitating. *Letters*, p. 83–4.

11. *Anthony Trollope: Aspects of His Life and Art*, p. 94. But see Roger L. Slakey: "to read [Trollope's] novels properly is to read all the plots of a given novel, not just one." "Trollope's case for Moral Imperative," *Nineteenth-Century Fiction* 28 (1973), p. 311.

12. *Saturday Review*, February 7, 1874. *Critical Heritage*, p. 383.

Chapter 5. The Eustace Diamonds: 'What is Truth?' Said Jesting Pilate

1. *Anthony Trollope: Aspects of His Life and Art* (London, 1958), p. 92.

2. Ruth ap Roberts, *Trollope: Artist and Moralist* (London, 1971), p. 21, and David Aitken, "'A Kind of Felicity': Some Notes About Trollope's Style," *Nineteenth-Century Fiction*, 20 (1966), p. 349.

3. A reservation is necessary here. Trollope's edition of Bacon's essays, with annotations, survives, and was described by Michael Sadleir in "Trollope and Bacon's Essays" in *The Trollopian*, I (1945), 21–34. Here he says of the essay "Of Truth" – discouragingly for my purposes – "There is nothing in this. He begins by accusing those who differ from him of being false in their search after truth. It is as though he shall declare that a man who did not believe revealed religion were a liar. His metaphor about the pearl and the diamond is not to the purpose" (p. 23). These notes date from 1879 or later, well after the writing of *The Eustace Diamonds*. Trollope would however have had a schoolboy's knowledge of Bacon, which could without his being conscious of it have contributed to his undoubted association of diamonds with lies; and besides, he could as easily have derived his image second-hand from his favourite novelist Thackeray, who recurrently uses diamonds as emblems of worldliness and falsehood. In a late novel, *An Old Man's Love*, he put these words into the mouth of Mr. Whittlestaff (who has been seen as a self-portrait), in a conversation with John Gordon, who deals in diamonds: "These things stick to the very soul of a man. They are a poison of which he cannot rid himself. They are like gambling. They make everything cheap that should be dear, and everything dear that should be cheap. I trust them not at all, – and I do not trust you, because you deal in them." (234). Elsewhere he uses the expression "a pearl of truth" (*DC*, II, 182); this in 1876 predates Trollope's notes on his Bacon essay, and shows him already using half of Bacon's metaphor as a standard figure of speech.

4. I am indebted to a student, Judy Flynn, for first pointing out this correspondence. See her "A Note on Trollope's *The Eustace Diamonds* and Bacon's Essay 'Of Truth,'" *Victorian Studies Association of Western Canada Newsletter*, 1:2 (Spring, 1973), 5–6.

5. Stephen Gill and John Sutherland have touched on this theme in their introduction to the Penguin edition of *The Eustace Diamonds* (Harmondsworth, 1973), pp. 13–15.

6. *Anthony Trollope: Aspects of His Life and Art* (London, 1958), p. 91. Polhemus, however, finds that Lizzie's differences from Becky are a mark of Trollope's subtlety. *The Changing World of Anthony Trollope* (Berkeley and Los Angeles, 1968), p. 173. Trollope also admitted to being worried by the Becky analogy in the *Autobiography*, p. 296.

7. If there was any influence here, again Trollope seems not to have been conscious of it, as he labels the Blanche temptation in Pen's development merely a "digression." See *Thackeray* (London, 1879) p. 111. He does however quote the passage on shams that I also single out below.

8. I have examined the operation of this theme in *Pendennis* in *Thackeray: The Major Novels* (Toronto, 1971), pp. 64–86.

9. Sadleir, in his introduction to the World's Classics Edition, calls this match "barely credible" (vi).

10. Polhemus finds the subject of this novel to be "nothing less than the loss of the self," and quotes this passage to show "how explicit Trollope's concern is with identity." *The Changing World of Anthony Trollope*, pp. 172, 177.

11. Not only did he have nothing to do with the robberies, as it turns out, but at the last he reproaches Mrs. Carbuncle with forcing Lucinda into marriage (635) – though earlier we have seen him too as determined to promote the match with Sir Griffin.

12. Sadleir points out in his introduction how even Trollope's beloved Glencora is in this novel tainted by the prevailing atmosphere of lies (vii).

13. Cockshut has interestingly explored some of the psychological implications of this relationship. *Anthony Trollope* (London, 1955), 192–6.

14. I have restored the manuscript reading at this point, in preference to the printed versions, which read ". . . chucking the necklace across the table to Frank, so that he was barely able to catch it. 'There is ten thousand pounds' worth, as they tell me. . . .'" I find it more appropriate that she should throw the diamonds "at" Frank (as she throws herself) rather than simply "to" him. The MS is in the Robert H. Taylor collection in Princeton University Library.

Chapter 6. *The Prime Minister:* Judgment, Pride and Prejudice

1. 22 July, 1876; *Critical Heritage*, p. 419.

2. *Anthony Trollope: Aspects of His Life and Work* (London, 1958), p. 98.

3. Exceptions are Robert Polhemus in *The Changing World of Anthony Trollope* (Berkeley and Los Angeles, 1968), pp. 197–209, and Helmut Klingler in "Varieties of Failure: The Significance of Trollope's *The Prime Minister*," *English Miscellany*, 23 (1972), 167–183.

4. Helmut Klingler undertakes the same task in his article cited above, but he comes to different conclusions. He develops a parallel between Lopez and Palliser, whom he sees as two men who take on enterprises for which they are constitutionally unfit, and he sees failure as the unifying theme. Robert Polhemus (see above) offers coalition as the central concept of the novel, which he reads as Trollope's delineation of "the dark new world." I find both studies convincing, but for me the most carefully developed parallel is

not between Palliser and Lopez but between Palliser and Emily; and the novel seems to me not centrally concerned with the changing social structure of the day, but rather with universal and enduring moral issues.

5. Trollope seems to have liked such neat divisions. His working sheet for this novel begins with the calculation: "Novel in 8 parts. 120 pages at 260 each page. 10 chapters at 12 pages ... at 40 pages a week – 24 weeks." Then follows his novel calendar, drawn up in advance for 24 weeks, and filled in as usual with his day-by-day record of the number of pages written. The calendar is filled in to the last day, with the final note of satisfaction, "finished in 24 weeks to the day." It may have fretted him that his total of hand-written pages came to 955, not 960 as it should have been at his calculated word count per page. He was half a percent out. See his working papers in the Bodleian Library, Oxford (MS Don. c. 9–10). I am grateful to Lloyds Bank limited, Trust Division, the owners of the copyright of these papers, for permission to quote from the manuscripts.

6. *Spectator*, July 22, 1876; *Critical Heritage*, p. 422. See also David Skilton's comments on the use of the term in *Anthony Trollope and his Contemporaries*, (London, 1972), pp. 90–91.

7. *Pride and Prejudice*, incidentally, Trollope considered to be the best English novel until the advent of *Henry Esmond*.

8. Here Trollope's choice of the character's official status for a title is almost capricious: The *Athenaeum* reviewer complained, "The Senator might be cut out of the book almost without affecting the story." June 16, 1877; *Critical Heritage*, p. 428.

9. I have emended the punctuation by the addition of a period, as seems necessary from the sense in the context. All editions read, "I won't deny that on general subjects ..." The manuscript in the Arents Collection of the New York Public Library confirms my reading.

10. Both novels deal with a stern, rich, professional father who resists the proposal of a fortune-hunting suitor for his daughter. Mrs. Roby and Mrs. Penniman, as the girl's aunt in each case, similarly get some vicarious sexual satisfaction in promoting the match. And the scene between the doctor and his daughter at chapter 18 is certainly reminiscent of that between the barrister and his daughter from which I have quoted above. Dr. Sloper asks Catherine:

> 'Don't you suppose that I know something of men: their vices, their follies, their falsities?'
>
> She detached herself, and turned upon him. 'He is not vicious – he is not false!'
>
> Her father kept looking at her with his sharp, pure eye. 'You make nothing of my judgment, then?' ...
>
> 'I wish to explain – to tell him to wait ... till you know him better – till you consent.'
>
> 'Don't tell him any such nonsense as that. I know him well enough, and I shall never consent.'

11. The Duchess, for all her exasperation at Lopez for avoiding punishment by rushing into eternity, ultimately pulls off the same trick herself, as we learn in *The Duke's Children*: "Whatever cause for anger the Duke might have

against Mrs. Finn, there had been cause for much more against his wife. But she had freed herself from all accusation by death" (I, 121). It is one of those tiny echoes and corroborations from one novel in the series to another on which Trollope prided himself. See the *Autobiography*, p. 310.

12. For one discussion of Trollope's subtle use of significant allusion, see Ruth ap Roberts, "Emily and Nora and Dorothy and Priscilla and Jemima and Carry," in *The Victorian Experience: The Novelists*, edited by Richard A. Levine (Ohio University Press: Athens, 1976), pp. 116–18.

13. I use North's Plutarch, from the life of Themistocles.

14. *The Changing World of Anthony Trollope*, p. 200.

15. As Polhemus notes, p. 199, we have here a mild Trollopian version of the execremental vision; it is an extension of the implications of the name of Dickens's swindler Mr. Merdle, and incidentally a possible source for Conrad's equally suggestive references to the guano cargo in *Lord Jim*. But lucre is filthy in more than one Trollope novel – a comic version of the same image is Mr. Cheesacre's pride in his dunghills.

16. I have enlarged elsewhere on this topic: see "The Equation of Love and Money in *Moll Flanders*," *Studies in the Novel*, 2 (1970), 131–144.

Chapter 7. The Duke's Children: Past and Present

1. See Robert Polhemus: "The tensions between the Duke and his children and, within the Duke's own mind, between the impact of the present and the psychological effects of the past on him bring us right to the heart of important problems of change in Victorian and modern life. The book could be subtitled *Letting Go*. Palliser, growing old, loses control over his children and his world. To live in the present, he must learn to let go of the past." *The Changing World of Anthony Trollope* (Berkeley and Los Angeles, 1968), p. 219. Polhemus only briefly enlarges on this major comment, however, and does not pursue the theme as it is worked out not just in the Duke but in all the major characters.

2. In the novels between *Can You Forgive Her?* and *The Duke's Children* Alice Vavasor, now Mrs. Grey, gets only very brief mention. But in the first and uncut version of *The Duke's Children* Trollope included a fairly extensive reference to her and her concerns, presumably to remind his readers of the close connection between the two novels. This had to be cut, as dispensable material, when Trollope was asked to reduce the length of the novel from four volumes to three. See the Manuscript in the Beinecke Rare Book and Manuscript Library, Yale University, (No. 1, pp. 7–8).

3. "*The Duke's Children*: Trollope's Psychological Masterpiece," *Nineteenth-Century Fiction*, 13 (1958), 1–21.

4. Barry A. Bartrum has suggested that Trollope was not consistent through the series in his characterization of Madame Max, alias Marie Goesler, alias Mrs. Finn: "During *Phineas Redux*, and especially *The Prime Minister*, the more exotic side of her character disappears, and she becomes increasingly like the typical Trollopian heroine." *The Parliament Within: a Study of Anthony Trollope's Palliser Novels*. Unpublished dissertation, Princeton, May, 1976, p. 125. But the Duke, who argues with himself "Had he not known from the first that the woman was an adventuress?" (I, 67), clearly retains some

vestiges of the prejudice against her that made Glencora once think of her as "a thin, black-browed, yellow-visaged woman with ringlets and devil's eyes, and a beard on her upper lip, – a Jewess" (*PF*, II, 267). This element in his feeling for her was more clearly present in the original unshortened version of *The Duke's Children*: a cancelled passage in the manuscript runs "She had been in some degree mysterious, and, in the same degree, objectionable" (No. 2, pp. 24–6). Madame Max has not been entirely Englished, or radically changed – she still provokes the same prejudice, and exercises the same energy and delicate judgment in countering it.

5. See George Butte, "Ambivalence and Affirmation in *The Duke's Children*", *Studies in English Literature*, 17 (Autumn, 1977), p. 711.

6. Op. cit, p. 724.

7. See Pamela Hansford Johnson, "Trollope's Young Women," in *On the Novel: A Present for Walter Allen on his Sixtieth Birthday*, ed. B. S. Benedikz (London, 1971), pp. 20–21.

8. "The Divided Mind of Anthony Trollope," *Nineteenth-Century Fiction*, 14 (1957), p. 25.

9. Early in the novel, at chapter 7, there is this deleted passage in the manuscript: "No doubt the conservative party would like it, and in order to seduce from his allegiance the heir of the Duke of Omnium would take care that arrangements should be made so that the family borough of Silverbridge should help him to his apostasy" (No. 1, p. 93). It is a pity this passage should have been sacrificed, since Silverbridge's naiveté here has given way to an astute assessment of the situation at the end of the novel, and the retention of both passages would more neatly have marked his progress.

10. Tregear is treated more hostilely in the uncut version of the novel, from which Trollope cut some of the more acid comments on him. In chapter 3, for instance, we hear how Tregear rejected a number of possible professions, including that of barrister: "He did not, he said, like the duplicity. He did not, in truth, like the labour. He liked to be a gentleman at large."

11. See George Butte on the comic consummation that is achieved in this union. "Ambivalence and Affirmation in *The Duke's Children*," p. 726.

12. *Anthony Trollope: Aspects of His Life and Art* (London, 1958), pp. 102–3.

Chapter 8. The Men and Women

1. Trollope's notes in his copy of *Emma* show how much pleasure he took himself in the reading of proposal scenes: "I cannot but notice Miss Austens timidity in dealing with the most touching scenes which come in her way, and in avoiding the narration of those details which a bolder artist would most eagerly have seized. In the final scene between Emma and her lover, – when the conversation has become almost pathetic, – she breaks away from the spoken dialogue, and simply tells us of her hero's success. This is a cowardice which robs the reader of much of the charm which he has promised himself. August 17, 1864." Trollope's copy of *Emma* is in the Robert H. Taylor Collection at Princeton, and I quote with his permission.

2. See David Aitken, "Anthony Trollope on 'The Genus Girl.'" *Nineteenth-Century Fiction*, 28 (1974), p. 427.

3. "Anthony Trollope," *Century Magazine*, July 1883; *Critical Heritage*, p. 541–2.

4. Riverside edition (Cambridge, Mass., 1957), p. x.

5. See R. P. Utter and G. B. Needham, *Pamela's Daughters* (New York, 1937) and George Orwell (who is in this context referring to Agnes Wickfield) "Charles Dickens," *Inside the Whale* (London, 1940), p. 83.

6. Anthony Trollope, *Four Lectures*, ed. M. L. Parrish (The Folcroft Press, 1938), p. 74.

7. See Charles Blinderman, "The Servility of Dependence: The Dark Lady in Trollope," in *Images of Women in Fiction*, ed. Susan Koppelman Carnillon (Bowling Green, Ohio, 1972), 55–67; and David Aitken, op. cit.

8. Mill's views on women were of course "in the air" and quoted by people who never read his work, like the American Minister in *He Knew He Was Right*, well before 1869. Harriet Taylor's essay, "Enfranchisement of Women" in the *Westminster Review* of 1851 was generally attributed to Mill, and was reprinted in his *Dissertations and Discussions* (1859), and republished and sold in large numbers to the working classes by George Holyoake under the title *Are Women Fit for Politics? Are Politics Fit for Women?* (1856). After his election to Parliament in 1865 Mill was identified as the champion of women's rights, and his speech in the Commons, "On the Admission of Women to the Electoral Franchise," delivered on May 20, 1867, and printed immediately as a pamphlet, was probably the immediate occasion for the use of his name as a household word on women's rights by Violet Effingham (*PF*, II, 145, 243). I am grateful to my friend John M. Robson, general editor of *The Collected Works of John Stuart Mill* (University of Toronto Press, 1963–) for his informed advice on Mill.

9. I use the Oxford World's Classics Edition, *On Liberty, Representative Government, The Subjection of Women: Three Essays by John Stuart Mill* (Oxford, 1912). Subsequent references are included in the text.

10. George Levine has interestingly commented on this and similar passages in "Can You Forgive Him? Trollope's *Can You Forgive Her?* and the Myth of Realism," *Victorian Studies* 12 (1974), 5–30.

11. *The Noble Jilt*, ed. Michael Sadleir (London, 1923), p. 92.

12. Sadleir finds that "in Mary Thorne is embodied the true essence of the Trollope heroine." He goes on, of this Trollopian maidenly type, "Modest of mein, low-voiced, by modern standards strangely feminine, each of these young women yet proves herself the ultimate despot of her social world. Claiming nothing of equality she achieves supremacy." Fond though he is of these girls, Sadleir acknowledged this ideal of womanhood "is, of course, a masculine one." *Trollope: A Commentary* (London, 1927), p. 382–3.

13. See also Aitken, op. cit.

14. *Paradise Lost*, IV, 1, 299.

15. See, for instance, Steven Marcus, *The Other Victorians: A Study of Sexuality and Pornography in Mid-Nineteenth-Century England* (New York, 1964), p. 29ff., or Eric Trudgill, *Madonnas and Magdalens: The Origins and Development of Victorian Sexual Attitudes* (New York, 1976), p. 56ff.

16. John Sutherland has made this connection in his introduction to the Penguin edition of *Phineas Finn* (Harmondsworth, 1972), p. 23ff.

17. The World's Classics Edition reads ". . . hard to manage?" I restore the MS and first edition punctuation.

18. Trollope thought it was no favour to women that they should "be thrown into the labour market, and hustle and tustle for their bread amidst the rivalry of men." ("Higher Education of Women," p. 76). In the same lecture however he singled out the occupation of governess for special mention: "There cannot be any doubt . . . that the difficult and delicate work of a governess is becoming a profession to which more and more care is being given year after year" (p. 77).

19. See the *Autobiography*, p. 251.

Chapter 9. The Places and Things

1. See the *Autobiography*, chapter 1.

2. A rare personal note occurs in the set of proofs of Millais' illustrations for *Orley Farm*: underneath the plate of Orley Farm itself, Trollope noted "This is Julians Hill (so called then) – where I lived when at Harrow School." The proofs are in the Robert H. Taylor Collection at Princeton.

3. See Alistair M. Duckworth, *The Improvement of the Estate: A Study of Jane Austen's Novels* (Baltimore and London, 1971), where he shows how for Jane Austen "the estate is symbolic of an entire inherited culture" (p. 55), and Barbara Hardy, "Properties and Possessions in Jane Austen's Novels," in *Jane Austen's Achievement*, ed. Juliet McMaster (London, 1976), 79–105.

4. *Jane Austen's Letters to her sister Cassandra and others*, ed. R. W. Chapman, second edition (London, 1952), p. 401.

5. Several critics have elaborated on the Sotherton episode in *Mansfield Park* as a major instance in Jane Austen's work of symbolic foreshadowing. See, for instance, Charles Murrah, "The Background of *Mansfield Park*," in *From Jane Austen to Joseph Conrad*, ed. Robert C. Rathburn and Martin Steinmann, Jr. (Minneapolis, 1958), pp. 33–4.

6. In the manuscript Trollope had given Phineas's age here as "twenty-six," possibly to vary it from the quarter century since Kennedy stood there and made his resolution. But on reflection, and presumably at the proof stage, he changed Phineas's age to twenty-five, which conforms with his figures in the first chapter. See the MS in the Beinecke Rare Book and Manuscript Library, Yale University.

7. Edmund Wilson in his Freudian reading of the tale first noted the sexual imagery of tower and lake, and since then the ground has been covered again numerous times. "The Ambiguity of Henry James," *Hound and Horn*, 7 (April-June, 1934), p. 387.

8. See "Bring Back *The Trollopian*," *Nineteenth-Century Fiction*, 31 (1976), p. 9.

9. The fact that he nearly always mentions teeth has been noted by James Pope Hennessy, who posits that Trollope felt the need to mention the good teeth of his heroines because poor dental care made them a rarity. *Anthony Trollope* (London, 1971), pp. 329–30. But teeth are only one item in a fairly standard catalogue. I had always thought Trollope was a hair man myself.

10. An interesting passage at the beginning of *An Old Man's Love* testifies to Trollope's not very highly developed visual sense. There he wrote, (or rather dictated, as Florence Bland was here his amanuensis), in the first version, while warming up to a description of Mary Lawrie: "Of Thackeray's Beatrix

I have a vivid idea, because [Thackeray absolutely drew her portrait as well as provided her character]." Then he must have recalled that Thackeray did not illustrate *Esmond* after all, for he deleted the words I have bracketed, and substituted "she was drawn for him by an artist under his own eye." In fact he was still wrong, as *Esmond* appeared initially with no illustrations, and Du Maurier's did not appear until the edition of 1868, well after Thackeray's death. Trollope, though he writes as though he feels at a disadvantage in having "no artist who will take the trouble to learn my thoughts and to reproduce them," had evidently responded to Thackeray's verbal power so strongly that he thought visual aids had been supplied. See Chapter 3 of the MS of *An Old Man's Love*, in the Robert H. Taylor collection.

Chapter 10. The Author

1. James Pope Hennessy, *Anthony Trollope* (London, 1971); and C. P. Snow, *Trollope: His Life and Art* (London, 1975).
2. *Trollope: His Life and Art*, p. 166.
3. *A Portrait of the Artist as a Young Man*, ch. 5.
4. " 'A Kind of Felicity': Some Notes About Trollope's Style," *Nineteenth-Century Fiction*, 20 (1966), p. 345.
5. Trollope at this time was actually living in the country at Waltham Cross; but Onslow Crescent may be a reminiscence of another large literary man (though no hunter), Thackeray, who lived at 36 Onslow Square from 1854 to 1862.
6. James R. Kincaid, "Bring Back *The Trollopian*," *Nineteenth-Century Fiction*, 31 (1976), 12ff. "He reminds us always that art is art" (p. 12).
7. *Nation*, September 28, 1865, or *Critical Heritage*, p. 249; "The Art of Fiction," *Longman's Magazine*, 4 (September, 1884), p. 504.
8. David Aitken perceptively notes that in his frequent use of repetition Trollope is "inviting us to regard his characters with affectionate sympathy. The trick induces a kind of warmth of feeling which is like the irrational, sentimental warmth that nursery talk can sometimes inspire even in adults." " 'A Kind of Felicity': Some Notes About Trollope's Style," p. 348.
9. "The Art of Fiction," op. cit., p. 504.
10. *Anthony Trollope* (London, 1928), p. 109.
11. "Anthony Trollope," *Partial Portraits* (1880); *Critical Heritage*, p. 527.
12. It is a byword that Trollope was read avidly and compulsively in the underground shelters in London during the second world war. Those who have fallen under his spell, in those or other circumstances, will sympathize with General Liddament, the Trollopian in Anthony Powell's novel, *The Soldier's Art* (London, 1966), who "read from a small blue book that had the air of being a pocket edition of some classic" (familiar prop!):

> "What do you think of Trollope?"
> "Never found him easy to read, sir." . . .
> *"You've never found Trollope easy to read?"*
> "No, sir.'
> He was clearly unable to credit my words. (45–6)

13. See José Ortega y Gasset, "On Point of View in the Arts," *The Dehumanization of Art and other Writings on Art and Culture* (New York, 1956).

Index

The entry for Trollope has been reserved for references to his life and general comments on his art. Discussions of his novels, and of characters and places in them that receive more than passing mention, are indexed separately under titles and names. Reference to works by other writers are indexed under the writers' names. Italicized page numbers indicate sustained discussion.